Social
budgeting

QUANTITATIVE METHODS IN SOCIAL PROTECTION SERIES
A series on financial, actuarial and statistical aspects of social security prepared jointly by the International Social Security Association and the Social Security Department of the International Labour Office

Modelling in health care finance: A compendium of quantitative techniques for health care financing
by Michael Cichon, William Newbrander, Hiroshi Yamabana, Axel Weber, Charles Normand, David Dror and Alexander Preker
ISBN 92-2-110862-7   1999

Actuarial mathematics of social security pensions
by Subramaniam Iyer
ISBN 92-2-110866-X   1999

Social budgeting
by Wolfgang Scholz, Michael Cichon and Krzysztof Hagemejer
ISBN 92-2-110861-9   2000

Actuarial practice in social security
by Pierre Plamondon, Anne Drouin, *et.al.*
ISBN 92-2-110863-5   Forthcoming

Other titles are in preparation

QUANTITATIVE METHODS IN
SOCIAL PROTECTION SERIES

Social budgeting

Wolfgang Scholz,
Michael Cichon
and
Krzysztof Hagemejer

A joint technical publication of the
International Labour Office (ILO) and the
International Social Security Association (ISSA)

 International Labour Office • Geneva

Scholz, W.; Cichon, M.; Hagemejer, K.
Social budgeting
Quantitative Methods in Social Protection Series
Geneva, International Labour Office/International Social Security Association, 2000
Social expenditure, social security financing, social protection, national accounting, economic model, forecasting technique. 02.01.0

ISBN 92-2-110861-9

ILO Cataloguing-in-Publication data

Printed in the United Kingdom

ALD

FOREWORD

This book is intended to be a practical guide on how to establish a rational tool for information about social protection expenditure and revenue. It addresses the past and the future; thus it shows how to set up a methodologically reasonable statistical basis on the financing of social protection, and it explains how to develop a meaningful mathematical projection instrument that allows a useful look into the future.

This book also aims at contributing to improving governance. It is a well-known fact that the success or failure of handling public finances through governments and public or semi-public institutions has directly correlated impacts on economies and on the well-being of people. Social budgeting is part of the routine management of public finances. Governments that fail to use such instruments and the information they provide will inevitably tend to mismanage any new or existing social protection systems.

The book is based on the authors' long-standing financial advisory experience in the field of social protection in developed as well as developing countries. Thus, it approaches its subject pragmatically, offering output-oriented guidelines for interested professionals. Much emphasis is placed on setting up a sound and methodologically clear database. The manual remains "basic" in order to maintain its purpose of practical guidance, although it sometimes bridges gaps between quantitative economics, classical budgeting procedures and more sophisticated projection methods of an unorthodox kind.

This volume is written mainly for those elaborating short- to medium-term financial planning, management and monitoring – those who have a planning horizon of two to five, sometimes of up to ten, years. It is part of a series on quantitative techniques in social protection being published by the Financial, Actuarial and Statistical Branch of the Social Security Department of the ILO, together with the International Social Security Association (ISSA). Other volumes already published in this series are:

- *Modelling in health care finance: A compendium of quantitative techniques in health care financing*

v

- *Actuarial mathematics of social security pensions*

The following title is in preparation:

- *Actuarial practice in social security*

Other volumes are expected to follow within the next two years. The objective of this series is to provide a full set of compendiums on the quantitative analysis of national social protection systems. It is also hoped that they will find their way into university and professional training courses, where material on these issues is notably scarce. They will be used in ILO and ISSA training courses as required reading.

<table>
<tr><td>Colin Gillion</td><td>Dalmer D. Hoskins</td></tr>
<tr><td>Director</td><td>Secretary General</td></tr>
<tr><td>Social Security Department</td><td>International Social Security Association</td></tr>
<tr><td>International Labour Office</td><td>Geneva, Switzerland</td></tr>
<tr><td>Geneva, Switzerland</td><td></td></tr>
</table>

CONTENTS

Contents

Contents

List of tables

Notes: E = Example (e.g. table E8.9 is found in example 8.9, in Chapter 8)
      A = Appendix (e.g. table AVI.4 is found in Appendix VI)

List of figures

Notes: E = Example (e.g. figure E8.1 is found in example 8.1, in Chapter 8)
     A = Appendix (e.g. figure AI.1 is found in Appendix 1)

Contents

ACKNOWLEDGEMENTS

This volume is the result of a team effort, as are the other books in the series. Many of the results could not have been presented without the direct or indirect input of others. A very first version of the Social Budget model, called ESTEEM, was developed in 1994 for Slovakia with the collaboration of the ILO multidisciplinary advisory team for Central and Eastern Europe in Budapest, ILO headquarters staff and Michael Hopkins.

However, the initial idea of designing a relatively small and compact model was overtaken by the requirements of reality. At present, the Social Budget model consists of a number of different models. It has turned into a complex model family. The ILO Social Budget family, or stand-alone versions of members of this family, has been applied to many different country cases and, thus, has been tested and improved by several users. Kenichi Hirose, actuary in the Financial, Actuarial and Statistical Branch (SOC/FAS) of the ILO's Social Security Department, designed and continues to polish up the demographic model, thus ensuring that the population projections are trustworthy. Anne Drouin, formerly an actuary in SOC/FAS and now social security specialist in the ILO's multidisciplinary advisory team for East Asia in Bangkok, applied the pension model to many different situations, thus testing its validity in a broad variety of demographic, economic and labour market circumstances. The same was done by Kenichi Hirose, and by Rüdiger Knop, a senior actuary seconded from the German Federal Ministry of Labour and Social Affairs to SOC/FAS. Axel Weber, consultant to the ILO, and Hiroshi Yamabana, who worked for over two years as an actuary in SOC/FAS but subsequently has returned to the Japanese Ministry of Welfare, tried and tested health models in several countries. Karuna Pal, computer specialist in SOC/FAS, contributed significantly to the development of a generic version of the Social Budget model. Often, she is the person of last resort when it comes to solving tricky programming problems or when the model family, during a country application, becomes too cumbersome and has to be cleaned up in order not to lose the overview. In many cases, the users of the model family were supported by young students of economics, mathematics or the actuarial profession. Often, this turned out to be a substantial direct investment by the ILO in the younger generation, but in a few cases it was also a transfer of fresh ideas to the ILO.

The authors are responsible for the layout of the Social Budget modelling structure and the conceptual development of much of the social budgeting approach to quantitative governance of social protection. The complexity of the model family, as it has become a reality over time, requires permanent checks and balances within a team of users. The authors would like to express their gratitude for the excellent support they received from their colleagues in preparing the presentation of the results of the past years' efforts in this book.

Many thanks go to Sandie Maksud, who turned the initial German–Polish phraseology of the first draft into standard English. She also gave useful hints for improving the layout of the book and the sequencing of some of its chapters. We are grateful to Paul Johnson, who compiled the Index.

We wish to express our appreciation also to the pre-reviewers (Cornelis Gorter and Peter Heller of the International Monetary Fund, Washington, DC, and Claus F. Hofmann of the Federal Ministry of Labour, Bonn) of the first edited draft version of the book. Their comments were most welcome and given effect whenever possible.

Finally, any remaining oversights or flaws in this book remain the responsibility of the authors.

ABOUT THE AUTHORS

Wolfgang Scholz holds a Masters degree in Economics (University of Bonn, Germany). From 1978 to 1994 he held different posts in the Planning Department of the German Ministry of Labour and Social Affairs, Bonn; ultimately he was head of the Ministry's Social Budget Division. In 1984 he initiated the development of a macroeconometric projection and simulation model, mapping the German social protection system, and was later responsible for the model's routine application in policy advice. In 1985 he worked for the German Permanent Representation to the European Commission, Brussels, and in 1986 joined the Department of Health and Social Security, London, for six months. After 1986 he supervised the German Ministry's feasibility study on a satellite system for the national accounts of the German health sector. During German reunification, 1989 to 1992, he was particularly involved in shaping national wage and employment policies aiming at an economically and legally consistent merger of the two different German social protection systems. Since 1994, he has been seconded to the ILO, Geneva, in order to support the Social Security Department. In this position he has contributed to short- and long-term financial evaluations of the social protection systems of several ILO member countries. From 1991 to 1995, he was appointed to a lectureship in social policy at the Social Academy of the City of Dortmund (Germany). He has published articles on interdependencies between social protection systems, public finance, labour markets and macroeconomic developments.

Michael Cichon holds a Masters degree in Pure and Applied Mathematics (Technical University, Aachen, Germany), a Masters degree in Public Administration (Harvard University) and a Ph.D. in Health Economics (University of Göttingen, Germany). He is a member of the German Actuarial Association (DAV), and worked in the Planning Department of the German Ministry of Labour and Social Affairs as an actuary for eight years before joining the Social Security Department of the ILO in 1986 as senior actuary and health economist. Between 1993 and 1995 he served as social security specialist in the ILO's multidisciplinary advisory team for Central and Eastern Europe in Budapest, with responsibility for social security projects in the region, including the first ILO Social Budget project in Slovakia. In 1995 he was appointed Chief of the Financial, Actuarial and Statistical Branch of the ILO's Social Security Department. He writes on financial and economic issues in social security, with occasional excursions into governance. He has undertaken technical co-operation assignments in more than 15 ILO member countries.

Krzysztof Hagemejer holds a Masters degree in Econometrics and a Ph.D. in Economics (Warsaw University, Warsaw, Poland). Before joining the Social Security Department of the ILO in 1993 as a policy analyst, he worked as an assistant professor at the Department of Economics, Warsaw University, and as an adviser to the Minister in the Polish Ministry of Labour and Social Affairs. During the period 1993–95, he was involved in social protection economic and financial modelling exercises in Bulgaria, Slovakia, Thailand, and Turkey. Between 1995 and 1998, he served as social security specialist in the ILO's multidisciplinary advisory team for Central and Eastern Europe in Budapest, with responsibility for social security projects in the region, including Social Budget modelling projects in Lithuania, Poland, Slovakia and Ukraine. From 1998, he has been senior social security statistician in the Financial, Actuarial and Statistical Branch of the ILO's Social Security Department, with responsibilities covering the ILO International Inquiry into the costs of social security, social protection accounting and budgeting. He writes on various economic issues in social security, particularly on problems related to the transition countries of Central and Eastern Europe.

LIST OF ACRONYMS

CEE	Central and Eastern Europe
CPI	Consumer price index
ESSPROS	European System of Integrated Social Protection Statistics
EU	European Union
Eurostat	Statistical Office of the European Communities
GAP	General average premium
GDP	Gross domestic product
GNI	Gross national income
GNP	Gross national product
ILO	International Labour Organization
NDP	Net domestic product
NHS	National Health Service
NPISH	Non-profit institutions serving households
NSSI	National Social Security Institute
OECD	Organisation for Economic Co-operation and Development
PAYG	Pay-as-you-go
PSRE	Past service reference earnings
RoR	Rate of return
SAIL	Social assistance intervention line
SAM	Social accounting matrix
SAS	Social accounting system
SNA	System of National Accounts
TFR	Total fertility rate
UF	Unemployment Fund
UIF	Unemployment Insurance Fund
UNDP	United Nations Development Programme
UNICEF	United Nations Children's Fund

PART I

OVERVIEW

WHERE DO WE WANT TO GO?

1

Social protection is a major item in total public spending. As such it faces constant political challenges. In the domain of globalized mainstream thinking, it has become equated with an obstacle to flexibility and a cost factor of production that limits income growth rather than enhances it.

Not surprisingly, in many countries there are concerns that the sheer aggregate amount of expenditure on existing social protection programmes is too high to be economically sustainable, or that their present moderate volume might outgrow economic possibilities in the near or distant future owing to system-inherent expansionary forces. Some countries have retained social security at relatively low levels for a long time – giving priority to (normally insufficient) individual private measures. Many countries have limited social protection to those better off in the formal sector – leaving further social protection against possible life contingencies to the "extended family". In such cases, social protection tends to be rather for the "haves" than for the "have nots".

Yet, there is renewed evidence – proved by developments in many countries – that economic success cannot be maintained over long periods, even when initially launched successfully, if not bolstered by reliable and sound social protection systems which redistribute a meaningful amount of the nationally produced income. The failure of market capitalism – many years ago in Africa, in the late 1990s in Southeast Asia, repeatedly in Latin America, and in recent years increasingly in the Russian Federation – is more and more related to a growing ignorance of fundamental regulatory requirements of market economies, in which substantial social protection is a prominent element.

One of the major reasons why social protection was in the past increasingly regarded as an obstacle to higher growth – a destabilizer rather than a stabilizer – was the fact that many governments seriously mismanaged the finances of social protection systems that were initially well designed.

Whatever the economic, societal, cultural and political positioning of social protection in a country may be, a rational discussion about its scope and future

3

direction, and its actual and potential stabilizing influence on general economic developments, is only possible if that discussion can be based on sound quantitative information about the past and possible future progress of social protection expenditure and revenue.

Governments continuously face the need to adapt their social protection systems to ever-changing economic, demographic and social environments. This applies to governments in the established industrialized economies facing globalization and demographic challenges, countries still in transition in Central and Eastern Europe, Asian and Latin American countries in structural adjustment processes, and developing countries in Asia, Oceania and Africa. The role of governments and parastatal agencies is more and more often challenged, and their spending is subjected to critical scrutiny.

In addition, almost everywhere social transfers account for an increasing share of gross domestic product (GDP), and social spending is often among the largest single expenditure items in government budgets. More than ever, governments need to develop steering mechanisms for the social sector to make sure that scarce resources are allocated where they are most needed. One prerequisite for developing a system of governance for the social sector is to know what the present overall level of expenditure is, where monies are spent, where needs are unmet, and how the overall national social expenditure and the financial burden for the different financiers of the systems (employers, workers and the government) would develop under different economic scenarios and under different reform options. Social budgeting, which comprises a clear social accounting and a meaningful projection system, is – or better, should be – one of the factual bases for national social policy.

1.1   TWO QUESTIONS

Before the central objectives of this book are presented, two key questions should be answered:

- What is social budgeting?
- Why do countries need social budgeting?

1.1.1   What is social budgeting?

Social budgeting consists of two basic components. The first is the statistical basis, i.e. the methodologically consistent compilation of the revenues and expenditures of a country's social protection system. We call this component the *social accounting system* (SAS). The second is the forecast of income and expenditure (budget projection), normally for a medium-term period, and/or simulations of social expenditures and revenues under alternative economic, demographic and/or legislative assumptions. This component is called the *Social Budget*. We use this notion in a comprehensive way. It comprises all analytical and interpretative work centred around the SAS *plus* its transformation into a concrete mathematical model application. Social budgeting is a critical aspect of the overall government budgeting and mid- to long-term planning process. A full round of social budgeting is completed when (a) the SAS has been established, *and* (b) the projection has been carried out and interpreted.

By its structure, the Social Budget is not a classical institutional (government) budget. Its SAS part, which defines the basic table structures for the statistical presentation and for the projection results, acts as an accounting concept for compiling the flows of funds of the *totality of all social programmes*. It is compatible with the one used by the European Union (EU) and its member countries which, at regular intervals, compile total national social expenditure and its revenue. Hence, a Social Budget encompasses social expenditure and income (which may or may not be legally earmarked to cover social expenditure) of independent social institutions as well as at all levels of government. Also, private sector transfers to private households are included in the Social Budget as long as they comply with certain characteristics attributed to the word "social", for example, if publicly mandated.[1] The exact contents of national Social Budgets might vary from country to country, depending on the traditional organization of national social protection systems, as well as the range of benefits offered. However, there are core elements which are represented in all national Social Budgets. On the expenditure side, these core elements include, among others:

- employment-related social security expenditure on:
  - pensions (by different institutions and/or the government)
  - health care
  - unemployment benefits
- publicly financed social protection expenditure on:
  - family benefits
  - health care
  - social assistance
  - tax benefits (e.g. tax rate reductions because of children)
- private sector/collective agreements based on social protection expenditure on:
  - occupational pensions
  - other enterprise-based social benefits.

A systematic classification will be introduced in Part II.

The income side accounts for all resources used to finance the above expenditure. The most important are social security contributions, taxes (whether general or earmarked; whether imposed by central, regional and/or local governments) and investment income. This Social Budget is first of all an accounting summary of the past and expected financial status of a pluralistic social benefit delivery system.

1.1.2 Why do countries need social budgeting?

Depending on their state of development, countries redistribute between 5 and 30 per cent of GDP through national social protection systems. All these systems are income redistribution systems of potentially vast dimensions; they place financial burdens on the financiers, for they collect social security contributions or taxes, and they transform these burdens into cash income (social assistance, sick pay or pensions) or in-kind transfers (social assistance, social or health services) to private households (the beneficiaries).

This redistribution has a fundamental impact on income distribution, the level and structure of production and its costs, the government budget, and the level and allocation of aggregate demand, hence on the economic behaviour of financiers and beneficiaries and therefore on economic and social development itself. Social protection systems can pull people out of poverty (such as those left without sufficient means of income or without means to earn their own income) and can prevent them from falling into poverty. They support, for example, elderly people who retired from work and who depend on an old-age pension as income, or people who are chronically ill and who have to have medical care provided. Social protection systems provide persons temporarily and involuntarily out of work with income, and they may also protect those who are generally in need of income support. In all such cases, social protection can alleviate a variety of hardships and/or guarantee individual participation in a country's overall income, even if the person no longer participates in the income-generation process.

Social protection systems also support economic growth through a positive impact on factor productivity, as in the preservation of social peace, a positive impact on workers' health, early retirement schemes or rationalization effects of prevailing financing provisions. At the same time, these systems might have detrimental effects on economic performance. High labour costs (caused, among other things, by high social security contributions), if not compensated by high labour productivity, may cause a compression of the demand for labour. Inconsistent provisions for legal contribution and tax rates can result in perverse marginal rates and, thus, contribute to an informalization of the workforce or segments of it. The effect of such impacts is different in all economies and is often subject to extensive theoretical debate. But, however circumstantial the evidence might be in specific cases, there is little doubt that the social protection system as a whole has a profound effect on any country's social fabric and economic performance. The aim of all policy should be to maximize the positive social and economic impacts and minimize the negative side effects of social protection systems.

Finding a proper balance between the positive impacts and the negative side effects is a matter of values and priorities, and of economic and cultural effects. There can be no general rule as to how a system should be designed. Independently of the system design and the level of protection, however, administrative systems with a fundamental impact on economic and social developments need to be planned and operated prudently. One of the most powerful tools for the quantitative management of a national social protection system is social budgeting.

Social budgeting serves two main purposes. *It is (a) part of the general social policy planning process and (b) part of any meaningful medium-term financial planning process.* Social budgeting is thus a macro device in national financial planning. National financial planning, which is essentially the attempt to reconcile public and semi-public expenditure with tax and contribution revenues, is an indispensable part of responsible governance in any society under any economic system.

Social budgeting supports the political decision-making process at the increasingly sensitive intersection between social policy and national financial planning. It allows:

- the evaluation of how the social protection system, in terms of its finances, behaved in the past in comparison to macroeconomic and general government budget developments;

- a description of how the present system of social protection would behave in financial terms in the future if the provisions governing the financing and benefit expenditure did not change (status quo projections); this would force decision-makers to define what level of expenditure, and hence social protection, they want the country to afford. It would provide indications on how to assess whether the present system could be maintained in the light of assumed future demographic and economic developments, and

  - if so, which funds have to be set aside at which time by which financiers to finance them, and

  - if not, to identify social subsystems which would need adjustments to avert potential financial and social problems;

- the exploration, by way of simulations, of which modifications of present financing and benefit provisions might help to improve the financial performance, or alter the social and economic impact of the social protection system as a whole or of its subsystems; simulations are most powerful tools of policy support, as such modifications cannot generally be tested in the real world without taking major social and financial risks.

As mentioned, the social protection system as a redistributive system collects money from some economic actors (employees, employers, other tax- and contribution-paying individuals or institutions/enterprises) and allocates it in the form of a generally complex and multifaceted benefit (in cash or in kind) delivery system to defined recipient population subgroups. A social budgeting model[2] describes the main quantitative characteristics of this redistribution in systematic terms and consolidates the effects in the form of accounts. A model is thus a systematic, often simplified but sometimes complicated, mapping of a complex real system of relations between different financial entities.

Without such systematization and consolidation, social protection and national financial planning are prone to errors and inconsistencies. If, for example, a government wished to change the retirement age for its active population, it would not suffice – as is regrettably often done – to reduce the cost of old-age pensions in order to assess the financial impact on the pension system. While the likely effect on the labour market is much discussed and often used to oppose such a measure, other second-round effects are hardly ever fully evaluated in quantitative terms. In reality, a mono-dimensional measure such as increased retirement ages triggers off a series of second-round indirect effects. Total employment might or might not react to the change in the retirement age. If it does not, then unemployment benefit expenditure will increase, as well as expenditure levels of social assistance, housing and tax benefits. Health insurance and unemployment insurance contributions, on the other hand, might be positively affected (owing to the partial or total replacement of young low-level contributors by older high-level earners). The number of invalidity pensioners might increase. What might first look like a positive reduction of expenditure in one branch of social security might be (partially, fully or more than) offset by increases in other branches, or be reinforced by interdependent effects in other branches. It might still leave the government with an increasing share of the overall financing of social protection, as tax-financed benefits (housing, social assistance, etc.) might increase as contribution-financed benefits are reduced. As modelling means delving into a comprehensive understanding of the interdependent operations of a system, a well-designed Social Budget model may give early warnings concerning what should be expected in case of legislative changes.

1.2   CONTENTS AND CENTRAL OBJECTIVE OF THIS BOOK

In *Part II* we describe a conceptual framework for design options of an SAS. This framework addresses methodological proposals as to how a country's social protection system can be conceptualized as an accounting system on the basis of the prevailing institutional, organizational and financial structures. This part is as hard reading as are all accounting handbooks. However, it cannot be avoided. No meaningful financial model of any institution can be built without a clear understanding of the definitions of its flows of funds. *Part III* shows how the relationships between the economy and the social protection system can be translated into a pragmatic quantitative model which allows projection and simulation of national social expenditure and revenues under status quo conditions, alternative economic scenarios and possibly alternative social policy options.[3] *Part IV* explains two concrete country applications.

The central objective of this book is to provide social policy planners with a pragmatic reference for the social budgeting process. It should thus be read as a self-contained "How to build a Social Budget guidebook", with the aim of providing guidelines to a quantitative social protection expert on how to build an SAS and how to use this in social budgeting. Reference should be made to the "Issues brief" (Annex I) on interdependencies between the economy and the social sector in order to support a proper understanding of such relationships in a model. However, the "Issues brief" cannot replace a complete textbook on the economics of social security. This has been provided elsewhere.[4] The focus of this book is on the concrete creation of Social Budgets as an operational tool of governance. Figure 1.1 provides a road map of activities for readers who want to establish a Social Budget model for their country. Each step in the social budgeting process is mirrored by the relevant chapters in the book (depicted by the shaded areas in the boxes). Thus, the road map to the establishment of a Social Budget is at the same time a road map to reading this book.

After perusal of this volume, readers should be able to establish with some confidence a national social accounting system and a Social Budget model. They should be able to simulate the financial effects of alternative social protection policy strategies, ranging from changes in retirement ages to changes in social insurance financing patterns or in benefit eligibility criteria. In a nutshell, they should be able to establish a set of quantitative information for policy makers which would all culminate in the compilation of a summary such as given in table 1.1.

The table shows a short-term forecast of a Social Budget in a typical middle-income country. The social budgeting specialist in that country, which has fairly low social expenditure when measured as a percentage of GDP, could indicate to the government, for example, that the social protection sector's required income from general revenue is growing faster than GDP. This might have negative impacts on the financial equilibrium of the government budget. As a consequence, the government might want to deploy some expenditure consolidation measures which would contain overall or specific expenditure in the medium-term future. On the other hand, the social sector specialist might want to alert the government to the fact that the present anti-poverty benefits only consume a tiny percentage of GDP, which might be inappropriate given the level of poverty in the country. A proper social expenditure exercise would permit very detailed analysis of each of the lines in the summary table. The pension component, for example, would reveal the number of present and future contributors, the number and structure of pensioners, insured wages by age, pensions by age and sex of the recipients, and so on. The level of detail in each component of an overall Social Budget has to be sufficient to

Figure 1.1   The road map to establishing a Social Budget

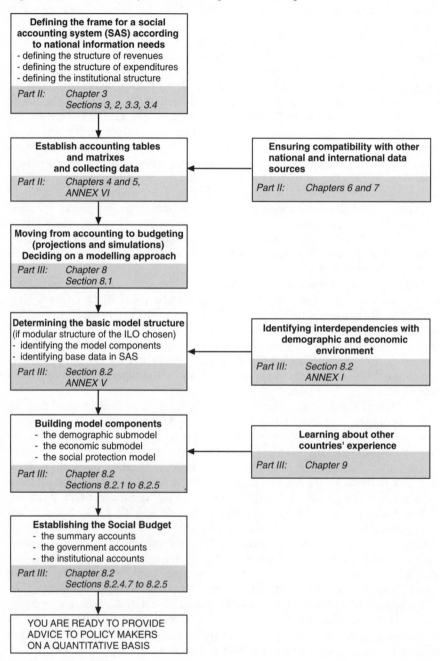

Table 1.1 A typical summary of a national Social Budget

Item	1995	1996	1997	1998	1999	2000
	% of nominal GDP					
Expenditure						
1. Pensions	3.4	3.6	3.7	3.9	4.1	4.3
1.1. Pension insurance benefits	3.3	3.5	3.6	3.8	4.0	4.2
1.1.1. Old-age pensions	2.6	2.8	2.9	3.0	3.2	3.4
1.1.2. Invalidity pensions	0.1	0.1	0.1	0.1	0.1	0.1
1.1.3. Survivors' pensions	0.4	0.4	0.4	0.5	0.5	0.5
1.1.4. Orphans' pensions	0.2	0.2	0.2	0.2	0.2	0.2
1.1.5. Grants	0.0	0.0	0.0	0.0	0.0	0.0
1.2. Administration	0.1	0.1	0.1	0.1	0.1	0.1
2. Unemployment expenditure	0.0	0.0	0.1	0.1	0.1	0.1
3. Short-term benefit expenditure	0.2	0.2	0.2	0.2	0.2	0.2
4. Social assistance expenditure	0.3	0.2	0.2	0.2	0.2	0.2
5. Health expenditure	4.2	4.3	4.3	4.4	4.5	4.6
6. Social expenditure on military personnel	0.8	0.7	0.7	0.7	0.7	0.7
7. Other social benefit expenditure	1.2	1.1	1.1	1.2	1.2	1.2
8. Change of reserves	–	0.4	0.5	0.6	0.4	0.3
Total	**10.0**	**10.6**	**10.8**	**11.3**	**11.4**	**11.6**
Revenue						
1. Social insurance contributions	2.5	2.8	2.8	2.9	2.9	3.0
1.1. Pension scheme	2.0	2.0	1.9	2.0	2.0	2.0
1.2. Health scheme	0.6	0.6	0.6	0.6	0.7	0.7
1.3. Unemployment scheme	0.0	0.3	0.3	0.3	0.3	0.3
2. Other income (including imputed contributions)	2.8	2.7	2.7	2.8	2.8	2.9
3. Investment income	0.0	0.1	0.3	0.4	0.2	0.2
3.1. Pension scheme	0.0	0.0	0.0	0.0	0.0	0.0
3.2. Health scheme	0.0	0.0	0.0	0.0	0.0	0.0
3.3. Short-term benefit scheme	0.0	0.0	0.0	0.0	0.0	0.0
3.4. Unemployment scheme	0.0	0.1	0.3	0.4	0.2	0.2
4. Income from general revenue	4.7	4.9	5.0	5.2	5.4	5.6
Total	**10.0**	**10.6**	**10.8**	**11.3**	**11.4**	**11.6**

Note: Totals may not add up exactly because of rounding.

permit the simulation of alternative policies and to satisfyingly explain the results. In the pension case, contributors and pensioners have to be displayed by individual ages, and age- and sex-specific pension amounts. Otherwise the analyst would not be able to simulate and explain, for example, the effects of a reduction or an increase of the pension age, which normally differs for men and women.

Modelling is a process rather than an event. Models change constantly and continually have to be adapted to national circumstances. No two Social Budgets for two different countries look completely alike in their SAS and projection parts. The structures, objectives and modes of operation of national social protection systems, their economies and labour markets are normally too different to be "squeezed" into one concrete single model structure. Some aspects could simply be irrelevant ("missing the point") or relevant aspects might be lacking for a reader with a specific country's background. That is why in Part III we only outline broad modelling techniques, sometimes relatively concrete, sometimes rather abstract. Still, we assume there is considerable material left to trigger inspiration for solving concrete modelling problems.

In any case, interested readers might wish to contact the Financial, Actuarial and Statistical Branch of the ILO's Social Security Department for copies of the latest ILO generic version of a *Social Budget model*, including the latest version of the accompanying technical guide. They might then take the version described as a basis for the development of a specific national model. The provision of the model and the manual is a service of the ILO to its constituents and is free of charge.

Notes

[1] See Annex III, "Glossary of the social accounting system", Section 4, "Expenditures by social function".

[2] For example, the ILO's Social Budget Model. There are other examples.

[3] Considerations on basic interdependencies between economic and social protection system developments have been added to Annex I, "Issues brief".

[4] See, for example: Nicholas Barr: *The economics of the welfare state* (London, Weidenfeld and Nicolson, 2nd edition, 1993).

PART II

DESIGNING A SOCIAL ACCOUNTING SYSTEM

INTRODUCTION

2

The availability of a social accounting system (SAS) is an indispensable part of the data basis required for a Social Budget model. It comprises the flow of funds data of the social protection system as observed in the past, systematically and consistently processed under a unified methodology that allows for structural analyses at a certain point of time, for time series analyses and for meaningful international comparisons. The SAS is one statistical basis for social budgeting.

Processing data means shaping past observed reality. Understanding the past depends on how the data are presented. The following chapters propose several possibilities of structuring available information. Ideally, the statistical data bank of a Social Budget should be organized so that it allows for each proposed approach.

In making different proposals, we try to offer a range of equivalent options. It is the users' choice as to which proposal (or group of proposals) they prefer and, thus, realize in a concrete country application. Among other things, this will depend on the available statistical information, on the "statistical tradition" of a country, on its political stability and so on.

In Part II the reader will learn that there are some trade-offs between the information content and the details of the SAS. It is well known that a too-detailed presentation of data may be "hiding" as much information as data that are presented only on a highly aggregate level. One presentation might be as much an obstacle to political decisions as the other. Therefore, all data-processing proposals aim at some degree of disaggregation. If, in special cases, more detailed information were required for modelling purposes, then reverting to the source database would be advisable.

The design of an SAS and, thus, a Social Budget depends on its purposes, which may be manifold. Initially, the SAS is a tool of governance for planning, monitoring and analysing social policy decisions at macro levels. It is a comprehensive formal account of the revenues and the expenditures of the social protection system of a country. Such an account is not an end in itself. For it serves many purposes as an information basis for a country's government, its general public, its politicians, its economic actors (for example, employers and employees), the social protection system's beneficiaries, the taxpayers, its scientific institutions and others who all might use the same information for different purposes. They might want to evaluate the social protection system's financial flows in an economic context; they might want to know about the existing social security institutions' relative sizes in terms of their aggregate expenditures; they might want to know about the structure of social protection expenditures and their financing, for instance, how much of total resources goes into different programmes and what is the relative weight of different revenue sources. All these issues might be addressed vertically, for a certain year, or horizontally, under a dynamic time perspective. And, last but not least, the addressees of this information might want to use it for international comparisons.

Given its basic character as a tool of governance and information, it is hoped that the implementation of an SAS serves to enhance rationality in public discussions on social protection, and supports the government in taking reasonable decisions on future social protection legislation by taking into account the aspirations and needs of the general public, as well as future financial and economic constraints.

As the potential different users of an SAS normally might want to address different aspects of the social protection system, it is advisable to clarify from the beginning that an SAS, whatever its final set-up might be, reflects just one, though an important, aspect of a social protection system, which is its fiscal flows of funds, disaggregated by different categories. Therefore, an SAS primarily provides information to those who are interested in a detailed financial picture of the social protection system in a macroeconomic and macrofinancial context. An SAS does not address microsocial or microeconomic issues. Important questions, such as adequacy of individual benefit levels, equity of benefit provisions, equivalence between individual contributions paid and benefits received, the impact of social expenditures and their financing on individual private households' income distribution, and many other questions will have to be investigated by using other sources of information. Still, such issues might only be addressed satisfyingly if seen in an SAS context. Furthermore, a comprehensive interpretation of the results of an SAS can be accomplished only if such micro and other structural and legal information is also taken into account. In fact, it will be seen later in this book that abundant information on micro issues is required when aiming at sensible projections of the Social Budget on the basis of the SAS.

Having set its scope and limits, the design of an SAS should be based on the following principles:

2.1 BASIC GUIDELINES FOR THE FORMAL CONSTRUCTION OF A SOCIAL ACCOUNTING SYSTEM (SAS)

1. The SAS should be designed so that it allows for methodologically prudent links to other information systems, most importantly the *System of*

National Accounts (SNA) which is in use worldwide as a methodological basis for the compilation of national accounts.

2. The SAS statistical scope should cover the social protection system in a comprehensive and significant manner:

- with respect to comprehensiveness: it should include *all* social expenditures (and their related revenues) irrespective of their sources of financing; and

- with respect to significance: it should only cover *social* expenditures; private voluntary provisions not financed on a mandatory basis, joining which is the individual's choice, should not be included (private savings accounts, life insurance).

3. The SAS should reflect "conventional a priori wisdom" of possibilities as to how to structure social protection finances; thus revenues should either reflect the payments to the institutions of the system by legal categories (employers, employees, government, others) or categorize revenues by their economic "sources" (enterprises, private households, the public sector, others) or both, and expenditures should be presented by all institutions administering the system, or by the social "functions" of the benefit provisions, or both.

4. The SAS design should allow for international comparisons. (Such "methodological pragmatism" is essential in order to guarantee this.)

These four guidelines may seem very abstract to readers who have not been involved before in social and/or national accounting. National accounts specialists will probably be able to immediately understand some of the points made. Others, even readers with some advanced methodological knowledge, would need further in-depth explanations.

This chapter aims at a comprehensive methodological step-by-step explanation of how an SAS could be designed most rationally, taking into account the four guidelines. In order to support the reader's understanding, a *Glossary* of the SAS will be found in Annex III. It might be helpful to refer to these definitions from time to time.

Two important aspects should be noted here. The first is a caveat. Methodological explanations and definitions, especially when written in an international perspective, tend to produce the dilemma of being either too abstract or too concrete. The advantage of abstractness is that such definitions and explanations may cover realities in a maximum of countries. Its disadvantage is that some readers might find it difficult to apply such definitions and explanations to their own concrete country case because they lack significance. This problem could be avoided by being as concrete as possible in the set-up of definitions. But a drawback could then be that readers might miss their own issues because they were not specifically addressed. Then, again, the application of definitions would be difficult in a country-specific context. In this chapter, we try to find a median solution in order to avoid definitions that are too abstract or too concrete.

The second point is that readers who are acquainted with the methods and definitions of the SNA will realize that many of the following methodological explanations and definitions with respect to the SAS resemble equivalent aspects of national accounting, with one exception, which is the proposed *functional* structure of the SAS. While abundant statistical information required for setting up an SAS can usually be found in the national accounts, this is most often not the case for the functional breakdown. In fact, international experience in those countries which have developed an SAS (most notably, the EU member States) shows that the functional breakdown of their respective accounts is a "specificity" which distinguishes the information contents of the SAS from the information as contained in the national accounts.

METHODOLOGY AND DATABASE

3

3.1 STANDARD CLASSIFICATIONS OF REVENUE AND EXPENDITURE

Setting up the database for a Social Budget, the SAS, is not as simple as it might seem at first glance. The basic problem is to define a meaningful set of categories of incomes and outlays which describes, under identical headings, the differing revenue and expenditure items of different institutions. These identical headings, on the one hand, have to allow for a reasonable and in-depth interpretation of the results of the SAS (and the Social Budget) but, on the other hand, must not be too detailed in order to maintain a significant degree of explanatory potential. In principle, the possibilities of categorization range from the most detailed information as reflected, for example, by the single budget lines of the government or the social security accounts to the most aggregate information, which would be total social expenditures or total revenues of that institution. Thus, in order to keep the data basis of the Social Budget manageable, a degree of categorization has to be found somewhere in the middle of these two extremes.

For a more profound understanding of this issue, look at tables 3.1 and 3.2. They reflect the revenue (3.1) and expenditure (3.2) items as they were included in the institutional budgets of the Bulgarian National Social Security Institute (NSSI) and the Bulgarian Unemployment Fund (UF) in 1996.

When trying to set up an SAS on the basis of this information, a number of problems arise, for example:

- Obviously the number of budget lines of the NSSI and the UF are different. On the revenue side, the NSSI budget distinguishes 29 different items, the UF only 12 (totals and subtotals not counted). On the expenditure side, the NSSI budget comprises 63 lines, the UF 42.

- On the revenue side, the main reason for these vast differences is that the NSSI contributions are much more differentiated than those of the UF, and that the NSSI receives transfers on many more grounds than the UF.

Table 3.1 Revenue budget lines of the Bulgarian National Social Security Institute (NSSI) and the national Unemployment Fund (UF), 1996

Revenue NSSI	Revenue UF

1. Social security revenue
  1.1 Employers' contributions
  1.2 Employees' contributions
  1.3 Contributions from self-employed
  1.4 Employers' contributions for work injury
  1.5 Additional contributions (Decree 35/1982)
  1.6 Contributions for working pensioners
  1.7 Fines and interest
2. Other revenues
  2.1 Payments from public enterprises
  2.2 Interest income on bank deposits
  2.3 Liquidation of shares
  2.4 Bonuses
  2.5 Dividends and donations
  2.6 Carry-over from the previous year
3. Received transfers
  3.1 Transfers from the privatization fund
  3.2 Subsidies (deficit coverage) by the State
  3.3 Reimbursements from the State and other public institutions
    3.3.1 Social security contributions
    3.3.2 Pension payments under articles 6 and 7 of the Pension Law
    3.3.3 NSSI war veteran pension payments
    3.3.4 State war veteran pension payments
    3.3.5[1] COOP war veteran pension payments
    3.3.6 Child-birth lump-sum payments
    3.3.7 Payment of child supplements on wages
    3.3.8 Payment of child supplements on NSSI pensions
    3.3.9 Payment of child supplements on State pensions
    3.3.10 Payment of child supplements on COOP pensions
    3.3.11 Payment of allowances to disabled children
    3.3.12 Reimbursement of COOP pensions
4. Temporary interest-free cash loans
  4.1 From the UF
  4.2 From other institutions
  4.3 From the state budget
	1. Employers' contributions
	2. Other revenues
	  2.1 Fines for violation of the Labour Law
	  2.2 Tax on work permits for foreigners
	  2.3 Grants
	3. Received interest on bank deposits
	4. Received budget transfers
	  4.1 For laid-off state employees
	  4.2 For young specialists and qualified workers
	  4.3 For child supplements on unemployment benefits
	5. Carry-over from the previous year
	6. Repayment of temporary interest-free cash loans
	  6.1 To the Ministry of Education
	  6.2 To the Ministry of Health
	  6.3 To the NSSI

[1] Social security fund of the rural cooperatives.

Table 3.2 Expenditure budget lines of the Bulgarian National Social Security Institute (NSSI) and the national Unemployment Fund (UF), 1996

Expenditure NSSI	Expenditure UF
1. Administration cost	1. Unemployment benefits
1.1 Central directorate	1.1 Paid to laid-off state employees
1.1.1 Salaries	2. Unemployment assistance for young
1.1.2 Social security contributions	specialists and qualified workers
1.1.3 Scholarships	3. Child benefits for unemployed persons
1.1.4 Support	3.1 Child allowances
1.1.4.1 Food	3.2 Other allowances
1.1.4.2 Medicines	5. Retraining measures for employed and
1.1.4.3 Business travel	unemployed persons
1.1.4.4 Office and business expenditure	6. Employment creation programmes
1.1.4.5 Bedding and clothing	7. Employment promotion measures
1.1.4.6 Education and research	7.1 Subsidies on interest payments
1.1.4.7 Repairs	7.2 Job-placement measures for young
1.1.4.8 Other expenditures	people
1.2 Regional offices	7.3 Promotion of entrepreneurship
1.2.1 Salaries	7.4 Promotion of part-time work
1.2.2 Social security contributions	8. Reimbursement of travel expenses for
1.2.3 Scholarships	unemployed persons
1.2.4 Support	9. Wage subsidies for employment of disabled
1.2.4.1 Food	persons
1.2.4.2 Medicines	10. Administration cost
1.2.4.3 Business travel	10.1 Wages
1.2.4.4 Office and business expenditure	10.2 Social security contributions
1.2.4.5 Bedding and clothing	10.3 Business travel
1.2.4.6 Education and research	10.4 Office maintenance
1.2.4.7 Repairs	10.5 Staff qualification measures
1.2.4.8 Other expenditures	10.6 Equipment
1.3 Health prevention and recreation	10.7 Repairs
1.3.1 Salaries	10.8 Clothing
1.3.2 Social security contributions	10.9 Other activities
1.3.3 Support	10.9.1 Social assistance for personnel
1.3.3.1 Business travel	10.9.2 Conferences and seminars
1.3.3.2 Office and business expenditure	10.9.3 External collaborators
1.3.3.3 Bedding and clothing	10.9.4 Guests
1.3.3.4 Educational and research	10.9.5 Payments under articles 222 and 224
expenditure	of the Labour Code
1.3.3.5 Acquisition of long-term assets	10.9.6 Additional staff expenditures
1.3.3.6 Repairs	10.9.7 Social contributions on payments
1.3.3.7 Other expenditures	under budget line 10.9.6
1.3.3.8 Health prevention	11. International agreements on labour force
2. Social security and welfare	exchange
2.1 Pensions	12. Labour market research expenditures
2.1.1 NSSI pensions	13. Investments
2.1.2 Pensions under articles 6 and 7 of the	14. Measures to improve the implementation of
Pension Law	labour legislation
2.1.3 Supplements to NSSI pensions for	14.1 Staff qualification measures
children and war veterans	14.2 Technical equipment for labour
2.1.4 Supplements to state pensions for	legislation monitoring
war veterans	15. Other expenditure

Table 3.2 Continued

Expenditure NSSI	Expenditure UF
2.1.5 Supplements to COOP pensions for war veterans	16. Transfers to the Promotion of Entrepreneurship Fund
2.1.6 COOP pensions	17. Temporary interest-free loans
2.1.7 Flat-rate emergency pension to each pensioner	17.1 To the NSSI
	17.2 To the Ministry of Education
2.2 Allowances under section III of the Labour Code	17.3 To the Ministry of Health
2.2.1 Sickness compensation	18. Advertisements, publications
2.2.2 Compensation for injuries at home	19. Further payments
2.2.3 Compensation for caring for a sick person	20. Other paid transfers
2.2.4 Compensation for occupational diseases	21. Development support to the national tobacco industry
2.2.5 Wage differences in special cases	22. Promotion of youth employment
2.2.6 Maternity benefits	
2.2.7 Wage differences for pregnant women	
2.2.8 Payments for taking care of a small child	
2.2.9 Death benefits	
2.2.10 Reimbursement of purchased orthopaedic devices	
2.2.11 Payments for persons being on a special diet	
2.3 Decree on increasing the birth rate	
2.3.1 Childbirth lump-sum payments	
2.3.2 Child benefits	
2.3.2.1 On wages	
2.3.2.2 On NSSI pensions	
2.3.2.3 On state pensions	
2.3.2.4 On COOP pensions	
2.4 Payments for disabled children	
2.5 Other social security expenditures	
2.6 Contributions to national and international organizations	
3. Acquisition of long-term assets	
3.1 Central directorate	
3.2 Regional offices	
4. Repayment of temporary interest-free cash loans	
4.1 To the UF	
4.2 To other institutions	
4.3 To the State	

- Not surprisingly, the paid benefits differ very much with respect to their social policy purpose. The NSSI covers pensioners and persons actively employed, while the UF covers the unemployed and the potentially unemployed.

- The differences between the two institutions have to be considered in a time perspective. With respect to most of its expenditure items, the NSSI is historically based on a long-standing and well-established spending structure, whereas the UF is a new institution.

Setting up an SAS under these conditions means to "invent" a robust methodological framework (classification) that allows for a meaningful economic and social interpretation of the structure and development of the finances of the NSSI and the UF, aggregate or separate, at a given point of time and/or over longer periods (as time series), over the past or projected into the future. In other words, some identical categorization has to be found for different budget lines, guaranteeing not only reasonable comparison of different institutions but also methodological stability over time. Time stability of definitions is especially important for a successful set-up of an accounting system such as the SAS. Without wishing to overemphasize the Bulgarian example, it is worthwhile mentioning that the country, like many of its neighbours in the region, was still in the process of separating budgetary institutions in 1996, most notably making social security institutionally independent. Not surprisingly, the new budget structures were still lacking stability: they were prone to "erratic" changes from year to year. Furthermore, both institutions might have to change their respective expenditure structures considerably in terms of relative amounts paid – the NSSI because it has to adapt its benefits to market economy conditions, and the UF because it has to react to the possibly changing labour market developments in Bulgaria. Such possibilities clearly call for a stable methodological SAS framework that is widely independent of changes. But other, non-transition countries might also be in the process of reforming their social protection systems, requiring new budget structures from time to time, and thus the headings and number of institutional budget lines might change over time because of changes in social protection legislation. As, in the context of a classical institutional budget, such changes make sense (just *because* they reflect changes in legislation), they might, at the level of abstraction of a Social Budget (SAS), still belong to identical categories of expenditure or revenue.

In order to be able to respond easily to these and other related problems, it has proved to be good statistical practice to introduce so-called *types of revenue* and *types of expenditure*. These *data types* represent the smallest data category of revenues and expenditures used for the compilation of an SAS. In other words, these data types are the basis for setting up the SAS from different points of view. There are:

- revenue by:
  - legal category
  - sources

and

- expenditure by:
  - economic category
  - function

The data types are also necessary in order to "institutionalize" the SAS. In doing so, the methodology used draws heavily (but not solely) on the methodology as developed for the SNA. It will later become obvious that a full understanding of all statistical and methodological aspects of an SAS might only be achieved when accompanied by a simultaneous understanding of important features of the SNA. An understanding of the SNA methodology not only facilitates access to an understanding of the SNA-related methodological similarities of an SAS but also helps to comprehend those aspects of an SAS that might distinguish it from the information provided by the SNA. It should be stressed that a full understanding of the SAS methodology is not an end in itself, but helps the full understanding of the statistical and projected results of a Social Budget, and avoids misinterpretations of such information. For the reasons, Part II will be completed by a chapter on some essential features of the SNA (see Chapter 6). In that chapter we focus on those SNA aspects that are directly or indirectly of importance for a full understanding of social budgeting.

3.1.1 Types of revenue

A possible list of types of revenue might comprise the following categories:

List 1: Types of revenue

- *Contributions*
  - Employees' contributions
  - Employers' actual contributions
  - Employers' imputed contributions[1]
  - Beneficiaries' contributions
  - Contributions by self-employed persons
  - Contributions by the government (including parastatal agencies) in lieu of beneficiaries
- *Subsidies*
  - State subsidies to social security institutions for deficit coverage
  - Regular ("formula-bound") state transfers to social security institutions
  - Transfers from international public bodies
  - Tax losses in case of indirect social expenditures ("tax benefits")
  - Other grants from public sources

- *Other revenues*
  - Special fees
  - Other grants
  - Returns on capital investments
  - Other income
- *Offsets*
  - Received offsets (reimbursements) of benefit payments from other institutions

In accordance with international practice and consistent with the SNA methodology, loans and credits are not taken into account.

It is important to note that the "summarizing headers" (in italics) at the top of the above groups of revenue types only intend to support the reader's understanding of their structure. They can serve as a preliminary guide for naming subaggregates of revenues of the Social Budget; but this structure, of course, would have to be designed for each country separately, based on its specific prevailing circumstances.

It should be stressed that the proposed list represents just one possibility out of many. In a specific country, the actual list of types of revenue might include more items or less. This depends on the concrete social protection legislation. For example, some countries have introduced compulsory contributions on benefits (pensioners pay contributions for their health insurance or unemployed persons pay contributions for their health and pension insurance). Others do not have such regulations. Some countries might have "regular" ("formula-bound") transfers from the state budget to the social protection system; others do not. Thus, this list will have to be adjusted accordingly in each concrete country case. Further, the list will depend on envisaged reforms of a country's social protection system. At a certain stage, countries might not have certain revenue items, but might propose to introduce them later; thus, when setting up the SAS methodology, provisions will have to be made accordingly. In summing up, any such list will be country specific, reform dependent and liable to variations over time. Once a country decides to establish a social budgeting routine, it will have to find a methodological and statistical solution which best fits into its own specific legislative situation.[2]

The reader will find comprehensive definitions of the data types as listed, including further explanations, in Annex III.

3.1.2   Types of expenditure

A possible list of types of expenditure might comprise the following items:

List 2: Types of expenditure

- *Pensions*
  - Retirement pensions

- Disability pensions
- Widows' and widowers' pensions
- Orphans' pensions
- Other pensions
- Lump-sum (pension) payments in case of retirement
- Lump-sum (pension) payments for other reasons
- Pensions paid abroad
- Funeral benefits/death benefits

- *Employment*
  - Cash payments in case of occupational training
  - Cash payments in other cases of labour market mobility support
  - Unemployment benefits
  - Other income support in case of unemployment
  - Other labour-market-related expenses

- *Rehabilitation expenses*
  - Cash payments in case of rehabilitation measures
  - Other expenses related to rehabilitation measures

- *Family-related benefits*
  - Child benefits
  - Youth-related expenditures
  - Family supplements on wages
  - Maternity benefits
  - Other family-related payments

- *Health*
  - Direct costs of out-patient (ambulatory) treatment
  - Direct costs of in-patient (hospital) treatment
  - Direct costs of dental treatment
  - Direct costs of dentures
  - Direct costs of pharmaceutical drugs
  - Reimbursements of health costs to private households
  - Reimbursements of health costs incurred abroad
  - Direct costs of public health services
  - Direct costs of other health-related expenses
  - Continued payment of wages in case of sickness

- – Sickness cash benefits
- – Other health-related cash payments
- *Housing*
  - – Rent allowances
  - – Allowances to reduce interest and annuity payments
  - – Tax reductions for owner-occupied dwellings
  - – Other direct or indirect housing-related support
- *Administration*
  - – Wages and salaries paid to persons administering the social protection system
  - – Expenses of the self-governing bodies of the social protection system
  - – Other expenses directly related to the administering of the social protection system
- *Other expenditure types*
  - – Other income-replacement benefits
  - – Other income-support expenses
  - – Costs of social measures
  - – Grants
  - – Other social-protection expenses abroad
- *Offsets*
  - – Paid offsets of institutions' benefit payments

Again, in accordance with international practice and consistent with the methodology of the United Nations SNA, loans and credits are not taken into account.

The reader will find comprehensive definitions of the data types as listed, including further explanations, in Annex III.

Again, the "summarizing headers" (in italics) at the top of the groups of the expenditure types are only intended to help the reader's understanding of their common meaning. Here, they might serve as a preliminary guide for the *functional* expenditure breakdown of the SAS. All other explanations that have been given with respect to the types of revenue are accordingly valid for the types of expenditure.

3.2 STRUCTURING THE REVENUE OF AN SAS

When considering the types of revenue as listed in the previous section, it is obvious that the different data types could, in principle, be grouped in numerous ways. As already indicated, however, there are some obvious ways for their aggregation. In this chapter, we describe two possibilities that have actually been implemented by countries and which have proved to be helpful for the potential users of the information contained in the SAS.

The first possibility describes a method of aggregation which will be familiar to most of the readers of this book. The second possibility is more sophisticated, requires well-established statistical reporting procedures and normally has to draw on estimation techniques.

3.2.1 Revenue by legal category

A well-established aggregation of the types of revenue results from the application of the following systematic nomenclature of revenue by legal category:

List 3: Revenue by legal category

- *Social contributions*
  - Contributions by the insured population
    Employees' contributions
    Contributions by self-employed persons
    Contributions by beneficiaries
    Contributions by other persons
    Contributions paid by public institutions in lieu of beneficiaries
  - Employers' contributions
    Actual contributions
    Imputed contributions
- *Subsidies*
  - Subsidies paid by the government
  - Subsidies paid by other sources
- *Other revenues*
- *Transfers from other institutions*

In order to comply with this nomenclature, each of the types of revenue has to be checked (List 1) to see which of these categories (List 3) it fits best. In many cases, this will be obvious, but in others, the correct placement might not be so clear. Thus a close investigation of the respective legislation would have to be undertaken, which normally helps to find a proper solution. The classification might have to be decided ad hoc in exceptionally few cases.

This structure according to legal categories would be applied to each of the institutions distinguished in the SAS.

The notion social "contribution" is used for any individual payment to a social security institution, be it mandatory or voluntary, of a certain percentage on the individual's income or a flat amount. This is calculated on the basis of the individual's total income, or of only an income bracket individually accounted and directly linked to the individual benefit potentially to be received. In case the contributions constitute a financial pool, thery are still not considered as a tax as long as this payment establishes an individual (sometimes constitutional) right to draw a benefit in case the "insured" contingency occurs. A certain style that has evolved in some economic literature in using "contribution" and "tax" synonymously has been avoided at present in SAS (Social Budget) contexts. Here, tax is understood only as a mandatory payment to the state authorities, not as establishing any well-defined entitlement to benefits.

A distinction between employers' and employees' contributions is to be made on the basis of the legislation, reflecting the obligation of payment. A contribution is called an "employee's contribution" if the legislation so stipulates, as well as if technical arrangements (legal or practical) stipulate that it is the employer *on behalf* of the employee transferring contributions to the social security institution.

Employers' *imputed* contributions have been introduced in order to reflect total labour costs correctly when compiling the primary distribution of gross domestic product (GDP). Assuming that an employer pays certain social benefits to (perhaps former) employees directly out of current business turnover (out of current tax revenue, in case the employer was the State), then no contributions are being levied on individuals' income. Such benefits are still to be regarded as part of the employer's total labour cost and, thus, should not be ignored. Imputed contributions are, of course, estimates. Their estimated level could be based alternatively on the assumption that the respective benefits are fully covered by these contributions on a "notional" pay-as-you-go basis or – in case an equivalent "parallel" system exists which actually collects contributions – the imputed contributions could be calculated according to that parallel system's legal regulations.

Subsidies are all transfers received by social insurance institutions – transfers in their own rights or in order to cover deficits – which effectively reduce the individual contribution rates that otherwise would have to be paid. These may come from the government budget or, for example, from public enterprises. The notion "subsidy" is here used in a broader sense than in the SNA, where "subsidies are current unrequited payments that government units ... make to enterprises ... and to public corporations"[3] in order to reduce prices charged.

Other revenues comprise capital income, fines, and so on, and the item transfers from other institutions reflect payments received from other institutions *within* the SAS framework.

A major advantage of this classification is that it is probably easy for the potential users of the SAS to understand because it reflects well-introduced elements of many countries' social fabric. Lawyers, journalists, politicians, economists and many others interested in the res publica will all have a direct understanding of the level and structure of the revenues of the SAS and the (projected) Social Budget. This information is important with respect to macroeconomic considerations for analyses of impacts of the financing structure of a country's social system on labour costs and on the disposable income of private

Table 3.3 Germany: Revenue of the SAS by legal category, 1960–97

Item	Year										
	1960	1970	1980	1990	1991	1992	1993	1994	1995p	1996p	1997s
Million DM											
Social contributions	39 188	108 690	310 577	521 083	614 982	672 250	699 373	747 626	790 402	819 243	844 410
Paid by the insured	14 727	42 051	124 577	222 469	267 532	294 791	318 091	341 834	364 293	385 655	404 261
– Employees	11 928	32 602	91 155	161 823	194 633	212 902	221 374	236 043	244 381	255 215	265 969
– Self-employed	367	10 050	5 109	8 415	9 178	9 938	10 781	11 713	12 865	13 110	13 699
– Beneficiaries	481	234	551	13 196	13 895	16 699	18 791	21 122	24 065	25 615	27 812
– Other persons	465	2 695	6 638	12 234	12 771	13 695	16 258	17 598	17 224	19 873	20 391
– Via social insurance institutions	1 487	5 469	21 123	26 801	37 054	41 558	50 887	55 357	65 757	71 842	76 390
Paid by the employers	24 461	66 639	—	298 614	347 451	377 459	381 282	405 792	426 109	433 588	440 149
– Actual contributions	15 775	37 602	110 761	189 906	227 405	246 919	257 504	275 214	284 656	293 833	304 352
– Imputed contributions	8 686	29 037	75 239	108 708	120 046	130 539	123 777	130 578	141 453	139 755	135 797
Subsidies	30 267	73 959	177 546	238 339	296 930	333 226	371 255	376 142	390 849	418 850	429 357
From public sources	26 978	68 726	165 761	225 039	282 506	318 051	355 482	364 393	377 499	404 866	415 079
From other sources	3 289	5 233	11 785	13 300	14 424	15 175	15 773	11 749	13 350	13 984	14 278
Other revenue	1 629	3 563	6 777	13 036	16 159	17 524	17 379	16 256	17 346	19 189	20 454
Total	**71 084**	**186 212**	**494 901**	**772 458**	**928 072**	**1 023 000**	**1 088 007**	**1 140 023**	**1 198 596**	**1 257 283**	**1 294 222**
Balancing item	**5 435**	**10 368**	**20 801**	**40 998**	**44 989**	**24 124**	**28 965**	**31 717**	**20 720**	**21 137**	**38 098**
Structure in %											
Social contributions	55.1	58.4	62.8	67.5	66.3	65.7	64.3	65.6	65.9	65.2	65.2
Paid by the insured	20.7	22.6	25.2	28.8	28.8	28.8	29.2	30.0	30.4	30.7	31.2
– Employees	16.8	17.5	18.4	20.9	21.0	20.8	20.3	20.7	20.4	20.3	20.6
– Self-employed	0.5	0.6	1.0	1.1	1.0	1.0	1.0	1.0	1.1	1.0	1.1
– Beneficiaries	0.7	0.1	0.1	1.7	1.5	1.6	1.7	1.9	2.0	2.0	2.1
– Other persons	0.7	1.4	1.3	1.6	1.4	1.3	1.5	1.5	1.4	1.6	1.6
– Via social insurance institutions	2.1	2.9	4.3	3.5	4.0	4.1	4.7	4.9	5.5	5.7	5.9
Paid by the employers	34.4	35.8	37.6	38.7	37.4	36.9	35.0	35.6	35.6	34.5	34.0
– Actual contributions	22.2	20.2	22.4	24.6	24.5	24.1	23.7	24.1	23.7	23.4	23.5
– Imputed contributions	12.2	15.6	15.2	14.1	12.9	12.8	11.4	11.5	11.8	11.1	10.5

Subsidies	42.6	39.7	35.9	30.9	32.0	32.6	34.1	33.0	32.6	33.3	33.2
From public sources	38.0	36.9	33.5	29.1	30.4	31.1	32.7	32.0	31.5	32.2	32.1
From other sources	4.6	2.8	2.4	1.7	1.6	1.5	1.4	1.0	1.1	1.1	1.1
Other revenue	2.3	1.9	1.4	1.7	1.7	1.7	1.6	1.4	1.4	1.5	1.6
Total	**100.0**	**100.0**	**100.0**	**100.0**	**100.0**	**100.0**	**100.0**	**100.0**	**100.0**	**100.0**	**100.0**
Share in GDP in %											
Social contributions	12.9	16.1	21.1	20.7	21.6	21.8	22.1	22.5	22.8	23.1	23.1
Paid by the insured	4.9	6.2	8.5	8.8	9.4	9.6	10.1	10.3	10.5	10.9	11.1
– Employees	3.9	4.8	6.2	6.4	6.8	6.9	7.0	7.1	7.1	7.2	7.3
– Self-employed	0.1	0.2	0.3	0.3	0.3	0.3	0.3	0.4	0.4	0.4	0.4
– Beneficiaries	0.2	0.0	0.0	0.5	0.5	0.5	0.6	0.6	0.7	0.7	0.8
– Other persons	0.2	0.4	0.5	0.5	0.4	0.4	0.5	0.5	0.5	0.6	0.6
– Via social insurance institutions	0.5	0.8	1.4	1.1	1.3	1.3	1.6	1.7	1.9	2.0	2.1
Paid by the employers	8.1	9.9	12.6	11.8	12.2	12.3	12.1	12.2	12.3	12.2	12.0
– Actual contributions	5.2	5.6	7.5	7.5	8.0	8.0	8.1	8.3	8.2	8.3	8.3
– Imputed contributions	2.9	4.3	5.1	4.3	4.2	4.2	3.9	3.9	4.1	3.9	3.7
Subsidies	10.0	11.0	12.1	9.4	10.4	10.8	11.7	11.3	11.3	11.8	11.8
From public sources	8.9	10.2	11.3	8.9	9.9	10.3	11.2	10.9	10.9	11.4	11.4
From other sources	1.1	0.8	0.8	0.5	0.5	0.5	0.5	0.4	0.4	0.4	0.4
Other revenue	0.5	0.5	0.5	0.5	0.6	0.6	0.5	0.5	0.5	0.5	0.6
Total	**23.5**	**27.6**	**33.6**	**30.6**	**32.5**	**33.2**	**34.4**	**34.3**	**34.6**	**35.5**	**35.4**

Notes: p: provisional; s: estimate.
Source: Federal Ministry of Labour and Social Affairs, Germany: *Materialband* [Statistical Annex] to *Deutscher Bundestag: Sozialbericht 1997* [Social Report 1997], Drs. 13/10142 of 17 March 1998. http://www.bma.de.

households. Because of its internationally accepted structure, this classification is probably the least controversial when used in international comparisons of social protection systems.

The definitions of the headers are methodologically linked to the SNA and, again, the reader will find comprehensive definitions and further explanations in Annex III. For example, on an aggregate level (aggregation over all institutions of the SAS), a concrete application could appear as shown in table 3.3, which provides an overview of the revenue of the German SAS by legal categories. The same structure of information exists for all 30 institutions presently included in the German SAS over a period of almost 40 years and thus builds a solid basis for (a) the empirical analysis of labour market and economic impacts on the revenue side of the system in the past, (b) its reaction to changes in legislation, and (c) the formulation of hypotheses on its future developments under assumed labour market, economic and legal developments (modelling). Apart from being helpful for modelling, this long-time series provides statistical in-depth information on the history of post-war social policies in Germany. One aspect, which is the significant increase of the share of employers' and employees' contributions in total revenue between 1960 and 1998, might be especially highlighted, as the constantly growing unemployment rate has been attributed by many observers to this change in the financing structure of the German social protection system, as it has contributed to growing labour costs.

3.2.2 Revenue by sector of the economy

A second possibility for classifying the types of revenue is by sector of the economy. In order to understand this classification, some reference has again to be made to the SNA, which is based, in principle, on the circuit theory of flows of funds within an economy and between economies.

In the SNA a national economy may be classified by the following sectors:

List 4: Economic sectors

- *Enterprises*
  - Enterprises of sector 1
  - Enterprises of sector 2
  - Enterprises of sector n
- *Government sector*
  - Central government
  - Provincial governments
  - Local governments (municipalities)
  - Social security institutions

- *Private households*
  - Private households of type 1
  - Private households of type 2
  - Private households of type m
- *Private organizations*
  - Private organization 1
  - Private organization 2
  - Private organization k
- *Rest of the world*

All these sectors are economically linked to the social protection system of a country by way of transactions (and, potentially, to social protection systems abroad).

A major statistical problem of this categorization is that it requires considerable numerical information, and normally many statistical estimations. For example, in order to allocate the employers' contributions to the different sectors of the economy, it is necessary to know the absolute or (at least) the relative shares of the paid employers' contributions in the different sectors. This information is normally only available when a sophisticated statistical reporting system exists at the national level. The lack of such information could be overcome by using statistics on the sums of wages subject to contributions as generated in the different economic sectors – if available from the national accounts – and then estimate the sectoral allocation of contributions accordingly. But the less information that exists about the sectoral structure of an economy, the more estimates would have to be used which, at a certain stage, would make the results unreliable.

Another problem that may occur is that one of the main purposes for compiling the SAS is for its use as a projection basis. In order to do so – in basing projections on the disaggregate data format discussed in this section – it is necessary to project a number of *other* variables of the different economic sectors (sectoral employment, sectoral average wages, sectoral productivity, sectoral contribution rates [if applicable], etc.). Sectoral projections of economies normally require an expensive and complicated infrastructure to support the econometric work involved, which might be too costly to sustain. Therefore, before introducing a sectoral categorization of the SAS revenues, check carefully whether the necessary information for doing so and the analytical tools to effectively "exploit" this information are available on a long-term basis. However, if this is the case, it is highly recommended that the SAS be designed accordingly, as this would significantly enhance the information content for the potential users. This revenue structure would then be applied to each of the institutions of the SAS.

Again, the German SAS is taken as an illustrative application. One of the most striking results of table 3.4 is that the enterprises and the (aggregate)

Table 3.4 Germany: Revenue of the SAS by economic sector, 1960–97

Item	Year										
	1960	1970	1980	1990	1991	1992	1993	1994	1995p	1996p	1997s
Million DM											
Enterprises	23 987	59 256	158 887	250 842	291 091	314 103	313 757	326 907	345 564	351 721	359 677
Federal government	17 875	43 977	110 667	144 694	182 563	199 611	226 394	231 015	238 407	245 520	252 999
State governments	9 635	25 436	56 718	78 539	93 318	104 407	110 707	116 382	118 251	135 714	139 194
Municipalities	3 503	12 453	35 743	60 553	74 615	88 564	96 096	100 026	106 362	111 125	111 088
Social insurance	115	376	1 135	1 851	2 422	2 811	2 959	3 076	3 265	3 396	3 421
Private organizations	677	1 570	5 305	10 170	11 906	13 430	14 374	15 832	17 065	18 085	18 445
Private households	15 292	43 091	126 324	225 667	271 852	299 869	323 327	346 560	368 985	390 107	408 688
Rest of world	–	52	122	143	305	205	393	225	698	616	711
Total	**71 084**	**186 212**	**494 901**	**772 458**	**928 072**	**1 023 000**	**1 088 007**	**1 140 023**	**1 198 596**	**1 257 283**	**1 294 222**
Structure in %											
Enterprises	33.7	31.8	32.1	32.5	31.4	30.7	28.8	28.7	28.8	28.1	27.8
Federal government	25.1	23.6	22.4	18.7	19.7	19.5	20.8	20.3	19.9	19.5	19.5
State governments	13.6	13.7	11.5	10.2	10.1	10.2	10.2	10.2	9.9	10.8	10.8
Municipalities	4.9	6.7	7.2	7.8	8.0	8.7	8.8	8.8	8.9	8.8	8.6
Social insurance	0.2	0.2	0.2	0.2	0.3	0.3	0.3	0.3	0.3	0.3	0.3
Private organizations	1.0	0.8	1.1	1.3	1.3	1.3	1.3	1.4	1.4	1.4	1.4
Private households	21.5	23.1	25.5	29.2	29.3	29.3	29.7	30.4	30.8	31.0	31.6
Rest of world	–	0.0	0.0	0.0	0.0	0.0	0.0	0.0	0.1	0.0	0.1
Total	**100.0**	**100.0**	**100.0**	**100.0**	**100.0**	**100.0**	**100.0**	**100.0**	**100.0**	**100.0**	**100.0**
Share in GDP in %											
Enterprises	7.9	8.8	10.8	9.9	10.2	10.2	9.9	9.8	10.0	10.0	9.8
Federal government	5.9	6.5	7.5	5.7	6.4	6.5	7.2	6.9	6.9	6.9	6.9
State governments	3.2	3.8	3.9	3.1	3.3	3.4	3.5	3.5	3.4	3.8	3.8
Municipalities	1.2	1.8	2.4	2.4	2.6	2.9	3.0	3.0	3.1	3.1	3.0
Social insurance	0.0	0.1	0.1	0.1	0.1	0.1	0.1	0.1	0.1	0.1	0.1
Private organizations	0.2	0.2	0.4	0.4	0.4	0.4	0.5	0.5	0.5	0.5	0.5
Private households	5.1	6.4	8.6	8.9	9.5	9.7	10.2	10.4	10.7	11.0	11.2
Rest of world	0.0	0.0	0.0	0.0	0.0	0.0	0.0	0.0	0.0	0.0	0.0
Total	**23.5**	**27.6**	**33.6**	**30.6**	**32.5**	**33.2**	**34.4**	**34.3**	**34.6**	**35.5**	**35.4**

Notes: p: provisional; s: estimate.
Source: Federal Ministry of Labour and Social Affairs, Germany: *Materialband* [Statistical Annex] to *Deutscher Bundestag: Sozialbericht 1997* [Social Report 1997], Drs. 13/10142 of 17 March 1998. http://www.bma.de.

government sector have significantly reduced their shares in the financial engagement in social protection over the past 40 years, whereas private households were obviously made to compensate for the resulting fiscal gaps.

Another possibility for using the sectoral breakdown of the economy for a more in-depth presentation of the structure of the SAS will be discussed later.

3.3   STRUCTURING THE EXPENDITURE OF AN SAS

The types of expenditure as classified in section 3.1.2 are the basis for aggregating the SAS expenditures. Theoretically, all data could be left disaggregated to the level as indicated by the list of expenditure types. But, again, this might not be supportive to the macro analyses as they are intended to be provided by an SAS. Over time, two different ways of looking at social expenditures have emerged in practice. The first is to structure expenditure by economic category. Technically, this means processing the database in a way that meets the methodology and definitions of the SNA. The second is to sort the statistical base by "social function". The functional breakdown is usually specific to SAS and social budgeting, in that it separates distinctly the information contents of a Social Budget from those to be found in national accounts. Detailed explanations of this approach will be given in section 3.3.2.

3.3.1   Expenditure by economic category

One established possibility for categorizing the SAS expenditure by economic category is as follows:

List 5: Economic expenditure categories

- *Income replacements (cash benefits)*
- *Reimbursements (cash)*[4]
- *Goods and services (in-kind benefits)*
- *General services*
    - Administration (in kind)
    - Measures (in kind)
    - Grants (cash/in kind)
- *Transfers to other institutions (cash)*

This breakdown is linked to the SNA as follows:

- Income replacements and reimbursements to beneficiaries of the social protection system are part of private household sector disposable income; goods and services, and administration and measures, are part of government consumption; grants may be part of the private household disposable income (if cash) or part of government consumption (if in kind).

• The item "transfers to other institutions" is included in order to have a full account of institutional expenditures (on the aggregate SAS level the transfers to other institutions and the transfers from other institutions are consolidated; their sum equals zero).

The practical application in the German case is shown in table 3.5.

3.3.2 Expenditure by social function

The expenditure by function aims at describing the SAS structure by the main social contingencies covered. The following list of functions describes one design possibility:

List 6: Social functions

• *Old age and survivors*
  – Old age
  – Survivors
• *Health*
  – Prevention and rehabilitation
  – Sickness
  – Work injury and occupational diseases
  – Invalidity
• *Family*
  – Children and youth
  – Maternity
  – Other family functions
• *Employment*
  – Occupational training
  – Mobility
  – Unemployment
• *Housing*
• *General neediness (poverty)*
• *Other functions*

It is important to note that the SAS applies the functional breakdown to all expenditure, including (in principle) the administration costs. As indicated earlier, current expenditure does not include the purchase of fixed capital assets or transactions in financial assets, such as the provision of loans. "In principle" refers both to non-autonomous administrations, where the costs cannot

Table 3.5 Germany: Expenditure of the SAS by economic category, 1960–97

Item	Year 1960	1970	1980	1990	1991	1992	1993	1994	1995p	1996p	1997s
Million DM											
Income replacements (cash benefits)	51 947	132 780	326 082	490 836	578 461	643 817	688 103	714 756	749 832	784 435	794 564
Reimbursements	2 620	9 370	32 929	48 180	62 585	72 048	82 816	87 254	105 156	121 252	132 247
Goods and services	7 724	25 611	91 069	155 301	191 300	224 582	228 864	247 798	260 598	266 834	262 699
General services and benefits	3 357	8 083	24 019	37 144	50 738	58 430	59 259	58 498	62 289	63 626	66 614
Grants	222	543	5 084	8 428	15 809	18 936	17 226	15 207	17 352	17 725	21 857
Measures	1 212	3 041	8 184	11 645	14 097	15 926	16 781	16 897	17 442	18 073	17 763
Administration	1 923	4 498	10 751	17 071	20 832	23 568	25 253	26 394	27 494	27 827	26 994
Transfers to other institutions	–	–	–	–	–	–	–	–	–	–	–
Total	**65 648**	**175 844**	**474 099**	**731 460**	**883 083**	**998 876**	**1 059 043**	**1 108 307**	**1 177 876**	**1 236 146**	**1 256 123**
Structure in %											
Income replacements (cash benefits)	79.1	75.5	68.8	67.1	65.5	64.5	65.0	64.5	63.7	63.5	63.3
Reimbursements	4.0	5.3	6.9	6.6	7.1	7.2	7.8	7.9	8.9	9.8	10.5
Goods and services	11.8	14.6	19.2	21.2	21.7	22.5	21.6	22.4	22.1	21.6	20.9
General services and benefits	5.1	4.6	5.1	5.1	5.7	5.8	5.6	5.3	5.3	5.1	5.3
Grants	0.3	0.3	1.1	1.2	1.8	1.9	1.6	1.4	1.5	1.4	1.7
Measures	1.8	1.7	1.7	1.6	1.6	1.6	1.6	1.5	1.5	1.1	1.4
Administration	2.9	2.6	2.3	2.3	2.4	2.4	2.4	2.4	2.3	2.3	2.1
Transfers to other institutions	–	–	–	–	–	–	–	–	–	–	–
Total	**100.0**	**100.0**	**100.0**	**100.0**	**100.0**	**100.0**	**100.0**	**100.0**	**100.0**	**100.0**	**100.0**
Share in GDP in %											
Income replacements (cash benefits)	17.2	19.7	22.2	19.5	20.3	20.9	21.7	21.5	21.7	22.1	21.7
Reimbursements	0.9	1.4	2.2	1.9	2.2	2.3	2.6	2.6	3.0	3.4	3.6
Goods and services	2.6	3.8	6.2	6.2	6.7	7.3	7.2	7.4	7.5	7.5	7.2
General services and benefits	1.1	1.2	1.6	1.5	1.8	1.9	1.9	1.8	1.8	1.8	1.8
Grants	0.1	0.1	0.3	0.3	0.6	0.6	0.5	0.5	0.5	0.5	0.6
Measures	0.4	0.5	0.6	0.5	0.5	0.5	0.5	0.5	0.5	0.5	0.5
Administration	0.6	0.7	0.7	0.7	0.7	0.8	0.8	0.8	0.8	0.8	0.7
Transfers to other institutions	–	–	–	–	–	–	–	–	–	–	–
Total	**21.7**	**26.0**	**32.2**	**29.0**	**30.9**	**32.4**	**33.5**	**33.3**	**34.0**	**34.9**	**34.4**

Notes: p: provisional; s: estimate.
Source: Federal Ministry of Labour and Social Affairs, Germany: *Materialband* [Statistical Annex] to *Deutscher Bundestag: Sozialbericht 1997* [Social Report 1997], Drs. 13/10142 of 17 March 1998. http://www.bma.de.

be separated from other outlays, and to units that cannot properly divide their administration costs by function.

The compilation of the functional SAS expenditure structure is not as easy as it might seem at first glance. For example, all social expenditure could be considered as aiming at alleviation or prevention of poverty; thus, it might be tempting to record all social expenditure under the heading "general neediness (poverty)". Or, as all social expenditure finally flows directly or indirectly to private households (or "families"), all social expenditure might be listed under the function "family". Another extreme would be, for example, to fully disaggregate social assistance expenditure (which is generally considered to aim exclusively at poverty prevention) by its different components. It would be found that part of the social assistance expenditure aims at supporting the elderly, part is spent on children, part is expenditure on rents, or on drugs, and so on. Accordingly, these different expenditures would be booked under the functions "old age", "family", "housing" and "health", respectively.

In order to find a practical solution to this methodological problem, it is necessary to have a clear understanding of a country's legislation and the intended legal *purpose*. But even then, the decision on where to book a specific benefit might not be easy to make. Let us refer to the case of social assistance again. Legislation might provide for benefits under certain conditions. For example, a law might *explicitly* stipulate that certain "cash benefits are to be paid to families or children in order to prevent poverty". Other parts of the law might, under certain conditions, stipulate special payments to the very elderly (for example, those 70 years of age and over) in order to prevent poverty. In these cases, the statistician setting up the SAS would still be left with a decision problem. Should these benefits all be booked under the function "poverty"? Or should they, in the first example, be booked under the function "family" and, in the second, under the function "old age"? Sometimes the prevailing statistical practice or the prevailing public discussion in a country might help to decide. If such guidelines are unclear or unreliable, then one might try to find out what the legislator had in mind when introducing a specific law. Was the intention, concerning these examples, *primarily* to foster (the cohesion of) families or *primarily* to prevent poverty? If this information remains unclear, then ad hoc booking decisions may have to be taken.

Sometimes another problem occurs: initial statistical information might not be disasggregated deeply enough in order to decide under which function to book a specific expenditure item. Then, either the full amount would be recorded under one function or estimates might be used in order to allocate certain portions of this item to different functions.

The reader might regard these issues as of minor importance. Indeed, if the SAS were designed only in order to provide a *national* information tool, then the actual practice of booking could be based on prevailing national conventions or on reasonable ad hoc decisions. But an SAS (Social Budget) usually also has *international* aspects in that it should allow for international comparisons of social expenditure levels by different functions. For this reason, it is necessary to coordinate the SAS booking practice (the methodology) internationally, at least within the broader region of a country or with its main trading partners. While this aspect is especially important for the coordination of the functional break-down, it should also be achieved with respect to the other classifications presented in this book.

In order to provide some assistance for decision-making, the reader will find at the end of the book proposals for definitions of functions (Annex III).

The German case is shown in table 3.6.

In-depth empirical and legal analyses would be required in order to draw detailed conclusions from this application. Apparently, family policies were in decline over the past 40 years, the main reason being the significantly reduced number of new-born babies annually since the late 1960s. Health gained consid-erable importance, mainly reflecting the successful lobbying and income policies of the providers of health care, a changing structure of the population demanding optimum health-care provisions, and technological progress. Spending on employment (creation) policies and unemployment benefits experi-enced the most dramatic increase as a share of total social protection, mirroring the social protection response to the ever-increasing cyclical and structural labour market problems. Finally, resources for old-age protection lost consider-able weight within total social protection expenditures, despite their growth as a share of GDP.

3.4 THE INSTITUTIONAL CLASSIFICATION

The institutional approach is intended to map social protection revenue and expenditure on the basis of the existing institutional structure of a social protection system. At first glance, this seems to be an obvious and easy approach. In countries where the social protection system is administered by institutions which are separate from the general government budget, the approach to be taken is clear: all information required for setting up the SAS is contained in the accounts (budgets) of these institutions. For example, such institutions might be public pension insurance, health insurance or unemploy-ment insurance.

But the predicament lies again in the details. Normally, besides social security institutions, there are social expenditures which are directly paid out of general government budgets, or by employers or through other channels such as municipality budgets. In effect, there are benefits which cannot always be easily related to "tangible" social institutions. Examples of these are social assistance, employers' benefits or pensions and other benefits to public employees and the armed forces (directly paid out of the budgets of the different state levels and financed out of taxation). In all these cases, in order to set up the institutions of the SAS, "notional" or "virtual" institutions have to be created. Criteria to do so would be the existence of a specific legislation, or of binding

Table 3.6 Germany: Expenditure of the SAS by social function, 1960–97

Item	Year 1960	1970	1980	1990	1991	1992	1993	1994	1995p	1996p	1997s
Million DM											
Total	**65 648**	**175 844**	**474 099**	**731 460**	**883 083**	**998 876**	**1 059 043**	**1 108 307**	**1 177 876**	**1 236 146**	**1 256 123**
Family	10 753	31 745	71 730	92 973	118 292	134 503	139 288	140 599	145 890	162 575	169 182
Health	18 187	50 854	152 145	250 818	301 074	341 956	351 095	373 907	406 396	422 056	418 744
Employment	1 806	5 862	28 782	62 095	99 172	123 020	144 493	142 141	148 317	164 252	169 444
Old age and survivors	29 119	73 897	188 291	294 317	330 855	361 052	382 801	406 009	430 129	439 895	452 670
Other functions	5 783	13 487	33 152	31 257	33 690	38 345	41 365	45 651	47 144	47 369	46 083
Structure in %											
Total	**100.0**	**100.0**	**100.0**	**100.0**	**100.0**	**100.0**	**100.0**	**100.0**	**100.0**	**100.0**	**100.0**
Family	16.4	18.1	15.1	12.7	13.4	13.5	13.2	12.7	12.4	13.2	13.5
Health	27.7	28.9	32.1	34.3	34.1	34.2	33.2	33.7	34.5	34.1	33.3
Employment	2.8	3.3	6.1	8.5	11.2	12.3	13.6	12.8	12.6	13.3	13.5
Old age and survivors	44.4	42.0	39.7	40.2	37.5	36.1	36.1	36.6	36.5	35.6	36.0
Other functions	8.8	7.7	7.0	4.3	3.8	3.8	3.9	4.1	4.0	3.8	3.7
Share in GDP in %											
Total	**21.7**	**26.0**	**32.2**	**29.0**	**30.9**	**32.4**	**33.5**	**33.3**	**34.0**	**34.9**	**34.4**
Family	3.6	4.7	4.9	3.7	4.1	4.4	4.4	4.2	4.2	4.6	4.6
Health	6.0	7.5	10.3	9.9	10.6	11.1	11.1	11.2	11.7	11.9	11.5
Employment	0.6	0.9	2.0	2.5	3.5	4.0	4.6	4.3	4.3	4.6	4.6
Old age and survivors	9.6	10.9	12.8	11.7	11.6	11.7	12.1	12.2	12.4	12.4	12.4
Other functions	1.9	2.0	2.3	1.2	1.2	1.2	1.3	1.4	1.4	1.3	1.3

Notes: p: provisional; s: estimate.
Source: Federal Ministry of Labour and Social Affairs, Germany: *Materialband* [Statistical Annex] to *Deutscher Bundestag: Sozialbericht 1997* [Social Report 1997], Drs. 13/10142 of 17 March 1998. http://www.bma.de.

agreements between employers and employees on the payment of certain benefits. (Voluntarily paid employers' benefits would establish a separate institution if the employer were bound to pay them to each employee, on the basis of legislation or by court decisions.) On the revenue side, virtual institutions would include all incomes required to finance their expenditures; on the expenditure side, they would include all benefit expenditures, plus the investments in real assets required to maintain the operational basis for paying these benefits, plus the respective administration costs. In some of these cases, information on investments and administration costs might not be available, so estimates would then have to be used in order to fill the statistical "gaps".

3.4.1 The institutions

The list of institutions to be included in an SAS depends on the concrete legal and practical situation in a given country. Here we will mainly refer to the example of the German SAS, which is one of the best developed, based on a tradition of nearly 30 years of compilation and publication. The German SAS is calculated in two different institutional versions. The first version reflects the national approach as shown in List 7.

List 7: Institutions based on the national classification of the German SAS[5]

- *General systems*
    - Pension insurance
        Wage-earners' pension insurance
        Salaried employees' pension insurance
        Miners' pension insurance
    - Health insurance
    - Occupational accidents and diseases insurance
    - Unemployment insurance and assistance
    - Child benefits
    - Child-raising allowances
- *Special systems*
    - Old-age assistance for farmers
    - Old-age insurance for the liberal professions
- *Statutory systems*
    - Civil service pensions
    - Civil service family supplements to wages and salaries
    - Civil service health assistance
- *Employer benefits*
    - Continued payment of wages in case of sickness

- Private employers' supplementary (occupational) pensions
- Public employers' supplementary (occupational) pensions
- Contractual and voluntary benefits
- *Compensatory systems*
  - War veteran pensions and related benefits
  - Reparations and related payments
  - Other compensatory benefits
- *Social assistance and services*
  - Public social assistance
  - Youth-related assistance
  - Promotion of training
  - Housing allowances
  - Public health services
  - Assistance to foster individual savings
- *Indirect (fiscal) benefits*
  - Income tax reductions for social purposes
  - Indirect subsidies to promote ownership of houses

The second version of the German SAS reflects its institutional structure as agreed upon between the member States of the EU (Eurostat classification) as follows:

List 8: Institutions based on the Eurostat classification of the German Social Budget[6]

- *Basic systems*
  - National systems
    Child benefits
    Child-raising allowances

  - General systems
    Health insurance
    Pension insurance
    Occupational accidents and diseases insurance
    Unemployment insurance
    Continued payment of wages in case of sickness

  - Special systems
    Statutory system
      Civil service pensions
      Civil service family supplements to wages and salaries
      Civil service health assistance

- Other occupation-related systems
    Old-age assistance for farmers
    Old-age insurance for the liberal professions
- Systems related to war victims and others
    War veteran pensions and related benefits
    Reparations and related payments
    Other compensatory benefits

- *Supplementary systems*

  - National systems
    Youth-related assistance
    Public health services

  - General systems
    Private employers' supplementary (occupational) pensions

  - Special systems
    Public employers' supplementary (occupational) pensions

  - Voluntary systems
    Employers' contractual and voluntary benefits

- *Other social protection systems*

  - Public social assistance

  - Promotion of training

  - Housing allowances

  - Unemployment assistance

The reader might want to consider the differences between the two classifications of the same system. While the German (national) classification more or less reflects the historically developed institutional structure of the system, it is important to understand that the Eurostat classification was introduced as a blueprint in order to allow for quantitative and structural comparisons between the EU member States. Again, setting up an SAS compatibility with similar international accounting systems should be the objective right from the beginning. By using electronic data bank software, both a national and an international version of the same national SAS can be produced.

Once the institutional SAS structure (either in its national or in its international classification or in both) has been set up, it is possible to present its revenue and expenditure by institutions and by the different revenue and expenditure classifications, as described in sections 3.2 and 3.3.

3.4.2   Revenue by category

Possible classifications of revenue have been described in sections 3.2.1 and 3.2.2 in terms of "revenue by legal category" and "revenue by sector of the economy". On this basis, for each of the institutions of a country their revenue might therefore be structured as follows:

List 9: Revenue of institution n

Revenue by legal category

- *Social contributions*
  - Contributions by the insured population
    Employees' contributions
    Contributions by self-employed persons
    Contributions by beneficiaries
    Contributions by other persons
    Contributions paid by public institutions in lieu of beneficiaries

  - Employers' contributions
    Actual contributions
    Imputed contributions

- *Subsidies*
  - Subsidies paid by the government
  - Subsidies paid from other sources

- *Other revenue*

- *Transfers from other institutions*

and alternatively or simultaneously as follows:

Revenue by sector of the economy

- *Enterprises*
  - Enterprises of sector 1
  - Enterprises of sector 2
  - Enterprises of sector n

- *Government sector*
  - Central government
  - Provincial governments
  - Local governments (municipalities)
  - Social security institutions

- *Private households*
  - Private households of type 1
  - Private households of type 2
  - Private households of type m

Table 3.7 Calculating the fiscal balance of institution *n*

A. Total institutional revenue by legal category
- Social contributions
  - Contributions by the insured population
  - Employees' contributions
  - Contributions by self-employed persons
  - Contributions by beneficiaries
  - Contributions by other persons
  - Contributions paid by public institutions in lieu of beneficiaries
  - Employers' contributions
  - Actual contributions
  - Imputed contributions
- Subsidies
  - Subsidies paid by the government
  - Subsidies paid from other sources
- Other revenue
- Transfers from other institutions

minus

B. Total institutional expenditure by economic categories
- Income replacements (cash benefits)
- Reimbursements (cash)
- Goods and services (in-kind benefits)
- General services
  - Administration
  - Measures
  - Grants
- Transfers to other institutions

equals

C. Institutional fiscal balance (net lending to/net borrowing from the money market)

- *Private organizations*
  - Private organization 1
  - Private organization 2
  - Private organization *k*
- *Rest of the world*

In case inter-institutional transfers exist, and on a single institution's level, the total amounts of revenue by legal category and by economic sector might not match, as the financial flows stemming from the economic sectors represent the receipts stemming from *outside* the social protection system, whereas the transfers represent fiscal flows *within* the system. In these cases, the difference

Table 3.8 Germany: Calculating the balancing item of the SAS 1960–97 (million DM)

Item	1960	1970	1980	1990	1991	1992	1993	1994	1995p	1996p	1997s
Income replacements (cash benefits)	51 947	132 780	326 082	490 836	578 461	643 817	688 103	714 756	749 832	784 435	794 564
Reimbursements	2 620	9 370	32 929	48 180	62 585	72 048	82 816	87 254	105 156	121 252	132 247
Goods and services	7 724	25 611	91 069	155 301	191 300	224 582	228 864	247 798	260 598	266 834	262 699
General services and benefits	3 357	8 083	24 019	37 144	50 738	58 430	59 259	58 498	62 289	63 626	66 614
Grants	222	543	5 084	8 428	15 809	18 936	17 226	15 207	17 352	17 725	21 857
Measures	1 212	3 041	8 184	11 645	14 097	15 926	16 781	16 897	17 442	18 073	17 763
Administration	1 923	4 498	10 751	17 071	20 832	23 568	25 253	26 394	27 494	27 827	26 994
Transfers to other institutions	—	—	—	—	—	—	—	—	—	—	—
Expenditure by economic category	**65 648**	**175 844**	**474 099**	**731 460**	**883 083**	**998 876**	**1 059 043**	**1 108 307**	**1 177 876**	**1 236 146**	**1 256 123**
Social contributions	39 188	108 690	310 577	521 083	614 982	672 250	699 373	747 626	790 402	819 243	844 410
Paid by the insured	14 727	42 051	124 577	222 469	267 532	294 791	318 091	341 834	364 293	385 655	404 261
– Employees	11 928	32 602	91 155	161 823	194 663	212 902	221 374	236 043	244 381	255 215	265 969
– Self-employed	367	1 050	5 109	8 415	9 178	9 938	10 781	11 713	12 865	13 110	13 699
– Beneficiaries	481	234	551	13 196	13 895	16 699	18 791	21 122	24 065	25 615	27 812
– Other persons	465	2 695	6 638	12 234	12 771	13 695	16 258	17 598	17 224	19 873	20 391
– Via social insurance institution	1 487	5 469	21 123	26 801	37 054	41 558	50 887	55 357	65 757	71 842	76 390
Paid by the employers	24 461	66 639	186 001	298 614	347 451	377 459	381 282	405 792	426 109	433 588	440 149
– Actual contributions	15 775	37 602	110 761	189 906	227 405	246 919	257 504	275 214	284 656	293 833	304 352
– Imputed contributions	8 686	29 037	75 239	108 708	120 046	130 539	123 777	130 578	141 453	139 755	135 797
Subsidies	30 267	73 959	177 546	238 339	296 930	333 226	371 255	376 142	390 849	418 850	429 357
From public sources	26 978	68 726	165 761	225 039	282 506	318 051	355 482	364 393	377 499	404 866	415 079
From other sources	3 289	5 233	11 785	13 300	14 424	15 175	15 773	11 749	13 350	13 984	14 278
Other revenue	1 629	3 563	6 777	13 036	16 159	17 524	17 379	16 256	17 346	19 189	20 454
Transfers from other institutions	—	—	—	—	—	—	—	—	—	—	—
Revenue by legal categories	**71 084**	**186 212**	**494 901**	**772 458**	**928 072**	**1 023 000**	**1 088 007**	**1 140 023**	**1 198 596**	**1 257 283**	**1 294 222**
Balancing item	**5 435**	**10 368**	**20 801**	**40 998**	**44 989**	**24 124**	**28 965**	**31 717**	**20 720**	**21 137**	**38 098**

Family	10 753	31 745	71 730	92 973	118 292	134 503	139 288	140 599	145 890	162 575	169 182
Children and youth	6 766	15 782	39 794	56 846	76 626	89 175	92 316	92 589	95 484	102 535	109 282
Spouses	3 375	14 668	28 179	30 848	35 597	38 670	39 890	40 803	42 905	51 786	51 535
Maternity	613	1 295	3 757	5 280	6 069	6 658	7 082	7 206	7 501	8 254	8 366
Health	18 187	50 854	152 145	250 818	301 074	341 956	351 095	373 907	406 396	422 056	418 744
Rehabilitation	1 369	3 733	9 367	15 867	18 618	21 522	23 395	25 423	27 631	28 709	24 675
Sickness	12 076	36 123	112 853	181 290	215 444	243 954	243 288	258 041	275 560	280 751	274 728
Work injury and occupational diseases	1 667	4 653	11 866	17 061	20 650	22 861	23 834	24 299	25 744	25 766	25 698
Invalidity	3 075	6 345	18 059	36 601	46 362	53 619	60 577	66 144	77 461	86 829	93 644
Employment	1 806	5 862	28 782	62 095	99 172	123 020	144 493	142 141	148 317	164 252	169 444
Occupational training	585	2 374	8 942	15 900	21 753	29 559	28 406	24 309	26 487	28 550	24 841
Mobility	344	1 780	5 960	8 240	15 852	22 704	22 978	20 519	21 932	21 224	25 530
Unemployment	877	1 708	13 879	37 955	61 567	70 758	93 110	97 313	99 898	114 478	119 073
Old age and survivors	29 119	73 897	188 291	294 317	330 855	361 052	382 801	406 009	430 129	439 895	452 670
Old age	25 723	67 644	175 309	280 321	315 663	344 883	365 398	387 471	411 193	420 971	433 301
Survivors	3 395	6 253	12 982	13 996	15 192	16 169	17 403	18 538	18 936	18 923	19 368
Other functions	5 783	13 487	33 152	31 257	33 690	38 345	41 365	45 651	47 144	47 369	46 083
Expenditure by functions	**65 648**	**175 844**	**474 099**	**731 460**	**883 083**	**998 876**	**1 059 043**	**1 108 307**	**1 177 876**	**1 236 146**	**1 256 123**
Enterprises	23 987	59 256	158 887	250 842	291 091	314 103	313 757	326 907	345 564	352 721	359 677
Federal government	17 875	43 977	110 667	144 694	182 563	199 611	226 394	231 015	238 407	245 520	252 999
State governments	9 635	25 436	56 718	78 539	93 318	104 407	110 707	118 251	118 251	135 714	139 194
Municipalities	3 503	12 453	35 743	60 553	74 615	88 564	96 096	100 026	106 362	111 125	111 088
Social insurance	115	376	1 135	1 851	2 422	2 811	2 959	3 076	3 265	3 396	3 421
Private organizations	677	1 570	5 305	10 170	11 906	13 430	14 374	15 832	17 065	18 085	18 445
Private households	15 292	43 091	126 324	225 667	271 852	299 869	323 327	346 560	368 985	390 107	408 688
Rest of the world	—	52	122	143	305	205	393	225	698	616	711
Revenue by sources	**71 084**	**186 212**	**494 901**	**772 458**	**928 072**	**1 023 000**	**1 088 007**	**1 140 023**	**1 198 596**	**1 257 283**	**1 294 222**

Notes: p: provisional; s: estimate.
Source: Federal Ministry of Labour and Social Affairs, Germany: *Materialband* [Statistical Annex] to *Deutscher Bundestag: Sozialbericht 1997* [Social Report 1997], Drs. 13/10142 of 17 March 1998. http://www.bma.de.

Table 3.9 Germany: Calculating the balancing item of pension insurance, 1960–97 (million DM)

Item	1960	1970	1980	1990	1991	1992	1993	1994	1995p	1996p	1997s
Income replacements (cash benefits)	16 938	43 726	120 452	206 037	235 012	260 877	279 489	302 273	324 639	337 437	347 480
Reimbursements	1 410	5 214	15 114	13 210	16 422	16 017	17 922	20 017	22 815	24 360	25 916
Goods and services	730	1 811	3 326	4 667	4 948	5 643	6 243	6 655	7 209	7 486	5 484
General services and benefits	426	987	2 563	3 573	4 304	5 101	5 680	5 973	6 444	6 360	5 822
Grants	6	3			0	30	29	31	31	30	22
Measures	57	155	396	572	666	810	911	977	1 041	1 065	983
Administration	363	829	2 166	3 001	3 638	4 261	4 740	4 965	5 373	5 265	4 817
Transfers to other institutions	47	410	1 015	1 414	1 606	1 935	3 908	4 674	2 636	2 656	2 646
Expenditure by economic category	**19 551**	**52 147**	**142 470**	**228 901**	**262 293**	**289 573**	**313 242**	**339 592**	**363 743**	**378 299**	**387 348**
Social contributions	14 450	43 610	112 980	187 825	214 170	230 030	237 180	264 180	272 130	287 580	304 288
Paid by the insured	7 240	21 770	58 370	96 835	111 683	120 402	125 417	139 416	147 381	159 088	168 345
– Employees	6 750	20 790	51 660	86 575	97 117	104 938	106 163	118 534	117 859	122 462	129 836
– Self-employed	160	280	780	886	1 070	950	1 180	1 370	1 440	1 460	1 533
– Beneficiaries				866	980	920	1 000	1 270	1 590	1 780	1 857
– Other persons	330	700	1 980	2 610	2 430	2 650	3 050	3 310	2 890	4 720	5 008
– Via social insurance institutions			3 949	5 898	10 087	10 943	14 025	14 931	23 603	28 666	30 111
Paid by the employers	7 210	21 840	54 610	90 990	102 487	109 628	111 763	124 764	124 749	128 492	135 943
– Actual contributions	7 210	21 840	54 610	90 990	102 487	109 628	111 763	124 764	124 749	128 492	135 943
– Imputed contributions											
Subsidies	5 696	10 716	30 027	49 422	57 306	61 159	65 617	75 188	78 176	82 359	87 981
From public sources	5 696	10 684	30 027	49 419	57 303	61 159	65 617	75 188	78 176	82 359	87 981
From other sources		32		3	3	0					
Other revenue	773	1 516	1 450	2 366	3 601	4 729	4 238	2 514	2 113	3 157	3 627
Transfers from other institutions			408	81	65	63	50	40	31	45	31
Revenue by legal categories	**20 919**	**55 842**	**144 865**	**239 695**	**275 142**	**295 981**	**307 085**	**341 921**	**352 449**	**373 141**	**395 926**
Balancing item	**1 368**	**3 695**	**2 396**	**10 794**	**12 849**	**6 408**	**–6 157**	**2 329**	**–11 294**	**–5 158**	**8 577**

Family	730	1 250	2 622	1 593	1 699	1 690	1 746	1 779	2 039	2 029	2 076
Health	2 836	5 406	11 979	21 086	24 976	28 384	32 096	34 709	37 894	39 491	38 051
Employment	16	493	1 517	3 671	3 872	3 498	3 694	5 731	9 450	15 147	15 563
Old age and survivors	15 484	44 066	124 183	200 628	229 820	253 654	271 343	292 144	311 202	318 465	328 759
Old age	13 202	40 441	117 229	192 659	221 093	244 350	261 157	281 006	299 860	307 244	317 087
Survivors	2 282	3 625	6 954	7 969	8 727	9 304	10 186	11 138	11 342	11 221	11 672
Other functions	438	522	1 155	510	320	412	455	555	522	510	254
Expenditure by functions	**19 504**	**51 737**	**141 455**	**227 487**	**260 687**	**287 638**	**309 334**	**334 918**	**361 107**	**375 642**	**384 703**
Enterprises	6 862	19 965	47 625	78 725	87 708	93 786	94 811	104 980	105 045	109 554	116 278
Federal government	5 779	11 280	30 995	50 983	59 110	62 131	67 031	77 217	80 060	84 269	90 002
State governments	236	947	2 982	4 758	5 748	7 215	7 183	7 436	7 366	7 579	8 035
Municipalities	261	571	1 722	3 125	4 217	4 764	4 731	4 770	4 517	4 418	4 662
Social insurance	50	148	336	568	761	864	913	1 024	1 029	1 062	1 121
Private organizations	131	462	1 749	3 655	4 107	4 555	4 857	5 709	5 972	6 423	6 805
Private households	7 600	22 438	59 047	97 797	113 423	122 604	127 509	140 745	148 430	159 790	168 993
Rest of the world	—	32	—	3	3	0	—	—	—	—	—
Revenue by sources	**20 919**	**55 842**	**144 457**	**239 613**	**275 077**	**295 918**	**307 035**	**341 881**	**352 419**	**373 096**	**395 895**

Notes: p: provisional; s: estimate.

Source: Federal Ministry of Labour and Social Affairs, Germany; *Materialband* [Statistical Annex] to *Deutscher Bundestag: Sozialbericht 1997* [Social Report 1997], Drs. 13/10142 of 17 March 1998. http://www.bma.de.

between both aggregates would be the *net* received transfer payments (the difference between an institution's transfers received and its transfers paid) of an institution. However, on the aggregate consolidated SAS level (received total revenue of national social protection) the difference would disappear, as this amount represents (only) the total revenue received from outside the social protection system, irrespective of its inter-institutional financial flows.

3.4.3 Expenditure by category

Possible classifications of expenditure have been described in sections 3.3.1 and 3.3.2 in terms of "expenditure by economic category" and "expenditure by social function". Accordingly, on this basis, the expenditure for each of the institutions of a country might be presented as follows:

List 10: Expenditure of institution n

Expenditure by economic category
- *Income replacements (cash benefits)*
- *Reimbursements (cash)*
- *Goods and services (in-kind benefits)*
- *General services*
  - Administration
  - Measures
  - Grants
- *Transfers to other institutions*

and alternatively or simultaneously as follows:

Expenditure by social function
- *Old age and survivors*
  - Old age
  - Survivors
- *Health*
  - Prevention and rehabilitation
  - Sickness
  - Work injury and occupational diseases
  - Invalidity
- *Family*
  - Children and youth
  - Maternity
  - Other family functions

Figure 3.1   Balancing item of the German social protection system[1] (million DM)

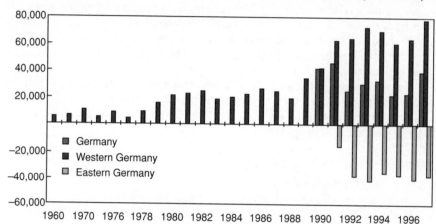

[1] From 1960 to 1989 figures refer to the Federal Republic of Germany; from 1990, see key.
Source: Federal Ministry of Labour and Social Affairs, Germany; *Materialband* [Statistical Annex] to *Deutscher Bundestag: Sozialbericht 1997* [Social Report 1997], Drs. 13/10142 of 17 March 1998. http://www.bma.de.

- *Employment*
  - Occupational training
  - Mobility
  - Unemployment
- *Housing*
- *General neediness (poverty)*
- *Other functions*

Again, in case of inter-institutional transfers, and on each single institution's level, the total amounts of expenditure by economic category and by social function might not match, as the functional financial flows represent the total amounts going directly or indirectly to private households (thus they "leave" the system completely), whereas the transfers represent fiscal flows *within* the social protection system. In these cases, the difference between both aggregates would be the *net* paid transfer payments of an institution (the difference between the institution's transfers paid and its transfers received). On the aggregate consolidated SAS level, the difference would again disappear (as is the case on the revenue side of the SAS).

The calculation of institutional fiscal balances should, therefore, be based on revenue by legal category and expenditure by economic category (table 3.7).

The fully-fledged application of these structures in the German SAS is illustrated in tables 3.8 and 3.9, which reflect the possible differences explained in calculating the fiscal balance. Table 3.8 shows the results for the total social protection system, whereas table 3.9 shows the results for public pension insurance (as a specific example). The reader might realize that on the *aggregate* SAS level (table 3.8), the balancing item is independent of whether calculated on the basis of revenue and expenditure contained in the *upper* part of the table or its *lower* part, whereas this is not the case in table 3.9 illustrating these explanations.

A graphical presentation of the balancing item of the German social protection system (figure 3.1) reveals that over the period of 40 years it has contributed to some limited degree to the economy's build-up of financial assets, as the balance was almost always positive.

Notes

[1] See Annex III, "Social contributions".

[2] Such country-specific approaches might sometimes set limits to international comparisons (cf. section 3.3.2.). Therefore, countries should continuously coordinate methodological specificities, at least on a regional level.

[3] *SNA 1993*, pp. 173–174. A social security institution is not a public corporation.

[4] The *SNA 1993* treats reimbursements as transfers in kind.

[5] Federal Ministry of Labour and Social Affairs, Germany: *Social security in Germany: Expenditure and revenue 1960–1993* (Bonn, 1994).

[6] Bundesministerium für Arbeit und Sozialordnung [Federal Ministry of Labour and Social Affairs]: *Ausgaben und Einnahmen des Sozialschutzes, ESSOSS 1993* [Expenditure and revenue of social protection. ESSOSS 1993] (Bonn, 1994).

BRINGING ALL OPTIONS TOGETHER: BLUEPRINTS FOR THE TABLE STRUCTURE OF A SOCIAL ACCOUNTING SYSTEM

4

Based on the classifications and categorizations introduced so far, this chapter gives a short formal overview of possible combinations of SAS data in table formats. We distinguish tables representing matrix information for each year *t* and tables representing information on a time-series basis. Blueprints of all tables are given in Annex VI. It is worthwhile recalling that any social protection system is multidimensional and, thus, the following proposals for tables are only partial representations of the full systems.

4.1 ANNUAL MATRICES

Annual matrices are rectangular (table) structures that, at a given point in time, allow for simultaneous cross-reference information on two different sets of classifications, as mentioned.

Revenue by legal category and institutions (year t*)* (Annex VI, figure AVI.1)

The left-hand column of this table contains the institutional breakdown of the SAS (Social Budget), and the top lines the institutions' revenue by legal category. When expressed as shares of total income or as a percentage of nominal GDP, the cells of this table allow for a direct comparison of the relative importance of different revenue categories for the system's institutions. Shares in total income can be calculated in two ways: either the sums of the single columns or the sums of the single lines add up to 100 per cent. Which one to use depends on the concrete issue under consideration.

Revenue by sector of the economy and institution (year t*)* (Annex VI, figure AVI.2)

In this table the left-hand column is the same as before; the top lines now contain the sectors of the economy. This table gives information about the different economic sectors' contributions to each of the social security institutions. However, when interpreting the results care should be taken to understand exactly the method of data compilation (the definitions) used – the results do not necessarily solve the incidence problem; they do not provide an answer to the question who *finally* pays the cost of social protection. Horizontal and vertical totals are calculated and can be used for intra-system structural analyses, or for the calculation of shares in GDP, or other meaningfully chosen macroeconomic aggregates.

Revenue by legal category, sector of the economy and institution i (year t) (Annex VI, figure AVI.3)

This alternative is a combination of the two given above but can only be compiled for each institution separately. The left-hand column contains the sectoral disaggregation of the economy and the top lines revenue by legal category. As the information in this table is, in fact, three-dimensional, each year t gives a number of n tables (n = the number of institutions), each table representing a different institution. When aggregating over the institutions, the SAS (Social Budget) is given for year t structured by economic sector and revenue by legal category. Again, horizontal and vertical totals are calculated and can be used for analyses.

Expenditure by economic category and institution (year t) (Annex VI, figure AVI.4)

This table now reflects on the expenditure side of the SAS, with the same structure as presented in Figure AVI.1 (revenues). The left-hand column again contains the different institutions of the social protection system, and top lines contain the economic expenditure categories, as defined. The horizontal and vertical totals can be used for relevant macroeconomic and financial analyses.

Expenditure by social function and institution (year t) (Annex VI, figure AVI.5)

This table is the equivalent of Figure AVI.2. The left-hand column contains the different institutions of the social protection system, and the top lines contain the different social functions. Again, the horizontal and vertical totals can be used for relevant macroeconomic and financial analyses.

Expenditure by social function, economic category and institution (year t) (Annex VI, figure AVI.6)

This table is an enlargement of the previous table. The left-hand column again contains the different institutions, and the functions are listed in the top lines. Furthermore, the functions are disaggregated by the different economic categories.

Expenditure by economic category, social functions and institution i
(year t) (Annex VI, figure AVI.7)

This table contains in its left-hand column the social functions, as defined, and
in its top lines the economic categories of social expenditure. Basically, it
contains the same information as the table structure shown in Figure AVI.6,
but now the information on the economic categories of expenditure is more
disaggregate.

Transfers between the institutions (year t) (Annex VI, figure AVI.8)

The dimension of this table is determined by the number of institutions. It is
quadratic, as the same institutions are contained in the left-hand column as
well as in the top line (in identical sequence). The left-hand column is defined
as containing the paying institutions, whereas the top line is defined as
containing the receiving institutions. Therefore, for each institution i contained
in the left-hand column and for every year t (statistics or projection), it is
possible to identify those other x institutions that receive transfers from the
institution i, including the respective amounts. The main diagonal of this
table is empty by intention.

4.2 TIME SERIES

The tables in time-series format are characterized by the fact that they
provide for information on the development of one type of budget data
classification over time, that is, the past and the projection period. Using this
method, cross references between two classifications, as described in the
previous section, are not possible. Whereas cross-reference tables allow for
structural analyses, data in a time-series format are open to the tools of time-
series analysis as, for example, the calculation of change rates over time,
elasticities, moving averages, and so on. Furthermore, if the results presented
are also calculated as a percentage of totals (=100 per cent) or as a percentage
of GDP, conclusions may be drawn from the development of such indices
over time.

Revenue by legal category (Annex VI, figure AVI.9)

The left-hand column contains all revenue items by legal category, and the
top lines reflect the observed period of statistical observation, as well as the
years over which the revenues are being projected. The projection period is
shaded.

Revenue by sector of the economy (Annex VI, figure AVI.10)

This table reflects the development of the financial contributions of the
economic sectors to the social protection system. The left-hand column contains
all revenue items "produced" in the listed economic sectors and transferred to
the social protection sector. Again, the top lines reflect the observed period of

statistical observation, as well as the years over which the sectoral contributions are being projected, the projection period being shaded.

Expenditure by economic category (Annex VI, figure AVI.11)

Now we switch to the expenditure side of the SAS. This table reflects the development of the SAS expenditure by economic category. A distinction between cash and in-kind benefits has been made. Although "general services" will normally consist mainly of in-kind benefits, they may also occur in cash; thus no distinction between cash and in kind has been made here. The left-hand column contains all expenditure items, and the top lines reflect the observed period of statistical observation, as well as the years over which the sectoral contributions are being projected, the projection period again being shaded.

Expenditure by social function (Annex VI, figure AVI.12)

The next table format mirrors the development of the SAS expenditure by social function. These results will probably attract the highest attention, especially when some extended time period can be covered by statistical results and through projections. The left-hand column contains all functional expenditure items, and the top lines reflect the observed period of statistical observation, as well as the years over which the sectoral contributions are being projected, the projection period again being shaded.

Expenditure by institution (Annex VI, figure AVI.13)

This table shows the SAS results in a classical institutional format. If calculated as percentage quotas of the total social expenditures or as shares of GDP, they may reveal information on the relative financial importance of different institutions and their development over time. The left-hand column contains all institutions' expenditures, and the top lines again reflect the observed period of statistical observation, as well as the years over which the sectoral contributions are being projected, the projection period being shaded.

The SAS fiscal balance (Annex VI, figure AVI.14)

The last table, figure AVI.14, shows two alternative methods of calculating the fiscal balance of the *overall* SAS. First, the difference may be calculated between total revenue by legal category and total expenditure by economic category; second, the difference may be calculated between total revenue by economic sector and total expenditure by social function. It should be remembered that, by construction, the results of the two alternatives only match if calculated on the aggregate total SAS results. When calculated for the single institutions, the two alternative approaches may differ in all those cases where an institution receives and/or pays transfers to/from another institution within the SAS framework. As explained earlier, the reason is that transfers received from within (paid to) the social protection system have been classified as "legal" and "economic" entities (see upper part of figure AVI.14), but not with respect to the "economic sector" origin or "social function". Thus, on the institutional level the calculated balances may differ for the net transfer amounts received (paid). On the total aggregate level, these differences are consolidated. The balance of the SAS is a first rough indicator for the development of the social protection system's fiscal position over time.

A WORK ROUTINE FOR DATA COMPILATION

5

A prerequisite for the successful set-up and maintenance of an SAS, structured as described, is a well-functioning, consistent and continuous reporting national statistical system. Much of the data and data sources will actually be the same as used for the compilation of the national accounts (Chapter 6).

The starting point is the available set of detailed basic statistics on social expenditures and their financing. Much of this information is normally available at the central government level; other information might be available at state or local levels only. When separate social security institutions exist, their data will be provided through them. In other cases, data might in principle exist, but no institution collects them systematically (e.g. social expenditures paid by enterprises). In these and other cases, either a data collection routine or a robust estimation technique has to be established.

Whatever the situation with respect to the availability of information, the administrative unit operating the SAS (Social Budget) will often itself have to establish a reliable routine of data collection and/or estimation.

The collected data have to be classified by institution as described in section 3.4. As previously noted, some of the institutional classifications will be self-evident, and other institutions will have to be "artificially" created ("notional institutions"). Only on this basis is it possible to establish, for each of the institutions so determined – be it a tangible or a notional institution – a "balance sheet" reflecting its revenues and expenditures.

These balance sheets are the basis for the classifications described above. First, revenues and expenditures have to be classified by type; then revenues have to be sorted by legal category and/or economic sector and expenditures by economic category and/or social function. The balance sheets might also represent the data level at which the projection techniques, as described in Part III, will normally be applied. A formal presentation of this process is provided in figure 5.1.

Figure 5.1   The SAS data compilation process

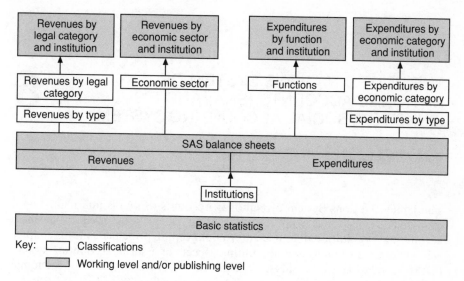

Key: ☐ Classifications

☐ Working level and/or publishing level

Source: Federal Ministry of Labour and Social Affairs, Germany: *Social security in Germany. Expenditure and revenue 1960–1993* (Bonn, 1994), p. 7.

THE UNITED NATIONS SYSTEM OF NATIONAL ACCOUNTS (SNA) AND ITS LINKS TO A SOCIAL ACCOUNTING SYSTEM

6

The United Nations System of National Accounts (SNA) is interrelated with economic theory[1] and with the accounting rules "long used in business accounting"[2] (traditional double-entry bookkeeping principle). In this chapter we only discuss some formal accounting aspects of a social accounting system (SAS) in relation to the SNA. Theoretical macroeconomic and economic policy issues are addressed in Annex I, "Issues brief".

6.1   THE RELATIONSHIP BETWEEN THE SAS AND THE SNA

The SNA has been broadly described as follows:[3]

> The System of National Accounts (SNA) consists of a coherent, consistent and integrated set of macroeconomic accounts, balance sheets and tables based on a set of internationally agreed concepts, definitions, classifications and accounting rules. It provides a comprehensive accounting framework within which economic data can be compiled and presented in a format that is designed for purposes of economic analysis, decision-taking and policy-making. The accounts themselves present in a condensed way a great mass of detailed information, organized according to economic principles and perceptions, about the working of an economy. They provide a comprehensive and detailed record of the complex economic activities taking place within an economy and of the interaction between the different economic agents, and groups of agents, that takes place on markets or elsewhere. In practice the accounts are compiled for a succession of time periods, thus providing a continuing flow of information that is indispensable for the monitoring, analysis and evaluation of the performance of an economy over time. The SNA provides information not only about economic activities, but also about the levels of an economy's productive assets and the wealth of its inhabitants at particular points of time. Finally, the SNA includes an external account that displays the links between an economy and the rest of the world.

Many of the issues as addressed in this characterization of the SNA also apply to an SAS. However, it should be clear from the above definition that the core issue of the SNA focus is the *economy* and its analysis. By contrast, an SAS aims at a comprehensive description of the flow of funds related to a national social protection system and provides a data basis for its projection. Much of the information contained in an SAS is also available in the SNA, but this information might only be found in different *loci* of the SNA. Other information might be missing, as the SNA partially follows different methodological rules, and aims at different purposes as compared to those of an SAS. The Inter-Secretariat Working Group on National Accounts, under whose auspices the *SNA 1993* was prepared, was well aware of such limitations of the SNA. That is why the *SNA 1993* allows for high flexibility as regards its implementation. But, "in some cases, working with the central framework [the SNA], even in a flexible way, is not sufficient."[4] In order to overcome the limitations set by the SNA, the introduction of "satellite accounts" is proposed, which are described as follows:[5]

> In certain types of analysis, the basic intention is...to focus on a certain field or aspect of economic and social life in the context of national accounts. The intent is to make apparent and to describe in more depth aspects that are hidden in the accounts of the central framework or surface only in a limited number of points.... In other types of analysis, more emphasis is given to alternative concepts.... For example, the production of domestic services by members of the household for their own final consumption may be brought within the production boundary.

And furthermore:

> The analysis of a number of important fields such as social protection, health or the environment may benefit from building a framework to accommodate elements which are included in the central accounts, explicitly or implicitly, plus complementary elements (either monetary or physical elements) and possible alternative concepts and presentations. In all cases, however, the links with the central framework are made explicit, there are a number of common elements and any contradictory features are introduced, not by chance, but after explicitly considering various ways of looking at reality. Those special constructs, which are semi-integrated with the central framework, are called satellite accounts.

This seems to be a fair description of the link of the SAS concept with the SNA – or, at least, what it should be. In other words, an SAS can be considered a satellite account of the SNA. It matches the definition of an SNA satellite account in many respects. For example, it has numerous definitional links with the SNA but also differs from that system, as in its functional breakdown of expenditures. Also, as the reader will see in Part III, the projection of a Social Budget requires (and, therefore, "produces") a quantity of information on physical entities which are not core elements of the SNA.

As this is not a book on national accounting, further explanations given on links between the SNA and an SAS can only cover some of the most relevant aspects. In order to enhance the reader's familiarity with the concepts of the SNA and the methodological concept of an SAS, the reader is advised to study especially the *SNA*: Chapters VII: "The primary distribution of income account", VIII: "The secondary distribution of income account" and IX: "The use of income account".[6] It is probably these areas in which the closest links between the SNA and an SAS exist.

6.2 THE SAS IN A SECTORAL ECONOMIC CONTEXT

The *SNA 1993* distinguishes the following institutional sectors of the economy:[7]

- Non-financial corporations
- Financial corporations
- Government units, including social security funds
- Non-profit institutions serving households (NPISHs)
- Households
- Rest of the world

The SNA describes the economic transactions (flows of funds) between these institutions and the resulting impact on the economy's wealth (acquisition and/ or disposal of financial and non-financial assets and liabilities by institutional units through transactions).

In principle, social protection[8] may be provided by each of these institutional sectors. Each sector might pay social expenditures to eligible households, and each sector might contribute financially to the social protection system. This is important, as it is one key to a comprehensive understanding of the purpose of a Social Budget. It is acknowledged that normally social protection is predominantly provided through the state and/or social security funds. The State, for instance, may pay child benefits or social assistance and may provide for health protection. Social security funds may cover unemployment benefits, pensions, occupational diseases, and so on. But the reality in various countries is often complicated. For instance, child benefits might not only be paid through the State, but also by corporations (such as "employers"). Social assistance might be provided by the State, but also through NPISHs. Countries might pay social benefits to the rest of the world (pensioners living abroad), and equally receive contributions from the rest of the world (from commuters). In an SAS, all these transactions (payments, receipts) are taken into account. There might be further benefits; for example, in many countries there are company-based social benefits, either legally defined or collectively agreed between employers and employees. Corporations might also pay social benefits on a voluntary basis and, if they do so, might have to pay these benefits to all their eligible employees or former employees, in which case they are included in the SAS database.

In other words, the SNA list of sectors may, from a specific SAS point of view, be more precisely rewritten as follows:

- Non-financial corporations, *including social protection related transactions*
- Financial corporations, *including social protection related transactions*

- Government units, including social security funds, *including social protection related transactions*
- Non-profit institutions serving households (NPISHs), *including social protection related transactions*
- Households, *including social protection related transactions*
- Rest of the world, *including social protection related transactions*

or by allocating the social protection related transactions of all sectors to the SAS:

- Non-financial corporations, *excluding social protection related transactions*
- Financial corporations, *excluding social protection related transactions*
- Government units, including social security funds, *excluding social protection related transactions*
- Non-profit institutions serving households (NPISHs), *excluding social protection related transactions*
- Households, *excluding social protection related transactions*
- Rest of the world, excluding *social protection related transactions*
- Social protection sector (Social Budget), *including the social protection related transactions of all SNA sectors*

From that aspect, an SAS just appears as another economic sector; by constructing an SAS, the social protection system of a country is looked at through a magnifying glass, broadly consistent with one other major statistical information system, which is the SNA. Again, an SAS's character as a "satellite account" of the SNA is obvious.

A simplified graphic representation of the SAS in a sectoral disaggregation of the economy is provided in figure 6.1.

Figure 6.1 Flows of funds between economic sectors and the SAS

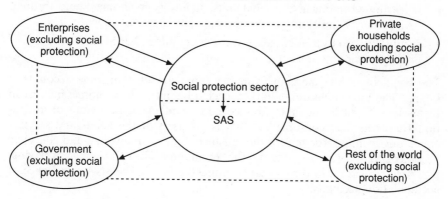

6.3 THE SAS AND REDISTRIBUTION OF INCOME

For all SNA sectors mentioned in section 6.2, only by including any "social protection sector" is it possible to compile the full sequence of the following SNA accounts.[9]

6.3.1 Current accounts

These accounts record the production of goods and services, the generation of incomes by production, the subsequent distribution and redistribution of incomes among institutional units, and the use of incomes for purposes of consumption or saving, of which:

Production account

The production account records the activity of producing goods and services as defined within the SNA. Its balancing item, gross value added, is defined as the value of output less the value of intermediate consumption, and is a measure of the contribution to GDP made by an individual producer, industry or sector. Gross value added is the source from which the primary incomes of the SNA are generated and is therefore carried forward into the primary distribution of income account. Value added may also be measured net by deducting consumption of fixed capital.

Distribution and use of income accounts

These consist of a set of articulated accounts showing how incomes are:

- generated by production;
- distributed to institutional units with claims on the value added created by production;
- redistributed among institutional units, mainly by government units through social security contributions and benefits and taxes;
- eventually used by households, government units or NPISHs for purposes of final consumption or saving.

The balancing item emerging from the complete set of income accounts is saving. The income accounts have considerable intrinsic economic interest in themselves. In particular, they are needed to explain the behaviour of institutional units as final consumers – that is, as users of the goods and services emanating from production for the satisfaction of the individual and collective needs and wants of households and the community. The balancing item, saving, is carried forward into the capital account, the first in the SNA's sequence of accumulation accounts.

6.3.2 Accumulation accounts

These are flow accounts that record the acquisition and the disposal of financial and non-financial assets and liabilities by institutional units through transactions, or as a result of other events, of which:

Capital account

This account records acquisitions and disposals of non-financial assets as a result of transactions with other units, or changes in inventories and consumption of fixed capital.

Financial account

This account records acquisitions and disposals of financial assets and liabilities through transactions.

Other changes in assets accounts

This account records (a) changes in the amounts of the assets and liabilities of units (sectors) as a result of factors other than transactions, such as destruction of fixed assets by natural disasters and (b) changes in the value of assets and liabilities that result from changes in their prices.

The link between the accumulation accounts and the income accounts is provided by the fact that saving (equals disposable income not spent on consumption) must be used to acquire financial or non-financial assets of one kind or another, if only cash, the most liquid financial asset. When saving is negative, the excess of consumption over disposable income must be financed by disposing of assets or incurring liabilities. The *financial account* shows the way in which funds are channelled from one group of units to another, especially through financial intermediaries.

6.3.3 Balance sheets

The balance sheets show the values of the stocks of assets and liabilities held by institutional units or sectors at the beginning and at the end of an accounting period.

It should be noted that, although it is necessary to present the SNA accounts in a particular order,

> the activities they describe should not be interpreted as taking place sequentially in time. For example, incomes are generated continuously by processes of production, while expenditures on the outputs produced may also be taking place more or less simultaneously. An economy is a general equilibrium system in which interdependent economic activities involving countless transactions between different institutional units are carried out simultaneously. Feedbacks are continually taking place from one type of economic activity to another.[10]

In order to avoid misunderstandings, some explanations should be given with respect to the "positioning" of social protection within this sequence of accounts.

First, it might be helpful to understand why, in principle, the social protection sector should show up in the production account. Of course, it does produce something: social security. But what is the "gross value added" to be booked in the production account? For example, it should definitely not be confused with the total annual social expenditure of a country, or total contributions collected. These are just "tools and instruments" of the social security production. In fact, social security has no market price which could be used to assess the sector's value added as, by contrast, is the case with goods and services available on markets. To circumvent the underlying valuation problem, national accounting normally assumes that the value added of the social protection system is directly linked to the wages and salaries paid to the employees of that sector.

Whether this practice is judged appropriate or not, one outcome is that the sector's contribution to GDP is largely correlated to its administration costs. The higher the sector's efficiency (by reducing staff and/or increasing per capita productivity), the lower its value added and vice versa. When the social protection system's employees are obliged to pay the same social contribution rates as the employees in the other sectors of the economy, then the social sector's own share in financing social protection depends on the number of staff, their average insurable salary and the contribution rate. In other words, if operating efficiently, the social protection sector's contribution to GDP, as well as its financial share in social protection, should be expected to be comparatively low.

The SAS accounts show how the social protection sector redistributes primary income. This process co-determines – in combination with the effects of taxation and the government's non social protection transfers to private households – the economy's secondary income distribution. The core of the SAS is positioned between primary and secondary distribution. In accounting terms, it is not the secondary distribution itself.

In so far as the SAS co-determines the amount of disposable income available to private households, it equally relates to the SNA use of income accounts. Obviously, private household savings, that part of disposable income unspent on goods and services, directly affect the accumulation accounts. But also, by way of transactions of the social protection sector itself (as an "institution"), the capital, financial and other changes in assets accounts will be affected – both the private households' and the institutional decisions affecting the respective balance sheets.

6.4 THE SAS AND THE *SNA 1993* SOCIAL ACCOUNTING MATRICES

The SNA predominantly focuses on T accounts, but it also allows for other methods of presentation of data – one of which is the presentation of national accounts in a matrix. One of the most prominent matrix formats is the input–output table (the basis for I-O-analysis).

Over time, another variant of matrix presentation of national accounts has developed, the social accounting matrix (SAM). This concept is briefly touched upon in this book in order to avoid confusing the SAS concept with the social accounting matrix concept of the SNA, but also in order to mention some of the common grounds of both.

SAMs have been traditionally applied to analyses focusing on causes and consequences of inequality among different private household groups. They provide a consistent framework for economic models with detailed classifications of actors, such as categories of employed persons or institutional subsectors. Thus, they have often been used to contribute additional information to the analysis of the level and composition of employment and/or unemployment, for example via a subdivision of the compensation of employees by type of person employed.[11] "This subdivision applies to both the use of labour by industry and the supply of labour by socioeconomic subgroup."[12]

Generally, the concept of social accounting matrices aims at obtaining more general insights into the state of human development without sacrificing a systems approach. Here, a SAM has a clear common basis with the SAS introduced in this book. Although the SAS has its primary focus on fiscal issues, it is often necessary to reconcile the respective information with related data from other sources in order to allow for meaningful interpretation of compiled data. Both systems aim at formal modelling and monitoring, and projecting the impact of alternative government policies or external influences on monetary (SAS) or non-monetary (SAM) variables. A SAM typically needs disaggregated information (on a meso level) on labour force participation rates, employment and wage levels by different socio-economic categories and/or by industries and national aggregates for these variables, which are consistent with the more detailed data.[13] So does the SAS. Thus, in many cases, both statistical systems might have a wide common data basis, although different analytical focuses.

Therefore, wherever in a country a SAM approach has been established, it is relatively straightforward to establish an SAS. Also, once an SAS has been solidly introduced, it may conveniently serve as a platform for the development of a SAM. Furthermore, like the SAS, a SAM can be considered the nucleus of a satellite system to the national accounts through incorporating related data from all kinds of dispersed sources.

For more details, it is recommended to study Chapter XX, "Social accounting matrices", in the *SNA 1993*.[14]

Notes

[1] *SNA 1993*, op. cit., p. XXXVII.

[2] ibid., p. 11.

[3] ibid., p. 1.

[4] ibid., p. 51.

[5] ibid., p. 51.

[6] ibid., p. 157 ff.

[7] ibid., p. 3.

[8] Social security funds are only a sub-component of the social protection system.

[9] *SNA 1993*, p. 2.

[10] ibid., p. 1.

[11] ibid., p. 468.

[12] ibid., p. 468.

[13] ibid., p. 469.

[14] ibid., pp. 461–488.

THE SOCIAL ACCOUNTING SYSTEM AND OTHER STATISTICAL DATA SYSTEMS RELATED TO SOCIAL PROTECTION FINANCES

7

7.1 OTHER NATIONAL STATISTICAL DATA SYSTEMS

The social accounting system (SAS) as described here is closely linked in its statistical approach to the approach followed in the national accounts (SNA concept). However, much of the social expenditure and revenue discussed is part of general government spending and expenditure, and thus has links to other data systems registering government finances. Social financial accounts use government finance data, and require knowledge of government finance statistics. The International Monetary Fund (IMF) has developed guidelines on such statistics. Unfortunately, only a draft version of the selected chapters of the new publication, *A manual on government finance statistics*, was available at the time when this book was finalized; the new version[1] introduces significant changes to the recommended methodology, compared to the previous one.[2] Here, we only summarize some of the major issues.

Differences in data systems usually reflect differences in their objectives. At the same time, such systems are normally interlinked, and data derived from one system are often reorganized to meet objectives of the other statistical system.

National accounts are primarily oriented towards measuring the utilization of productive factors (labour and capital), production of goods and services. They attempt to measure flows of goods and services, matching them with parallel financial flows (actual or imputed).

There are various administrative accounts and accounting procedures of different general government institutions (including social security institutions), each with a system of statistical data. The major objective of these accounts is control and monitoring accountability of the respective organizational units. All the social security institutions have (or should have) separate accounting systems and their own statistical bases. Other general government institutions, where provision of social protection benefits is only one of the many functions, also have their own accounting systems, where the social part of the accounts is more or less easy to identify.

The main functions and objectives of government finance statistics differ both from those of national accounts, and those of government accounts. The focus is on financial transactions (taxing, borrowing, spending and lending) and not on the physical flows. The objective is not registering and controlling individual transactions, but rather analysis, planning and policy making.

In many respects, government finance statistics have to utilize administrative accounts as inputs. At the same time, as stated in the 1986 IMF *manual*:

> It is desirable for the government finance statistics to follow the conventions and classifications utilized in construction of the national accounts.... This should permit the subsequent incorporation in the national accounts of data compiled as government finance statistics after appropriate reconciliation with the concepts and data for other sectors.[3]

As stressed throughout this book, the main objective of the social accounting system is not just to record particular transactions, nor to monitor accountability of the individual institutions responsible for different social protection schemes. The main objective is planning and policy analysis through social budgeting. As social budgeting has to be done within the context of the full economic environment, it is convenient to establish a social accounting system compatible with the national accounts. On the other hand, social protection finances are a major part of government finances. Thus, when the fiscal and monetary aspects of social policy are analysed, it is important to have the data system compatible with the one developed for government finance analysis.

Government finance statistics usually focus on outlays made during the current period (while national accounts seek to measure production, income, consumption, capital accumulation and finance arising during the current period, whether from current, past or future outlays). Government finance statistics tend to measure only actual gross flows of payments to and from government, rather than estimate or impute – which are additional methods utilized in compiling national accounts. Until now, government finance statistics have been recording transactions on a cash basis. In the national accounts, they are recorded on an accrual basis (as the times at which payments take place may diverge significantly from the economic activities and transactions to which they relate, and which economic activities and transactions the SNA attempts to portray).[4] Government finance statistics often call for classifications and groupings of transactions adequate for the specific government functions, while the SNA attempts to group them in a similar way for all sectors.

Significant efforts have been made in recent years to harmonize the IMF approach to financial statistics with that of the SNA "to the fullest extent possible".[5] The new approach recommends the accrual basis for recording most of the transactions. It also introduces significant changes in groupings and classifications related to sectors, units, types of expenditure and revenues, and its economic and functional classifications, adopting in most cases SNA principles. For government functions it adopts the United Nations Classification of Functions of the Government. This means introducing a "social protection" function, with the further classification of its functions following the one of the European System of Integrated Social Protection Statistics (ESSPROS).

Depending on the particular purposes of the social budgeting exercise, different approaches may exist for building a social accounting framework. When the full economic picture of social protection finances is aimed at, transactions which are not just measures of "actual flows from and into" the general government should also be taken into account. For example, items such as tax revenues foregone because of the "tax benefits" provided through various tax deductions and exemptions should be estimated. But when the purpose is to concentrate on the purely financial aspects of social protection, the social accounts may be built exactly following the IMF guidelines.

7.2 INTERNATIONAL STATISTICAL DATA SYSTEMS ON SOCIAL PROTECTION FINANCES

Three major international data compilation systems exist, all built to enable a comparison of social protection finances among different countries.

* ESSPROS is the instrument of statistical observation of social protection in the EU member States developed by Eurostat.[6]

* The OECD developed SOCX, the social expenditure database used to provide an accounting system for social expenditure in its member States.[7]

* The ILO has been conducting its Inquiry into the costs of social security from after the Second World War, collecting data on social protection expenditure and revenue from over 100 countries.[8]

With respect to the methodology and classifications used, the social accounting system presented in this book is close to the ESSPROS. It is a comprehensive statistical system which can be used both at the national level as well as for international comparisons. The OECD database uses national source data on expenditure grouped by individual social protection programmes, according to an agreed classification to provide internationally comparable social policy indicators of levels and patterns of social spending. It does not aim, as ESSPROS does, to establish a common statistical system. While Eurostat and OECD data frameworks cover a limited number of countries with well-developed statistical systems and differentiated – but extensive – social protection programmes, the ILO Inquiry aims at covering all countries of the world: those with well-developed social security schemes, and those where such schemes were established only recently, and which cover relatively small groups of the population. It is obvious in such circumstances that the statistical approach also has to be different. The ultimate objective of the ILO Inquiry is not only to collect data which can be used for international comparisons, but also in developing countries to promote a comprehensive approach to social protection statistics which would enable social policy planning at the national level. The recent revision of the Inquiry's methodology brings it closer to Eurostat's approach; however, the contents of the data actually collected reflect not only a differentiation of the social protection system, but also different capacities of the national statistical systems.

Notes

[1] http://www.imf.org/external/pubs/ft/gfs/manual

[2] IMF: *A manual on government finance statistics* (Washington, DC, 1986).

[3] ibid., p. 1.

[4] ibid., p. 81 (3.92).

[5] *SNA 1993*, p. 9 (1.46).

[6] Eurostat: *ESSPROS Manual 1996 (The European System of Integrated Social Protection Statistics)*, (Luxembourg, 1996).

[7] OECD: *Social expenditure statistics of OECD member countries*, Labour Market and Social Policy Occasional Paper No.17 (Paris, 1996).

[8] ILO: *The Cost of Social Security, Nineteenth International Inquiry* (Geneva, 1997).

PART III

THE SOCIAL BUDGET

MODELLING EXPENDITURE AND REVENUE

8

Social accounts are social expenditure and its financing. They identify how much a country is spending on different social benefits and how they are financed. They thus help to pinpoint potential imbalances and gaps in the contemporary social protection system. A social accounting system (SAS) is an essential part of the quantitative basis for policy planning, but it is not the policy-planning instrument itself. To arrive at a comprehensive policy-planning instrument, a further step has to be taken. The accounting frame has to be projected into the future, and used for the simulation of alternative future benefit and financing structures. In short, the transition from statistical analysis to budgeting has to be made.

In complex financial systems this is best done with the help of a model. Models are simplified images of reality. The degree of simplification depends on the amount of detail in available statistical information, and on the purpose of the model, which results in the political decision-making process. The statistical basis described in Part II provides for a high degree of detailed information; it is at this level of disaggregation that a model should generally operate. This "working level" has to be distinguished from the "display level". Social policy-makers, who need to assess the development of the overall national social expenditure, or the expenditure of major components of the overall national social expenditure, generally do not need every detail of the institutional budget of each and every social security institution. They are normally interested in information of higher aggregation. Thus, although the database for a Social Budget model is usually highly disaggregated, its results normally have to be displayed on a more aggregate level in order to achieve understanding. The aggregation procedure should always be well documented, so that the results of model projections or simulations can be traced back to every detail if need be.

Modelling means linking the expenditure and revenue mathematically to certain determinants, such as the demographic development and/or development of economic variables, including employment, unemployment, wages or

Figure 8.1 The social budgeting process

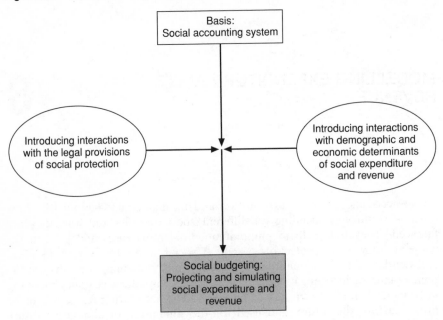

prices, as well as the legal provisions which govern the national social protection system. In many cases, such links between social finance variables and exogenous determinants are obvious, whereas in others they might have to be based on detailed empirical research. Once the complete set of interlinks between the social accounting system and the exogenous determinants has been established, projection techniques for revenue and expenditure items can be devised, and can be compiled into a simulation and projection model. This linking of expenditure and revenue to determining variables embodies the crucial step from accounting to budgeting, that is, projection and simulation (figure 8.1).

Part III is closely linked to Part II. It explores possibilities ("techniques") to project Social Budget revenues and expenditures, based on available statistical, legal and political information. In other words, we are now engaged in "model-ling" a Social Budget, finding meaningful methods that allow for an exploration of its future development. Thus, this part of the book extends the scope of the previous part. But its purpose is not to examine again all the projection methods that have been already extensively described, and their pros and cons as discussed in numerous books and articles. Nothing of methodological substance can be added to the literature in the context of this guide to the practice of social budgeting. Rather, it systematically tries to provide examples of how to plunge into the middle of a practical social budgeting process.

In doing so, we concentrate on what we call (as others have done before) "system approaches", and in that context provide a description of the model family which has been developed by the ILO. This has been done on the basis of experience with financial analyses of social protection systems around the world, including countries in Africa, Asia, the Caribbean, Europe and Latin America.

However, before we explain the ILO's approach to social budgeting in detail, we will show the reader some alternatives.

8.1 ALTERNATIVE MODELLING APPROACHES

This section serves as a reminder of the existence of other modelling approaches. We will mention their advantages and disadvantages in order to give readers a choice as to which approach might best fit their country's case. We start with the classical case, which most of us know well.

8.1.1 The classical budgeting approach

Historically, this is the oldest approach, and is still extensively used by practically all governments and institutions operating public resources. Projections of the first existing Social Budgets in Europe were based on this method. It is potentially very reliable in its results when applied to a time horizon of approximately one to two years.

Basically, this method consists of an expert inquiry. Each expert is responsible for operating, observing and/or analysing the developments of a limited set of financial items (of the social protection system). By means of their high specialization, they acquire detailed knowledge about the driving forces (including legislation) behind the observed financial developments and, thus, are ideally equipped to perform reliable heuristic projections of the variables under their "control".

In a Social Budget context, this method would result in experts' projections of each "type of revenue" and each "type of expenditure" as defined in Part II, sections 3.1.1 and 3.1.2, or aggregates thereof.

The projections would normally be based on "robust" extensions of time series, such that the last available statistical value of a variable Y_{t-1} (a specific expenditure type) would be multiplied by a factor k in order to calculate a value for Y_t:

Equation 8.1

$$Y_{t,i} = k_i * Y_{t-1,i}$$

the index i representing the "responsible" expert.

We call this approach "robust" because the factor k contains all the expert's condensed knowledge on the legislation and exogenous variables influencing the development of Y over time.[1] It may just be a simple growth factor of another variable, or a factor reflecting the combined impact of a set of other variables on Y. *Robustness* also means that projection results are "anchored" to statistically observed initial values. These initial *anchor values* are usually compiled in the accounting matrices for the initial year. Anchoring projection values to observed starting values avoids the model producing results in specific expenditure and revenue categories which are completely "aloof" from the values observed during the years preceding the projection period. Thus, potential unwarranted breaks in data series are avoided by recursive projections of each year's results on the basis of last year's results. By contrast, if such time-series breaks were to be expected – for example because of changes in legislation – then this method would be best suited to map such breaks. In fact, this simple calculation method with a high information content plays an important role in the ILO's "modular system approach", which will be explained later.

Other classical methods of time-series extrapolation might also be used, for example different types of trend extrapolation functions, auto-regressive equations (of which equation 8.1 is an example), or econometric single equation estimations. We will not address these in detail. The interested reader may search the ample literature on time-series analysis for further information.[2] The results can be compiled, sorted and aggregated in table formats along the lines described in Part II, and will then be open to analysis and discussion.

There are a number of obvious advantages to an approach that explicitly taps experts' knowledge. The first is its potentially high acceptance by politicians and the general public, as the projection is based on experts' knowledge, and thus if necessary can easily be defended in public. The second advantage is that the projected Social Budget, if combined with the projection of the normal government budget, is consistent with other public financial developments. A third advantage is that the Social Budget so projected can reflect policy goals – the political will of the government as far as it can be reflected in figures – if the expected revenues and expenditures contain politically intended "programme elements".

There are, of course, disadvantages to this approach. If the projection contained "too many political considerations" instead of sober analysis, then the budget projection might already be wrong in its *status nascendi*. The general public would possibly receive incorrect or biased signals through the information provided. Another disadvantage is the inherent danger of inconsistencies in the projection assumptions, and the potential failure of not taking interactions between different social protection subsystems into account. If the experts belong to different institutions, they may have long-standing, traditionally different or politically influenced views on social and economic developments. Labour market developments, for example, might be expected to develop differently, such differing expectations resulting in incoherent projections of Social Budget variables. The problem is not so much divergent views on the future development of the same variable – such differences can be arranged by discussion – but it occurs if two experts, responsible for disjunct sets of Social Budget variables, base their respective projections on the same set of labour market variables while disagreeing on their expected developments. A third disadvantage, linked to the previous one, is the decreasing reliability of such experts' projections if applied to longer projection periods, say a three- to ten-year time horizon. In that case, undetected differences in underlying assumptions become increasingly important because any resulting inconsistencies grow.

Another disadvantage which must be explicitly mentioned is that this method does not allow for policy simulations. For example, the probable financial impacts of proposals to change the social protection legislation may well be calculated for certain financial variables, but no comprehensive view on the total Social Budget could be made available within a reasonable time. The calculation of alternative scenarios and any impacts they have on the total Social Budget, its structure and future development, would be extremely time-consuming.

Still, despite these disadvantages, experts' inquiries can be a valid and solid projection method if a government introduces a social budgeting process just in order to mirror the impacts on the social finances of its general short-term budget and medium-term financial planning process. This method has been successfully used over long periods in many OECD and other countries. However, a precondition for a satisfactory operation is that the experts develop some culture of "independence", "prudence", bilateral and multilateral consultations, and a routine of recurrent thorough discussions. If political pressure is too obvious and often results in wrong projections, then the signals coming from these projections are no longer accepted by their addressees. In such circumstances, the whole projection effort becomes futile because it undermines public confidence.

The ILO has recently tried to marry a systematic modelling approach to the above classical modelling approach by convening national task forces (consisting of experts of all social security institutions, the ministries of social protection, labour, health and finance, as well as representatives from national statistical offices), and asking them to develop jointly a national Social Budget model. This approach usually results in a set of interlinked modules, each covering a major function or institution of the national social protection systems, or its economic and demographic environment. Thus, modelling and consultation take place simultaneously. Analytical system approaches (or microsimulation; see section 8.1.2) can thus be successfully applied to "back up" the classical approach given here.

8.1.2 Microsimulation

The modelling approaches described in the following sections are based in principle on macroeconomic, macrofinancial and/or "macrosocial" considerations. Sometimes their theoretical reasoning may satisfy, but occasionally ad hoc approaches dominate. Whatever degree of incorporated detailed specificity there may be, there is still some dissatisfaction with structural and individual economic and social effects. Furthermore, the theoretical basis of macro models is usually weak, as any explicitly or implicitly incorporated behavioural relations are usually drawn from microeconomic considerations, which are usually difficult to prove to be also valid for aggregate (group) behaviour.

On this basis, a "movement" has developed since the end of the 1950s which concentrates on the microrelations between individuals/households, and which has elaborated formal instruments to cope with the related modelling problems – well known as "microsimulation models".

Microsimulation models are based on representative individual data sets for the population. They usually include information on each individual's age, sex, formal education, occupation, living status (family, single, household), number of children, employment status, residence, gross/net income, ownership of wealth, durable consumer goods, and so on. The establishment of such data files normally takes considerable time and resources.

The basic idea of microsimulation is to describe mathematically the activities over time of each individual included in the data set. The starting period is the base (data) period $t = 0$; by applying appropriate mathematical formulae, a new data file for all individuals in $t = 1$ is produced which, in turn, becomes the data basis for the next step ($t = 2$). Theoretically, an unlimited series of data files is produced which, in essence, describes the dynamic behaviour of the system for all individuals.

For example, consider the case of social assistance. The projection procedure can be separated into the following steps:

- The available information on each individual is checked as to whether he/she is eligible for social assistance benefits under the legislation. The decision depends on the parameters defined in the law, for example on income, the size and composition of the family, the health status of the family members, and so on.

- By using a random variables processor, it is in $t = 1$ decided whether the eligible individual actually receives social assistance. The respective probability may be estimated by the actually observed take-up rate in the base year $t = 0$. For example, the statistical database might indicate that 80 per cent of the eligible population actually receive a transfer. Then the random processor would filter 80 out of every 100 eligible persons to receive a benefit. Now we consider a person actually receiving a benefit. We could, for example, assume that a new child is born and the person finds a job (the probabilities for these events must be known, of course). Furthermore, the social assistance legislation may have changed, for example the poverty line was increased (indexed to the CPI). It is now checked whether this person – under the new constellation of social and legislative variables – is still eligible for social assistance and, if so, by what amount.

- This kind of consideration is undertaken for each individual in the data set. Thus, at the beginning of the next period, $t = 2$, we have created a new set to start with. The person we considered in the previous period may now have a certain probability of dying; this again is decided with the help of a random processor – the probabilities for eligible persons dying being known. For those that die, the payment of benefit will be stopped. But their dependants' eligibility situation has now changed. They might get additional benefits (funeral grants) and/or benefits (higher monthly payments), or social assistance could be replaced by benefits from a different institution/legislation.

It is thus possible to pursue individuals from birth to death with respect to their "relation" to social assistance – how their life cycle behaviour would influence the financial development of social assistance (as a scheme) and how changes in social assistance legislation would change the individual's income situation, the financial situation of the scheme, and possibly that of other institutions. Depending on the size and structure of the data set available, social phenomena such as marriage, divorce, and children starting and leaving school, could also be simulated – if relevant to social assistance expenditure projections. The problems of operating such models will probably grow proportionally with increasing model size and the details covered.

With real data and information providers being available, microsimulation models have meanwhile been successfully developed by many governments/institutions in order to have a better understanding of certain partial aspects of legislation. Microsimulation models, for example, exist in Australia, Germany, Sweden and the United Kingdom. This list is by no means exhaustive.

These models are mostly used to establish the distributive effects of changes in social transfer schemes, for example to establish a sound winners' and losers' analysis before introducing modifications to existing benefit provisions. Models of this nature have not been used to establish full Social Budget simulations and projections. The number of individual behavioural functions which link different social security branches, as well as the national budget, to individual behaviour would simply be too large to handle. Longer-term forecasts are generally not the prime purpose of microsimulation models, and the numerous behavioural assumptions make long-term forecasting very uncertain. However, micro-analytical results could be used to improve the estimates of social expenditure and income (when these are due to changes in legislation), as well as aggregate social outcomes in some branches of the social protection system. The most important module is the social assistance module, where benefit eligibility depends on the individual household income situation, that requires the projection of income distributions, which is of course best done on a micro-data basis.

The ILO modelling approach (see section 8.1.3) in some areas tries to strike a balance between pure macro models which estimate highly aggregate behavioural equations and the micro-behavioural approach by using distributions when establishing the eligibility of certain categories of persons for social protection benefits, notably pensions and means-tested benefits.

8.1.3   System approaches

Using the nomenclature of system theory, a system generally consists of a set of interrelated elements. A system may be linked to other systems, may be nested in a supersystem, or may consist of a number of subsystems. Whether a subject of interest may be considered an element, a subsystem, a system or a supersystem depends mainly on the purpose of analysis, and this has to be determined in each concrete case. The *structure* of a system is established by the set of all the relations between its elements.

A social protection system and its Social Budget are *real* systems like, for example, a national economy or an enterprise, which can be systematically observed and analysed. Real systems may be contrasted by *formal* systems, which are constructed on a mere logical or theoretical basis. Here, we focus only on real systems.

Also, social protection (its Social Budget) is an *open* system (as opposed to a closed one), that is, it is characterized by the fact that impacts from outside change the behaviour of the system. Closed systems do not react to their environment. Open systems do.

Under this system's theoretical perspective, a social protection system can be visualized as follows:

Figure 8.2   Social protection as an open system

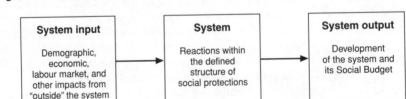

Its elements and relations are normally described by mathematical equations.

A *Social Budget model* is a simplified mathematical representation of the real social protection system, with a special focus on the system's finances. It covers the elements of the system (population, economy, labour market, social institutions and functions, etc.), as well as the relations between the system's elements. Building a Social Budget model means achieving a high degree of similarity between the reality of social protection and its simplified image. Simplification involves including in the model only those elements of reality and their (inter)relations that are regarded as relevant for the analytical purposes under consideration, that is, the analysis of the social protection system's finances. In other words, modelling a Social Budget means reducing reality but also describing this reduced version of reality as precisely as possible.

Such a model allows the analysis and projection of the existing social protection system under status quo conditions, as well as the comparative analysis of alternative policies under a clearly defined set of assumptions.

This is why a social protection model will be able to answer many questions, but not all, regarding social reality. More precisely, a Social Budget model will be able to answer many, but not all, *financial* questions concerning social protection. In fact, a good deal of the range of possible answers (and underlying questions) of a Social Budget model is more or less determined by the methodological structure and the database.[3]

It should be noted that the financial aspects of social protection systems are especially suitable to describing them by an image of reality, but also enable this "reduced reality" to be modelled very precisely. This is because social protection systems are normally highly formalized, and the behaviour of the systems' participants is often heavily regulated. The links between the system input and the system itself are also often more predictable than in other systems. For example, an increase in open unemployment will lead to an increase in the number of recipients of unemployment benefits. The more precise the labour market and wage projections are, the more precisely the expenditure can be estimated.

Still, there is no one specific model that can be applied to each single country around the world. There is too much variety in social systems, and any attempt at uniformity would mean putting constraints on most countries' social protection systems. As a consequence, the description of the ILO's modelling approach in section 8.2 will vary between higher and lower levels of abstraction. When describing submodels which the authors regard as more or less universally applicable, we try to be relatively concrete; when addressing submodels which will probably have to differ substantially from country to country, we will be relatively abstract. We hope to meet any reader's demand for more concrete information by offering the description of two applied country cases in Part IV.

8.2 THE MODULAR SYSTEM APPROACH OF THE ILO

The ILO's approach to Social Budget modelling is modular. This means that the overall Social Budget model consists of several submodels, which can be used simultaneously, or as stand-alone models for separate purposes, in which case they are models in their own right. Each of the models or submodels consists of several modules which map certain coherent parts of reality. Consistent with the considerations in the "Issues brief" (Annex I), the model consists basically of the following components:

- a demographic model, which is used for population projections;
- a labour supply model, which allows for projections of the supply of labour;

- an economic model, which is designed for projecting GDP, prices, wages, labour productivity, labour demand (equals actual employment) and unemployment – including a whole range of variables which have a direct impact on the social protection system, for example, the number of contributors, categories of beneficiaries and others;
- a government budget model, which describes revenues and expenditures of the different administrative levels of government;
- a social protection model, which consists of:
  - a pension submodel to project the different types of pension cases, average pensions by category, and revenues and expenditures of the pension system;
  - a health submodel, designed to project health-specific types of physical entities (hospitals, doctors, patients, etc.) and revenues and expenditures of the health system;
  - other submodels projecting the financial development of other social protection subsystems, for example, unemployment benefits or social assistance;
  - a Social Budget submodel, aggregating the fiscal results of all social protection models into an aggregated social accounting framework (which may reflect one of the display formats described in Part II).

In principle, the different components are subject to a hierarchical dependency structure: the results of the demographic model feed into the labour supply model, into all submodels or modules describing social protection, and into the government accounts model. The labour supply model results feed into the economic model, into the pension submodel and into the other social protection models. The economic model's results feed into all social protection submodels and into the government accounts model. As far as social protection finances are concerned, all results are finally compiled in the Social Budget component.

Due mainly to software limitations, any feedback, such as reverse impacts from social protection finances on the economy or the labour market, is normally not modelled explicitly. However, such feedback can principally be recognized within the ILO model family, although it is mainly for demonstration purposes.

Furthermore, the number of model components might vary considerably from country application to country application. The reasons are mainly differing legislation, institutional structures, formats of statistical information and/or modelling purposes and policy goals. Despite basic similarities in social protection the world over, the concrete modelling of social protection in Asia is different from the transition countries of Eastern Europe; Latin American countries are not the same as Africa; and Western European countries might differ from other OECD countries.

Figure 8.3   Hierarchical dependency structure of the ILO model

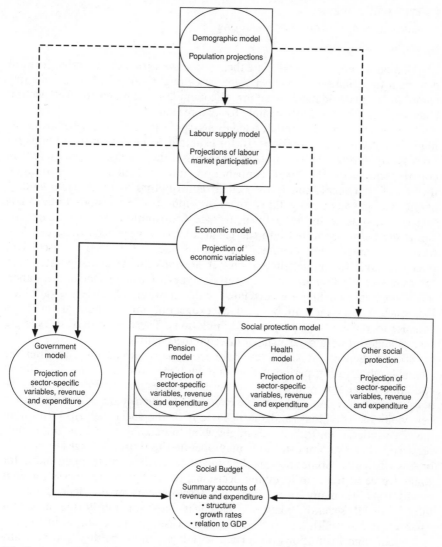

Note: Rectangular frames indicate a relative stability of the model structure in different country applications, whereas ovals indicate high variability due to country-specific circumstances.

An overview of the model components and the dependency structure is given in figure 8.3.

The calculation methods used are generally a pragmatic intersection of four quantitative disciplines:

- methods of quantitative economics
- actuarial techniques
- national and institutional accounting
- social accounting[4]

All model components calculate their respective variables by straightforward deterministic equations, which in some cases might still be of a considerably complicated mathematical structure. Econometric estimates of behavioural equations have been omitted mainly for two reasons.

First, many social protection regulations can be properly described by deterministic mathematical equations. If, for example, a social security administration is operating the institution efficiently, then wage development in combination with the legal contribution rate will describe contribution income of that institution fairly well. If contributors to the scheme tend to avoid their payment obligations, there are appropriate methods to calculate (externally, outside the model) an average contribution evasion factor that can easily be incorporated into the technical relation between wage development and contribution income. The evasion factor can then be used as a policy variable for model simulations. If previous knowledge stipulates that, for example, the take-up rates of certain types of benefit (social assistance, unemployment benefits) are correlated with variations of reference variables, then such knowledge can be used as exogenous model input in order to enhance its reliability of projections/simulations. There is no need to estimate such changes of parameter behaviour econometrically.

Second, there might be clear cases for econometric estimations, but often the available observation period is not long enough – owing to the difficulty of collecting consistent past data – to permit such estimates. For example, the development of a financial variable over time frequently depends on both the behaviour of individuals and the behaviour of the social security institution under consideration. Individuals might want to maximize the benefit amounts received, whereas administrations may operate the respective legislation more or less efficiently. Sometimes the law might be unclear, or it might allow for some degree of freedom in taking decisions, or contain more or less rigorous means tests. In many cases, financial developments might depend on the interaction of several "players", which is most obviously the case, for example, in the health sector. Thus, in many cases the behavioural impacts of individuals and institutions on certain variables cannot be distinguished; any attempt to separate the underlying behavioural structure by estimating statistically significant parameters fails.

As the ILO model components have been purposely developed in order to be applicable in different countries, that is, under varying statistical, legal and administrative conditions, a purely or predominantly econometric approach would have failed in practice. This is why focusing on such an approach has been avoided right from the beginning. There might be some resulting loss of insight, but not necessarily. Often, parameter estimates based on institutional a priori knowledge of system behaviour might even be more reliable than parameters estimated on the basis of econometric techniques. In mature social protection systems, and under status quo conditions, parameters are unlikely to change quickly. Thus, behavioural coefficients (for example, benefit take-up rates of sickness and maternity benefits) can, with some acceptable risk, be kept equal to observed last (average) values. Hence, in relying on external estimates for behavioural parameters, the model is by its nature mainly a tool to perform "if-then" types of analyses, projections and simulations.

Therefore, it is recommended to use the methods described in this book (section 8.2.1) as a launching platform for the construction of a national Social Budget model, especially if countries are in economic and/or social transition, or if they are at the beginning of a reform phase of, for example, intensified privatization and accompanying changes in social protection legislation and administration. In all such cases, the past observation period might be (too) short for a successful application of broader econometric modelling techniques. If the results are considered satisfying, then, in principle, no further model improvement will be necessary. But once countries have entered a "stable situation" (which could, for example, also mean a stable continuation of transition), then an intensified use of econometric techniques might be worth considering.[5]

8.2.1   The demographic submodel

Most social protection systems are redistributive mechanisms which collect money and resources from some economic actors and allocate these resources to defined subgroups of the population in the form of social protection benefits.[6] All systems require knowledge about the expected future number of financers (employers, employees, taxpayers) and beneficiaries (pensioners, unemployment benefit recipients, social assistance recipients, sick and disabled persons, etc.). Thus, in order to determine the number and structure of present and future financers, as well as of present and future beneficiaries, the Social Budget model needs a demographic basis. This may be provided by a national population census and projections, but it can also be generated with the help of population projections based on national censuses and the United Nations forecasting methodology,[7] which is incorporated in the ILO Social Budget model.

A disadvantage of using national population projections exogenously – instead of elaborating your own projections within the Social Budget model family – is that the sensitivity of the model to demographic change cannot be tested. Also, extended long-term population projections over several decades, which are sometimes considered helpful when analysing long-term patterns of pension systems or labour supply (or both in combination), may not always be available, or may be outdated. Again, an own population model within the Social Budget context seems to be useful.

The United Nations population model or some derivative version is normally applied at the statistical institute of most countries. This is why we give here only a short description of the ILO version, to the extent necessary for an understanding of the subsequent sections of this part of the book.

The ILO population model is based on the methodology developed by the United Nations Department for Economic and Social Information and Policy Analysis (Population Division). It was adapted, especially in terms of its software, to the social budgeting environment of the ILO.[8]

Movements over time in the size of the population depend essentially on the three following variables: (1) the number of births, (2) the number of deaths, and (3) net migration across borders. It is obvious that a population increases from observation in time t to observation in $t + 1$ if the number of births is higher than the number of deaths and vice versa (assuming zero net migration); or, assuming the same number of births and deaths, the population increases if the number of immigrants is higher than the number of emigrants (net inflow) and decreases in the opposite case (net outflow).

The ILO population model age-specifically applies initial fertility, mortality and migration rates[9] to an observed initial population. The model can accommodate alternative assumptions on the future development of fertility and mortality rates.[10]

The basic procedure of a population projection can best be described by figure 8.4.

Given a specific base population and its structure, it is the *choice* of future survival rates (equals inverse death rates), future fertility rates and future migration rates which determines future population development. Fertility and mortality changes have a direct impact on the age and sex structure of the population. The structure of a population in turn has a direct impact on social expenditure; for example, an ageing population will lead to a faster increase and higher levels of old-age dependency rates (not necessarily to increasing *total* dependency rates). Demographic dependency rates are usually defined as the ratio of persons over 65 or 60 (in exceptional cases, over 55) years of age, or those aged 19 and younger to the population in active age groups (usually 20 to 64, 59 or 54, respectively). Demographic dependency rates are one determinant of the number of beneficiaries in a national social protection system. However, it should not be overlooked that they do not wholly determine the so-called *system dependency rates* of social protection systems. The latter are also influenced to a large extent by such factors as labour market participation, employment and unemployment levels, retirement behaviour, and so on.

The actual development of mortality, fertility and migration rates in the past and for the future depends on numerous exogenous impacts, such as cultural habits, economic developments, education and health provisions, as well as on epidemics, wars and environmental catastrophes. With respect to the world population, since the Second World War the United Nations has distinguished different phases of population growth which might be described as

Figure 8.4 Basic procedure of the population projection model[11]

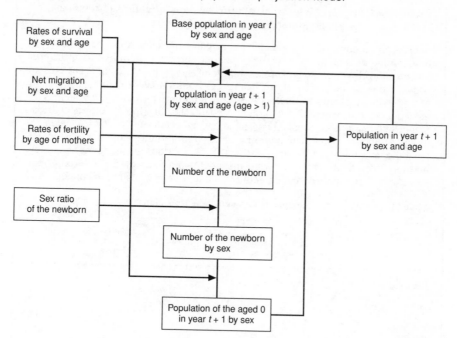

being "mortality-induced", "fertility-driven" or "stagnant" – each of these reflecting different constellations between fertility and mortality and, thus different patterns of population development. It is up to users of a population model in the Social Budget context to decide which pattern might in future be relevant for their own country's case. In addition, decisions on net migration have to be taken (which is irrelevant on the world population level). In order to choose meaningful assumptions, the United Nations has developed probable patterns of future fertility and mortality developments for different regions of the world, which can be applied in individual countries' cases.[12] Example 8.1 demonstrates the effect of alternative mortality and fertility assumptions on the demographic structure of the country case of Egypt.

8.2.2 The labour supply submodel

In principle, labour supply can be measured in persons ("heads") or in time ("hours"). If labour supply is measured in "heads", it is also called the labour force. (As reliable statistics [or estimation procedures] about working time offered by private households are not available in many countries, the head-count concept is used within the framework of the Social Budget model.) Another reason is that, in this context, a direct link was to be maintained

---

Example 8.1 Egypt[1]: Effects of alternative demographic assumptions on population projections

In order to demonstrate the effects of alternative mortality and fertility assumptions on the development of the total number of a population and its structural composition, two population projections for Egypt under two different sets of assumptions are undertaken here. Both projections start with an initial population of 58.7 million people in 1995. Table E8.1 summarizes the key demographic assumptions (life expectancy at birth and the total fertility rate) for both scenarios. Scenario A assumes a constant improvement of mortality up to a typical value for an upper-middle-income country and a decline of fertility down to replacement level (i.e. to a total fertility rate (TFR) of 2.1). Scenario B assumes that mortality and fertility will not change during the next two-and-a-half decades and that thus the country stays on the demographic pattern of a developing country.

Table E8.1 Egypt: Key assumptions for population projections

	Standard variant (scenario A) Intermediate mortality improvement and intermediate fertility	Alternative variant (scenario B) Low mortality improvement and low fertility
Initial population ('000)		
Under 15	22 997	
In % of total	39.2	
15–64	33 495	
In % or total	57.1	
Over 65	2 157.5	
In % of total	3.7	
Total	**58 650**	
Demographic indicators		
Initial life expectancy at birth		
Male	65	
Female	69	
Initial total fertility rate	3.93	
Assumed levels of:		
Life expectancy until 2020		
Male	71.4	65
Female	76.1	69
Fertility until 2020	2.1	3.93

The following graphs display the results of alternative projections based on the ILO population model. Figure E8.1a depicts the development of the total population. It shows that by the end of the projection period of 25 years the population under scenario A would be about 13 million smaller than under scenario B. Figures E8.1b–d describe the shift in the population structure in terms of classical demographic dependency ratios:

- Figure E8.1b, the ratio of the number of the population over 65 to the number of the population between 15 and 64 years of age, i.e. the so-called *demographic old-age dependency ratio*

- Figure E8.1c, the ratio of the number of the population under 15 to the number of the population in the active age group 15 to 64, i.e. the so-called *demographic youth dependency ratio*
- Figure E8.1d, the *total demographic dependency ratio*, which is the sum of the previous two ratios

Figure E8.1a   Egypt: Total population development

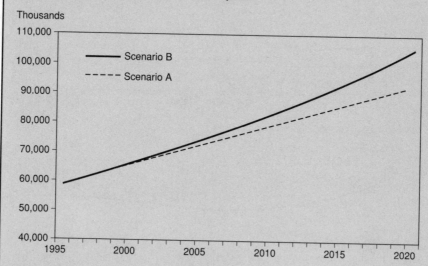

Figure E8.1b   Egypt: Old-age dependency ratios

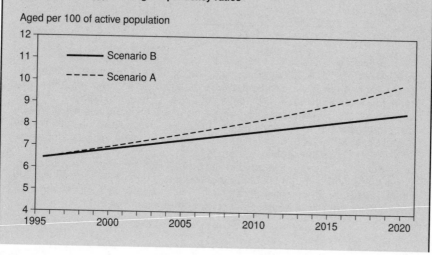

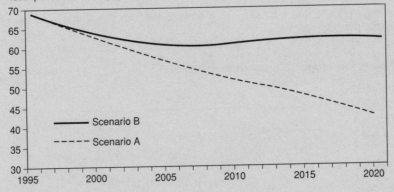

Figure E8.1c Egypt: Youth dependency ratios

Youth per 100 of active population

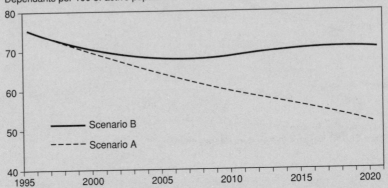

Figure E8.1d Egypt: Total dependency ratios

Dependants per 100 of active population

A preliminary analysis reveals that the dominant impact stems in both scenarios from the fertility assumption. The significantly reduced fertility rate of scenario A results in reduced total population growth and a significantly reduced number of youth. While the old-age dependency ratio increases, youth dependency decreases fast, resulting in a significant total dependency decline from about 75 dependants per 100 of active population in 1995 to only slightly over 50 in 2020. Such information has to be taken into account when, for instance, balancing public resources for old-age security and education.

Dependency ratios are of pivotal importance for an assessment of social protection systems. But it should be noticed that demographic ratios are only rough indicators for potential problems of social protection systems and their subsystems. We return to these aspects in other examples.

[1] The example has been taken from the database of ILO: *Social protection in Egypt*, a preliminary report (Geneva, Nov. 1998).

between the projected population and the projected age structure of the contributors to social protection. Social protection financing analyses focus mainly on the number of persons financing (contributing or paying taxes) and potentially receiving benefits – not so much on the hours worked backing the contribution payment.

Maximum labour supply is determined by the level and structure of the total population, and more precisely by the maximum number of potentially active persons, which is all persons between a minimum and a maximum age. Statistical programmes often fix the minimum age for potentially participating in the labour market at 15 years, sometimes at 12. At the upper end of the age scale, labour market measurement is often cut off for ages over 65 or 70, all those older ages still participating being summed up in the age group 66 (or 71) and over. In other words, the potentially active population comprises all persons, male and female, between the ages 12 to 15 and 65+ to 70+. The only other potential sources of labour supply are commuters across national borders. Whether commuters should be explicitly taken into account has to be decided for each case of actual model application on a country level. For the sake of simplicity, we disregard here any commuter effects on labour supply. In this submodel migration also does not influence labour supply, because that has been accounted for already in the population model.

For a number of reasons, not all of those who could potentially participate in the labour market will actually do so. For example, many younger persons may still be in education, and thus not available on the labour market. Others may never intend to work, or may not fit into the world of labour. Married women (and/or men) may retire from the labour market in order to raise children, or for other reasons. Older persons may receive a pension or live off personal savings, and thus decide not to participate in the labour market any longer. Those who actually participate or want to participate, that is those who offer their labour, are usually measured in (regular) labour market surveys. A core result of such surveys is the possibility of calculating so-called labour market participation rates. Labour market participation rates are, for each single age (or age group), equal to the total number of persons offering labour over the total potentially active in that same age group, expressed as a percentage.

A technically simple way to project the future development of labour supply is by leaving the age-specific participation rates constant during the projection period; any projected changes in the overall participation rate then only result from changes in the population structure. The simplicity of this approach is obvious. Its usefulness stems from the fact that it is considered worthwhile knowing what would happen in future under status quo conditions before assuming any future modification due to behavioural or policy changes. Leaving participation rates unchanged might be advisable because no better information is available; if past trends, changes in legislation or different developments in countries with comparable socio-economic environments indicate a different development pattern of future national participation rates, then the rates may be modified accordingly. In general, in recent decades, labour force participation rates for women have been increasing in most countries, notably in developed market economies, whereas the rates of older male workers have dropped. At the same time, it might be expected that prolonged unemployment has, in many parts of the world, discouraged labour market participation and that participation rates may drop further in certain age/sex groups.

Concerning the estimation of future social expenditure in the Social Budget framework, it must be kept in mind in particular that modelling policies of rising retirement ages have to be accompanied by simultaneous increases of labour force participation in older age groups and hence the total labour force, which in turn might lead to higher unemployment, and thus possibly higher expenditure on unemployment benefits. In addition, it is the peak participation rates in the age groups between 30 and 45 which are most liable to determine the size of the total number of persons with credits in pension systems, rather than the size of the employed population close to the retirement age bracket alone. This proves that the labour force is a pivotal element for the Social Budget.

To sum up, the calculation of the labour force can be made as follows:

Equation 8.2

$$TLF_t = \sum_{x,s}(POP_{t,x,s} * LFPR_{t,x,s}),$$

where:

$$TLF_t = \text{Total labour force in year } t$$

$$LFPR_{t,x.s} = \text{Labour force participation rates of sex}$$
$$s \text{ and age } x \text{ in year } t$$

$$\text{Exogenous} = LFPR_t$$

$$t = 1, \ldots, T \ (T = \text{end of projection year})$$

$$x = \text{Age } 0, \ldots, 100$$

$$s = \text{Male } (0), \text{ female } (1).$$

The following box provides another example (8.2) from Egypt. A further application of the technique will be provided later when describing the structure and calculation of the labour market balance.

8.2.3   The economic submodel

The economic model is designed to support the Social Budget projections. Thus it has two main purposes:

- to calculate labour demand, which is actual employment by its single components, and – as a residual – unemployment, both in order to establish a labour market balance; and

Example 8.2 Labour force projections in Egypt[1]

As in other developing countries, Egypt's measured labour force participation rates are traditionally low. But if Egypt succeeds in entering a high economic growth path, labour market behaviour can be expected to change accordingly, lifting female labour force participation especially within the next two to three decades. This would have a considerable impact on the composition and level of the country's total labour force.

In the base year, the following labour force participation rates were observed:

Table E8.2   Egypt: Labour market participation rates in the base year of projection

Age group	12–14	15–19	20–24	25–29	35–39	40–44	45–49	50–54	55–59	60–64	65–69	70+
	% of population in "active" ages											
Male	30.0	37.7	56.6	73.2	86.0	95.0	95.0	95.0	95.0	76.8	35.2	0.0
Female	8.7	12.8	28.6	29.2	29.3	25.9	25.9	16.3	16.3	6.7	2.1	0.0

Based on these initial rates (and on the scenario B population projection of example 8.1) two sets of labour force projections were undertaken. Variant I assumes that the age-specific participation rates remain constant throughout the projection period. Variant II assumes that female participation will increase by 1 percentage point per year, except for the "prime active age groups" between 35 and 49, where the participation rates increase by 2.5 percentage points annually. Male participation rates remain unchanged. The results are shown in figure E8.2.

Figure E8.2   Egypt: Total and female labour force development (variants I and II)

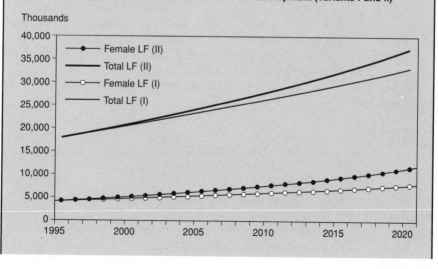

> The graph shows that an underestimate of future development in participation rates, for example that of women, could lead to a substantial underestimation of the future size of the workforce. In Egypt the increased participation of women leads potentially to an additional 3.8 million workers within two-and-a-half decades, offering ample room for additional economic growth or, if not absorbed by the labour market, additional open or hidden unemployment.
>
> [1] The example has been taken from the database of ILO: *Social protection in Egypt*, a preliminary report (Geneva, Nov. 1998).

- to project the key economic inputs for the social projection model, comprising mainly wages and prices, as well as the development of total GDP and its primary distribution on the production factors "labour" and "capital" which are pivotal comparators for the measurement of social expenditure and revenue.

8.2.3.1 Employment projections

The projection of actual employment is based on the following approach: first, an assumption is exogenously made on the annual growth of GDP in constant prices, starting from a suitable observation year (in short, we call this the growth assumption on "real GDP"). On the basis of this growth assumption, absolute real GDP is projected, starting in a base year t_0.

Second, another exogenous assumption is introduced, this time on labour productivity growth. Labour productivity is, for the same base year t_0, simply calculated as real GDP over actual total employment. Thus, it is the (annual) value of a certain amount of goods and services produced per employed person, expressed in "real" currency units. In the projections it is calculated as the previous year's value multiplied by an assumed growth factor.

Then, over all years of the projection period, total employment is calculated as a residual by dividing real GDP by labour productivity.

In formal terms the calculations can be presented by means of the following set of equations:

Equation 8.3

$$EMPL_t = GDP_t^r / LabProd_t,$$

where:

$$GDP_t^r = GDP_{t-1}^r * R_{GDP,t}$$
$$LabProd_t = LabProd_{t-1} * R_{LabProd,t}$$
$$GDP_t^r = GDP_t^n / DEFL_{GDP,t}$$

and

$EMPL_t = $ Total number of employed in year t,

$R_{GDP,t} = $ Exogenous growth factor of real GDP in t,

$R_{LabProd,t} = $ Exogenous growth factor of labour productivity in t,

$GDP_t^n = $ Nominal GDP in t,

$GDP_t^r = $ Real GDP in t,

$DEFL_{GDP,t} = $ GDP deflator in t.

Considerable tautology has thus been introduced for calculating one time series, which is actual employment: an assumption on GDP development combined with an assumption on labour productivity development in order to obtain employment.

Why not directly assume a certain growth rate for employment? The reasons are of mainly a political nature. Governments all over the world usually elaborate short-, medium- and long-term development plans. In the OECD world, these are generally short- and medium-term financial plans on a revolving basis, where the plans are being adjusted every year to actual developments, which might be slightly or significantly different from the planned figures. In other countries, there is a different tradition of planning: once a plan has been established covering, for example, a period of five years, ancillary government planning processes adhere to these plans. They are not always adjusted to actual developments, even if these differ significantly from the initial plan. Both options have their pros and cons, and differing backgrounds of governance. An advantage of the first option is that it adapts planning figures almost immediately to new, unforeseen developments and, thus, especially in case of comparatively unfavourable developments, satisfyingly performs an early warning function. A disadvantage is that eventually differences between initial plans and actual developments may easily disappear from the public's memory. This, in turn, is the main advantage of the second option: a detailed record can be kept of deviations between the initial plans and actual developments. However, a disadvantage is that governments might feel obliged to adhere to their initially planned figures, even if reality had long ago taken a different path.

Social budgeting cannot be left unaffected by such different patterns of policy attitudes. The projection of a Social Budget has inevitably to be nested in the general economic and financial planning procedures of governments. Very often these do not take specific account of social policy and social protection finance developments in the planned economic context, although social protection systems in many countries turn over larger amounts of monies than the regular government budget. Performing recurring projections of the Social Budget, on the other hand, aims at significantly upgrading the stance of social policy, among other things by proving its conformity with other planned economic and financial (fiscal) developments. In order not to counteract these efforts, it is of utmost importance to reveal the basic economic assumptions on which any Social Budget projection is based, especially when these are only implicit (hidden). Only then will the participants in the political decision-making process be provided with the explicit and (even more important) implicit conditions which have to be met in order to achieve certain politically defined income and/or social policy goals.

When the necessary statistical information on hypotheses for the future development of individual sectors of the economy is available, the development of total employment may be calculated on the basis of sectoral real value added and sectoral labour productivity. The same "tautological" procedure would then be applied to the single sectors of the economy, and resulting sectoral employment would be compiled to aggregate employment. Again, the major advantage of such a fairly disaggregate approach would be deeper insight into the conditions that have to be met in order to achieve certain goals.

As already mentioned, the ultimate purpose of the economic submodel is to support the Social Budget projections by providing necessary input. Thus, it is not mainly the projection of total employment we are interested in, but a breakdown of the labour market by employment category. These can be regarded as a "frame" for the structure and development of the "stakeholders" of the social protection system, who are mainly the contributors and groups of beneficiaries. For example, Part II, section 3.2.1, discussed a breakdown of contributions by legal category (see list 3). Thus, ideally, labour demand should be calculated using exactly the same categories, for the model calculations on contribution income can then be based on a solid labour market frame.

8.2.3.2 Establishment of a labour market balance

One of the core instruments used in analysing and forecasting a Social Budget in an aggregate labour market context is the so-called "labour market balance". A labour market balance is basically a table consistently[13] showing both an economy's labour supply and labour demand (both by different categories of person) over a certain past and/or future period of time. Unemployment is calculated as a residual of labour supply and demand. For purposes of social budgeting, the information provided is especially important, as the numbers of contributors or certain categories of beneficiaries might be interpreted as subsets of labour market categories. Thus, the labour market balance also establishes a general ("maximum") frame of important categories of social protection systems. For example, it is only within the limits of the labour market balance that the maximum potential number of contributors to a social protection scheme can be identified. Equally, the number of unemployed, so calculated, would provide for a maximum number of beneficiaries of unemployment benefits.

Figure 8.5   Blueprint for a labour market balance

Item	Unit	Year 1	Year 2	...	Year t	Year $t+1$	...	Year $t+k$
		Statistics				Projection		
Supply side of the labour market								
1. Population	No.							
2. Active population	No.							
3. Average participation rate	No.							
4. Labour force	No.							
Demand side of the labour market								
5. Total employed persons	No.							
5.1 Total self-employed persons	No.							
5.2 Total unpaid family workers	No.							
5.3 Total employees	No.							
Economic sector 1								
6.1 Employed persons in sector 1	No.							
6.1.1 Self-employed persons in sector 1	No.							
6.1.2 Unpaid family workers in sector 1	No.							
6.1.3 Employees in sector 1	No.							
Economic sector n								
6.n Employed persons in sector n	No.							
6.n.1 Self-employed persons in sector n	No.							
6.n.2 Unpaid family workers in sector n	No.							
Contributors								
7.1 Self-employed contributors	No.							
7.2 Contributing unpaid family workers	No.							
7.3 Contributing employees category 1	No.							
7.4 Contributing employees category 2	No.							
7.m Contributing employees category m	No.							
8. Other contributors	No.							
Residual								
9. Unemployed persons	No.							
10. Unemployment rate	%							
11. Unemployed contributors to the social protection system	No.							

Note: For analytical purposes, it is in many respects helpful to disaggregate all items further by sex. For instance, medium-term projections of unemployment benefits become more meaningful when taking different male/female unemployment rates into account, or long-term projections of pension expenditures become more reliable when differentiating the number of contributors by sex.

The general design of a labour market balance is presented in figure 8.5. The upper part of the balance (items 1 to 4) reports important variables of the supply side of the labour market.

Item 1 reflects the total resident population which represents the "maximum source" for the labour market supply. Item 2 is the potentially active population. It is defined as the total population minus children minus older people and others not potentially able to participate in the labour market. Children include all residents up to a certain age (for example, 12 or 14 or 16 years), depending on a country's relevant legislation on child labour protection;[14]

older people might be all or most of those beyond the minimum legal retirement age. Other persons might comprise, for example, prisoners or severely disabled people unable to work. In some countries, depending on the economic, social and legal circumstances, all older people are included in the active population.

As mentioned earlier, the labour force (item 4) covers all persons who participate in the labour market, that is those who are either actually employed or who are unemployed but looking for work.[15]

The participation rate (item 3) is calculated as the relative share of the labour force in the potentially active population. For purposes of labour market projections, this rate might be used as an exogenous variable to determine the development of the labour force. The potentially active population (item 2) serves as the maximum "boundary" for labour force development; the boundary would be achieved if the participation rates in all potentially active cohorts of the population were equal to 100 per cent.

Within the labour market balance, actual labour demand is reflected by all those who are actually employed (item 5). In practice, the total number of employed persons is subdivided into self-employed, unpaid family workers and (dependent) employees (items 5.1 to 5.3). Alternatively, the demand side might be broken down by sectors of the economy, each reflecting the structure of the employed as presented in the blueprint. In principle, the possibilities of breaking down the number of employed are numerous, depending on the statistics available, but also on their relevance for the analysis and projection of the Social Budget.

This is to say that the employed should normally be broken down by the same categories as the number of contributors (items 6 to 7). In other words, when conceptualizing the labour market balance for social budgeting purposes, priority should be given to establishing meaningful theoretical and statistical links between those persons who contribute to a country's Social Budget and those who are employed, which are not necessarily identical groups. Instead, it would normally be expected that the number of contributors be subgroups of (categories of) the employed. Such a careful modelling approach could provide important information for politicians responsible for the social protection system as to which degree the employed by different categories are registered as contributors and/or actively pay contributions. For projection purposes, this information would be helpful, because the projected level and structure of employment would clearly determine and limit the expected number of contributors. In many practical cases, however, labour market statistics and the statistics on the number of contributors are probably not compatible, because both were set up in order to serve different information purposes. In such cases, it is necessary to investigate which labour market breakdown of the number of employed fits (methodologically, statistically) best with the breakdown available with respect to the contributors. Such attempts might sometimes be in conflict with the requirement to reconcile the labour market balance with the available wage information (see below).

"Contributors" (item 7) has been added to the labour market balance in order to take account of those contributors who do not directly participate in the labour market. These may be voluntary contributors such as home-makers, students and others who may be indirectly linked to labour market developments.

Taking the difference between the total labour force and the total number of employed (labour force minus employed; item 4 minus item 5) results in the number of unemployed as a residual. The unemployment rate (item 10) is then calculated as the relative share of the number of unemployed in the labour force. The labour market balance, finally, might also include informa-tion on the number of unemployed persons contributing to the social protection system (if any). The calculation process for the labour force balance is summar-ized in figure 8.6.

An example of a projected labour market balance is presented in example 8.3. It contains preliminary interim results obtained in a social security evaluation project undertaken by the Social Security Department of the ILO for the Government of Panama during 1997 and 1998.

8.2.3.3 Wages, prices and interest rates

The population structure, labour force participation and employment – that is how many persons are potentially employed (and contributing or paying income taxes) versus how many persons are not actively employed (and possibly receiving benefits) – determines the potential demographic structure in any benefit system. This is what has been considered so far in this chapter. Now we turn to the economic model's "monetary frame".

Apart from labour market developments, the actual financial situation (income versus expenditure) of benefit systems is determined by variables such as wages and inflation. Their development, in turn, depends on the overall assumption of economic growth.

In order to cover a maximum range of possibilities of wage creation, the economic submodel of the ILO model family offers high flexibility in projecting average wage developments. The model's wage philosophy is based on the fundamental insight that there is only a certain share of national income which can be allocated to labour (the actively employed), whereas the other share has to go to (the owners of) capital, who might be private or public or both. Violations of this "law" (whether at the expense of labour income or at the expense of capital income) are only tolerable for very short periods, but even then they are most probably accompanied either by accelerating inflation or deflation.

This insight is not equivalent to saying that the labour income shares observed in concrete countries' cases are "naturally determined parameters" (similar to physical constants) and thus allegedly untouchable. On the contrary, labour income share is maintained as an exogenous policy variable and thus the

Figure 8.6 Calculating a labour market balance

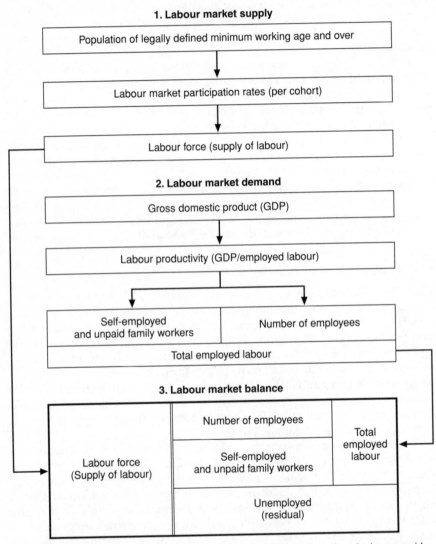

Note: Unemployment = labour force minus employees minus self-employed minus unpaid family workers.

users of the model are free to vary its level over time according to their own judgement – theoretically between the extremes of 0 and 100 per cent, 0 per cent meaning that labour gets no income and capital all national income, 100 per cent meaning that labour gets all and capital nothing.

In the OECD member States, labour income shares vary historically between around 60 and 70 per cent of national income, the share in nominal GDP being accordingly lower. For many countries, especially in the developing world, reliable statistics do not exist; further, the informal sector sometimes turns attempts of precise measurements into guesswork. However, preliminary and tentative estimates, undertaken by the ILO's Social Security Department in the mid-1990s in the context of social security financial evaluation projects, indicate that in many developing countries the labour income share is substantially lower and seems to vary between 25 and 40 per cent of GDP. For these countries, with the assumption of successfully sustained long-term economic

---

Example 8.3   A labour market balance for Panama[1]

The technical results presented in table E8.3 below have been introduced only for illustrative reasons. Thus, they reflect neither the authors' views on future long-term development of the Panamanian labour market, nor those of the ILO in its position as an organization, nor those of the Government of Panama. Bearing this disclaimer in mind, some explanations might help to better understand the results as presented.

Panama's population is at present very young on average, i.e. its population pyramid has a broad basis of children and youth while tapering off quickly at the older ages. The expected ageing of the population will first, over the next 20 to 30 years, produce increasing labour market problems and only later a general problem of how to support the aged. On this basis, a rational policy goal is to formulate the conditions under which the upcoming labour market problems could be solved, that is, how to create more employment. Technically, this was done as follows: labour market supply was calculated on the basis of constant 1995 age-specific labour market participation rates. Labour demand (actual employment) was based on the scenario assumption of *much* higher-than-in-the-past average GDP growth rates and only slightly improved average labour productivity growth rates, thus generating high employment growth (Southeast Asian 1970s to 1990s pattern). In fact, these calculations were undertaken on a sectoral basis (allowing for considerable variations of sectoral assumptions) in order to draw a consistent picture of possible future sectoral employment developments. Another policy assumption was that Panama would, over the projection period, pursue a policy of fostering private sector employment, resulting in much lower public sector employment increases.

The number of contributors to the social security institution was then linearly correlated with the number of dependent employees in order to calculate the annual current income basis of the social security institution, and also its potential current or (in case of the institution's pension branch) definite later number of beneficiaries. The degree to which the economic assumptions and the related labour market projections are mutually consistent and credible is important for a final judgement of the Social Budget projection results, especially when these results are meant to be the quantitative basis for major reform steps to be undertaken.

Table E8.3 Long-term labour market balance: The example of Panama

Item	1995	2000	2010	2020	2030	2040	2050
Population	**2 631 014**	**2 855 703**	**3 266 166**	**3 619 568**	**3 938 973**	**4 160 041**	**4 288 162**
Men	1 330 146	1 440 801	1 641 651	1 812 193	1 960 913	2 060 361	2 114 192
Women	1 300 868	1 414 902	1 624 515	1 807 375	1 978 060	2 099 680	2 173 970
Population age 15 and over	**1 632 355**	**1 837 901**	**2 254 457**	**2 630 391**	**2 973 162**	**3 210 798**	**3 349 947**
Men	809 546	906 169	1 106 919	1 286 290	1 455 336	1 568 186	1 629 002
Women	822 809	931 732	1 147 538	1 344 101	1 517 825	1 642 612	1 720 945
Labour force	**1 007 882**	**1 117 830**	**1 357 790**	**1 548 079**	**1 737 209**	**1 860 896**	**1 926 070**
Men	657 841	719 146	876 173	1 007 416	1 159 818	1 262 582	1 319 611
Women	350 041	398 684	481 616	540 663	577 392	598 313	606 460
Participation rate (%)	**61.7**	**60.8**	**60.2**	**58.9**	**58.4**	**58.0**	**57.5**
Employed by sex and region, total	**866 658**	**1 001 641**	**1 183 690**	**1 495 083**	**1 699 324**	**1 813 823**	**1 911 421**
Men	587 108	678 641	801 985	1 005 487	1 137 747	1 216 221	1 306 513
Share of total employed (%)	67.7	67.8	67.8	67.3	67.0	67.1	68.4
Women	279 550	323 000	381 705	489 596	561 577	597 601	604 909
Share of total employed (%)	32.3	32.2	32.2	32.7	33.0	32.9	31.6
Metropolitan	516 633	602 332	723 643	928 963	1 072 860	1 163 287	1 244 995
Share of total employed (%)	59.6	60.1	61.1	62.1	63.1	64.1	65.1
Rest of Republic	350 025	399 309	460 047	566 120	626 464	650 536	666 426
Share of total employed (%)	40.4	39.9	38.9	37.9	36.9	35.9	34.9
Employed by category of contract	**866 658**	**1 001 641**	**1 183 690**	**1 495 083**	**1 699 324**	**1 813 823**	**1 911 421**
Dependent employees	584 667	682 329	830 017	1 078 271	1 259 559	1 380 703	1 493 224
Government employees	161 421	186 083	212 830	235 858	256 672	271 077	279 425
Employees of private enterprises	354 297	439 951	555 656	771 004	928 895	1 038 303	1 146 704
Employees of the canal commercial/defence sites	17 012	2 337	2 501	2 830	2 843	2 636	2 357
Employees in domestic services	51 937	53 957	59 029	68 578	71 149	68 688	64 738
Self-employed and owners	247 023	281 310	314 683	375 040	400 784	400 581	393 464
Family workers	34 968	38 002	38 990	41 772	38 982	32 539	24 733
Employed by economic sector	**866 658**	**1 001 641**	**1 183 690**	**1 495 083**	**1 699 324**	**1 813 823**	**1 911 421**
Agriculture and fisheries	200 045	231 417	264 592	328 326	366 112	370 686	356 098
Manufacturing, electricity, related services	98 808	114 065	134 377	165 564	177 628	178 105	176 652
Construction and quarrying	53 799	52 499	40 805	23 376	8 544	2 900	968
Hotels, transport, communication	89 553	108 265	145 181	209 722	269 099	319 911	373 775
Financial intermediaries	19 039	21 239	23 791	26 223	23 240	19 078	15 389
Real estate, management and renting	25 558	29 516	34 987	42 604	44 142	42 505	40 331
Public services, health and other activities	133 390	152 333	173 659	208 836	222 352	224 187	225 529
Education	48 836	59 295	77 745	113 557	153 091	191 853	236 972
Private households' domestic help	54 155	62 969	76 614	98 558	113 561	119 229	120 077

Table E8.3 (Continued)

Item	1995	2000	2010	2020	2030	2040	2050
Unemployed	141 224	116 189	174 099	52 996	37 885	47 073	14 649
Unemployment rate (%)	14.0	10.4	12.8	3.4	2.2	2.5	0.8
Male	70 733	40 505	74 188	1 928	22 070	46 361	13 098
Unemployment rate, male (%)	10.8	5.6	8.5	0.2	1.9	3.7	1.0
Female	70 491	75 684	99 911	51 068	15 815	712	1 551
Unemployment rate, female (%)	20.1	19.0	20.7	9.4	2.7	0.1	0.3
Metropolitan region	102 545	87 943	124 314	48 670	31 159	32 363	6 013
Unemployment rate, metropolitan region (%)	16.6	12.7	14.7	5.0	2.8	2.7	0.5
Rest of the Republic	38 679	28 246	49 785	4 326	6 726	14 710	8 636
Unemployment rate, rest of the Republic (%)	10.0	6.6	9.8	0.8	1.1	2.2	1.3

[1] ILO: *Panama – Valuación financiera y actuarial integral de la Caja de Seguro Social y elaboración de un modelo de cuentals sociales* (Geneva, San José, Lima, 1998).

growth, increasing formal employment and structural changes resulting in higher dependent employment, it may be reasonable to assume a growing labour income share over time which might reach present OECD levels if the projection period were sufficiently long. Whether such an assumption is realistic or pure illusion depends on the specific country-related judgements of the model users.

The second fundamental insight is that labour income can, in principle, be allocated to different numbers of employed persons. At one extreme, only one employed person takes all labour income; at the other extreme, total labour income has to be distributed over as many as there are persons offering labour.

This is not to say that economies allow for a free choice as to how many "heads" provide total labour income. On the contrary, the level of labour income produced in economic reality depends on the prevailing production technology and the number and per capita productivity of the persons involved in the production process. But to some extent, the question of including people in or excluding them from the labour market seems also to depend on prevailing attitudes on how to organize societies. Otherwise, it is difficult to explain why many OECD countries with comparable levels of combined labour and capital productivity have significantly different unemployment rates. Again, the model is open to incorporating such considerations as long as they can be transformed into numerical developments, for example by adjusting the labour productivity assumption in order to "create" higher or lower employment growth "in return for" lower or higher average wage growth – such results in the model being guaranteed by the fact that the addressed modifications would leave nominal GDP growth and the labour income share unchanged.

In formal terms, the wage estimation approach might be described as follows:

Equation 8.4

$$WAGE_t = LI_t/EMPLD_t,$$

where:

LI_t = Total labour income in year t,

$LI_t = SHARE_t * GDP_t^n$

$SHARE_t$ = Percentage share of labour income in GDP in t,

$SHARE_{t_0+N}$ = Target value of $SHARE_t$ in the final projected year

$SHARE_t = (SHARE_{t_0+N} - SHARE_{t_0})/(N-1) + SHARE_{t-1}$,

$EMPLD_t$ = Dependent employment in year t

$EMPLD_t = EMPL_t - EMPLS_t$

$EMPLS_t$ = Self-employed (may be exogenous) in year t

N = Number of projected years

t_0 = Projection base year

$t = t_0, \ldots, t_{0+N}$

It should be noted that for reasons of simplicity $WAGE_t$ has here been defined as per capita gross wage, including employers' social security contributions and any other overheads paid by the employer (labour-cost concept). In the model application, per capita wages are defined more precisely as gross wages only (total labour income LI minus employers' social security contributions minus other overheads) per capita. The function for $SHARE_t$ has been arbitrarily chosen; any other suitably chosen functional relationship may be valid in case of a concrete model application.

While the described method might be called a top-down approach, the model also allows for a "bottom-up method"; in short, it works as follows. First sectoral nominal labour productivity is calculated and projected. Then sectoral average labour income (and/or sectoral average wages) is defined as a function of productivity (average labour income might be a linear function of productivity, based on elasticity estimates). The results are multiplied by the respective sectoral numbers of employees in order to achieve sectoral labour income (wage) sums. Aggregation of these sums leads to total labour income (total sum of wages) in the economy, and the labour income share (as a percentage) might then be calculated as a residual.

We would like to stress that both methods, as described, are just techniques – they do not at this stage involve any theoretical considerations on wage behaviour. Concrete projection assumptions will always have to be based on an in-depth empirical and theoretical investigation of the economy and its labour market.

Price development ("inflation") is equivalent to the measured differential between real and nominal income developments. At a given wage or social benefit level, the real purchasing power of that amount is higher the lower the prices and vice versa. Modelling of prices depends mainly on the availability of data. The general approach is to project either the consumer price index (CPI) or the GDP deflator, or both, exogenously – either as trend extrapolations of past data or on the basis of government-defined policy targets.

If nominal and real GDP expenditure data are available, then the deflator of one of the expenditure components can be made linearly dependent on the others. This one component can serve as an endogenously calculated consistency control variable for the "correct" exogenous fixing of the other deflators; for example, over very long-term projections, it might be considered correct that all deflators' growth rates converge to the (assumed) GDP deflator growth rate. In order to explain this procedure in simple mathematical terms, we assume a closed economy where GDP is spent on consumption and investment only. This results in the following set of equations:

Equation 8.5 Nominal GDP (definition)

$$GDP_t^n = C_t^n + I_t^n$$

where:

$$GDP_t^n = \text{Nominal GDP in year } t$$

$$C_t^n = \text{Nominal consumption in } t$$

$$I_t^n = \text{Nominal investments in } t$$

Real GDP (definition):

$$GDP_t^r = C_t^r + I_t^r$$

where:

$$GDP_t^r = \text{Real GDP in year } t$$

$$C_t^r = \text{Real consumption in } t$$

$$I_t^r = \text{Real investments in } t$$

Deflators (definitions):

$$DEFL_{GDPt} = GDP_t^n / GDP_t^r$$

$$DEFL_{Ct} = C_t^n / C_t^r$$

and:

$$DEFL_{GDPt} = DEFL_{GDPt-1} * RDEFL_{GDPt}$$

$$DEFL_{Ct} = DEFL_{Ct-1} * RDEFL_{Ct}$$

$$RDEFL_{GDPt} = \text{Exogenous growth of GDP deflator}$$

$$RDEFL_{Ct} = \text{Exogenous growth of } C \text{ (consumption) deflator}$$

then:

$$GDP_t^r = GDP_{t-1}^r * R_{GDPt}$$

$$C_t^r = C_{t-1}^r * R_{Ct}$$

$$I_t^r = GDP_t^r - C_t^r$$

$$GDP_t^n = GDP_t^r / DEFL_{GDPt}$$

$$C_t^n = C_t^r / DEFL_{Ct}$$

$$I_t^n = GDP_t^n - C_t^n$$

$$DEFL_{It} = I_t^n / I_t^r$$

$$RDEFL_{It} = DEFL_{It} / DEFL_{It-1}$$

Some explanations follow concerning incorporating an interest rate projection into the model. The correct choice of the interest rate depends on many factors. For example, it makes a significant difference whether a system is in deficit or in surplus. In the first case, the interest rate will be a borrowing rate, in the second a lending rate. Furthermore, it has to be decided whether the modelling situation refers to a short- or long-term borrowing situation or a short- or long-term lending situation. Are we looking for a short-term money market borrowing rate or a long-term rate of return (RoR)? Are we evaluating a large social security system that itself – by way of its borrowing/lending behaviour – might be able to influence market rates, or is the quantitative situation such that the social security system is fully dependent on prevailing capital market conditions? The following explanations may help to find a suitable approach in concrete cases.

For a national economy, on a macro level the annual real interest rate can be defined as the (measured) rate of return of the economy's capital stock (stock of productive tangible assets). If appropriately measured statistical information on the economy's capital stock is available, then the rate of return could simply be measured as follows:

1. Calculate the fictitious labour income component of the owners of the capital stock (the self-employed might be used as a dummy for the

"owners"). This step takes account of the fact that not all income of the owners of the capital stock is just "profits" but, partially, income to be attributed to the management of their enterprises.

2. Calculate total capital factor income (derived from national accounts) minus the labour income component of the capital stock owners; the labour income component may be based on the same average wage as the one measured for the dependent employed, but – according to the circumstances – it might be assumed lower or higher; call the result "profits".

3. Divide the profits by the capital stock.

The result is the real rate of return of the economy's capital stock as long as identical deflators were used for the calculation of the "real" capital stock and the "real" profits. The nominal rate of return could be defined either by adding the CPI change rate, or the GDP deflator change rate, or by another suitably chosen rate.

When calculated as proposed, the development of the rate of return depends on the development of:

4. GDP, consumption of the capital stock, gross investments into the stock.

5. The productivity of the capital stock.

6. The labour income share in national income.

7. The share of "owners" in total employment and their fictitious average labour income.

If historical data on all these variables are available, an estimation might be made of some structural parameters which could serve as starting values for medium- and long-term projections of the capital stock which, in turn, would be required to calculate the economy's overall rate of return endogenously. Regrettably, statistical institutions very often do not compile capital stock data. As, at the same time, the model was developed in order to provide policy advice, usually at relatively short notice, no special efforts were undertaken to include an "artificial" capital stock component. There were other reasons, which mainly reflect modelling consequences stemming from the broad variety of systems used around the world.

Within the Social Budget context, the interest rate plays a twofold role in co-determining either the income level and structure of the Budget, or affecting the government budget. Revenues are influenced if the social protection system is in surplus or if it is partially or fully funded. Then the system will receive capital income which is predominantly influenced by "the" interest rate. If the system is in deficit, then it needs financial support from the government, which may cover the necessary expenditures through taxation and/or deficit spending, by tapping the money and capital market(s). Then the interest rate is important for the projection of the government budget.

If the system is (partially) funded, the funds are broadly diversified, and pre-matured, and the annual inflow of additional funds is large in comparison to the country's overall annual savings, then the system itself might have an impact on the level of the interest rate, which could change over time. The same holds true if the same system were in a post-maturity situation, dissolving its capital stock. If the system has only small funds available, it may not be able to diversify very much; thus it may have to rely on specific sectors of the capital market(s).

Furthermore, the possible interest rate impact on the system finances changes with the degree by which the system is allowed to invest its funds nationally or internationally. Most countries stipulate that if their social protection systems create funds, they are only allowed to invest these monies nationally; often exceptions are made, but usually allowing for relatively small investment abroad.

After balancing all arguments, it appears that the most practical approach to medium- and long-term projections of the social system related interest rate/rate of return is to assume it exogenously in each single country case, based on thorough analyses of past interest rate trends, future investment policies and opportunities and, if applicable, future government policies concerning the public budget. In any case, financial and capital market experts' knowledge should be taken into account.

However, if the model is being tailored to reflect a specific country's case, it is recommended to develop a submodule that covers the interdependencies, as set out in points 4 to 7, above. Then, development time for such additional components should be available, and even when substantial information on the national capital stock is missing, plausible estimation techniques can be used in order to obtain preliminary estimates, which could later be replaced easily by more substantial estimates.

8.2.4 The social protection model

The social protection model is the core of Social Budget modelling. It maps the expenditure and income of all major branches of the social protection system. Depending on the system's organization, this may be made in the form of an institutional breakdown, or in the form of a functional breakdown, or both. The following descriptions follow basically a functional approach. They provide the reader with some basic techniques to simulate and project income and expenditure of major social protection functions, such as pensions, health care, unemployment benefits, social assistance, and so on. These techniques can then be used to model the main expenditure and income categories of different national institutions in concrete country cases. For example, in many countries pensions are provided by more than one institution. Often there is a general scheme for the private sector, and another separate scheme for government employees. Health-care systems are often even more fragmented, consisting of a set of social insurance and private insurance subsystems, as well as the government systems charged with certain delivery functions for the total population, and/or the provision of comprehensive services for those who cannot afford coverage under the other schemes. It is not possible to explain all the possible options for the institutional organization of a national social protection system. Thus, this chapter limits itself to the provision of major functional building blocks for the modelling of institutional budgets. In financial terms, pension and the health-care schemes are the most important subsystems of social protection, as in many countries they account for about two-thirds of all social expenditure.

8.2.4.1 The pension model

In many countries, models for the major components of the national social protection systems do exist. They are used by ministries or social security institutions. Most often, such models are in place for the pension and health components because these schemes traditionally turn over the highest amounts of resources of all institutions, and misplanning of their respective expenditure and revenue can easily lead to serious budgetary and economic consequences. A Social Budget model could therefore use the results of such models.[16] Firstly, this would simplify the modelling work for the Social Budget model considerably; secondly, the results of such models are often subject to clearance by different government agencies and social security institutions. Since two models rarely produce exactly the same results, it would be preferable to use the results of the known and broadly accepted model for the Social Budget simulations and projections, instead of producing competing results. In that case, an interface between the Social Budget model and the external model would have to be constructed.

Alternatively, integrated modules can be developed specially for the purposes of the Social Budget models. This option generally has the advantage that the linking of the model with the other components of the Social Budget model poses less problems than in the case of a stand-alone model, which has not been developed for the purpose of the Social Budget exercise.

In this section we introduce both options by taking advantage of the Social Budget and pension modelling experience of the ILO's Social Security Department, which includes both a stand-alone pension model and a version integrated into the Social Budget model.

Linking up to an external version

Stand-alone pension models are used for the financial management and planning of an existing pension scheme and/or the exploration of pension reform proposals.

The results of an existing stand-alone pension model can be used in the following way. First it is ascertained that the stand-alone model uses the same demographic and economic input data and assumptions as the Social Budget model, and then the results of the pension model are imported into a "pensions" spreadsheet of the Social Budget (sub)model. This pension spreadsheet is the "interface" between the external pension model and the Social Budget model.

The linking of the two separate models inevitably leads to some overlap and duplication of work. If, for example, the World Bank pension model[17] were to be used as an external model, then this model would calculate its own set of insured persons on the basis of population projections, even if it imported the same population matrix as the Social Budget model. It would also generate its own reference earnings for pension calculations. If the stand-alone ILO pension model (ILO-PENS)[18] were used, then this model would use the Social Budget model data on the insured persons, but would generate its own distribution of past credits.

The computation results of both external models are generally compatible with the (other) results of the Social Budget model as long as the former depart from the same initial year's input and identical assumption bases. However, scenario analyses are generally much more cumbersome than those of an integrated pension module. A modification of one basic assumption, for example on economic growth, would require a separate modification of the assumption, as well as all its dependent variables. The external model would then have to be re-run on the basis of these modified assumptions, and the results imported into the Social Budget model via the interface spreadsheet. This time-consuming procedure is acceptable when it comes to the projection of status quo conditions under rather stable exogenous assumptions, but not if a multitude of different test runs on different alternatives or reform proposals needs to be carried out.

Using an integrated version

For scenario analyses or sensitivity tests, it is generally simpler and faster to use an integrated pension model. Such a model tends to be less sophisticated than a large stand-alone pension model because the users of Social Budget results have different information needs with respect to pensions from the users of "pure" stand-alone pension models. Therefore, this option might provide slightly less detailed results which might not be fully compatible with other pension models that could be applied, but it reacts automatically and correctly to changes in assumptions.

The next section describes a relatively simple way to create a robust integrated pension model. The basic mathematical reasoning is nonetheless the same as that applied in most major pension models. However, compared to fully fledged national stand-alone pension models, the proposed modelling approach takes obvious shortcuts, in particular concerning the calculation of newly awarded pensions. Large national pension models, as well as the ILO standard pension model, normally use cohort-specific past service and earnings histories in order to derive average new pensions. The model proposed here does not keep a record of past service and earnings. Nevertheless, the basic philosophy of major actuarial pension models is described, without explaining every detail of pension modelling. This permits the user to assess the potential impacts of the pension module outlined here. The reader can find a fully detailed account of pension modelling theory and practice in two other volumes of the ILO/ISSA series on *Quantitative Methods in Social Protection*.[19]

All pension projections are based on one basic equation which describes the relative cost of a pension scheme in terms of total insurable earnings:

Equation 8.6   Basic pension cost equation

$$PAYGCR_t = (PENS_t/ACT_t) * (APE_t/AIE_t)$$

*"PAYG cost rate = demographic ratio * financial ratio"*

where

$PAYGCR_t$ = PAYG cost rate or contribution rate in year t

$PENS_t$ = Number of pensioners in year t (in all categories of pensions)

ACT_t = Number of active contributors in year t

APE_t = Average amount of pensions

AIE_t = Average amount of insurable earnings

The term $(PENS_t/ACT_t)$ is called the *demographic ratio* of the pension scheme. It describes the demographic burden of the scheme, that is, the ratio of how many pensioners per contributors have to be provided with pensions. The term (APE_t/AIE_t) is called the *financial ratio* (or often also the *average replacement ratio*) and describes the relationship between the average pension and the average insurable earnings of the active contributors. The PAYG cost rate is the central cost indicator for a pension scheme. It is also an indicator for the state of development (i.e. the age) of a pension scheme. It is usually very small in young schemes, since they hardly pay any benefits during the first two decades, because only a few persons qualify for old-age pensions. Pensions paid during that period mainly consist of invalidity and survivors' pensions. In a second phase, the PAYG cost indicator increases sharply, as the demographic ratio rises fast: more and more former contributors become eligible for a pension. This is compounded by a steady increase of the financial ratio, as the average pension entitlements of each new generation of pensioners also increases, owing to ever-longer "insured careers". In fact, the above basic equation is also the key equation for other cash benefits, such as unemployment benefits, and sickness and maternity benefits. Example 8.5 provides a typical life cycle cost curve for a pension scheme.

From the basic equation, it follows that all calculations of pension models can be grouped into three categories: demographic projections, financial projections and financing calculations.

Demographic projections

General principles

All pension schemes serve a certain defined population, consisting of persons registered as active or inactive members, and others registered as beneficiaries.[20] Together, these groups establish the demographic structure of a pension scheme. Demographic projections establish a new structure for each projection year.

Most pension models first establish the full initial demographic structure of a pension scheme by age and sex, and a full matrix of active contributors, inactive registered members, and beneficiaries of old-age, survivors' and invalidity pensions by age and sex is established. This matrix has obvious links to the general demographic and economic framework of the pension scheme, and covers the demographic structure, the labour force structure and the employment structure of the country. The methodological core of demographic projections is the iterative "moving forward" of the matrix on a year-to-year basis. This means that on the basis of a demographic matrix for year t, a matrix for year $t + 1$ of the same structure is produced. The transition from t to $t + 1$ is governed by a set of transition rules which are established on the basis of past experience or expected future conditions.

Table 8.1 provides a typical condensed demographic matrix for a young African pension scheme. Its non-matured status is indicated by the fact, for example, that the number of active contributors distributed around the age group 40 to 44 is (still) very much higher than the number of old-age pensioners around the age group 60 to 64. Once the active contributors around 40 to 44 have grown old (after 20 years), the relation between the then existing stock of pensioners and the then existing number of contributors will have significantly increased (assuming that the total number of active contributors will have remained at about the same level as 20 years before).

Based on the data in table 8.1, figure 8.7 demonstrates the typical transition by single ages from non-participation in the scheme during adolescence (until after the age group 10 to 14) to active participation (payment of contributions between, say, 20 and 54) and then into pensions (at around 50 to 54 and after) and finally to death.[21]

There are two basic methodological approaches for the "moving forward" of the demographic matrix. The first is the so-called *stock approach*. The basic methodology for the stock approach is demonstrated here projecting the number of active contributors by age and sex:

Table 8.1 Demographic structure of a young African pension scheme[1]

Age	Insured persons						Beneficiaries							Grand total (members and beneficiaries)
---	Inactive persons			Active contributors			Old-age pensioners			Invalidity pensioners			Survivors	
	Male	Female	Total	Male	Female	Total	Male	Female	Total	Male	Female	Total	Total	
Under 5	0	0	0	0	0	0	0	0	0	0	0	0	36	36
5–9	0	0	0	0	0	0	0	0	0	0	0	0	209	209
10–14	0	0	0	0	0	0	0	0	0	0	0	0	418	418
15–19	0	0	0	378	38	416	0	0	0	109	189	298	638	1 351
20–24	11	1	12	425	50	475	0	0	0	110	222	332	210	1 028
25–29	293	49	342	5 867	607	6 474	0	0	0	54	108	162	224	7 202
30–34	783	207	990	7 835	1 034	8 868	0	0	0	147	254	402	271	10 531
35–39	995	372	1 367	9 950	1 862	11 812	0	0	0	185	333	518	825	14 522
40–44	1 335	531	1 866	13 353	2 655	16 008	12	12	25	277	411	688	945	19 531
45–49	934	447	1 381	9 344	2 235	11 580	21	23	43	214	317	532	1 287	14 823
50–54	496	226	722	4 961	1 130	6 091	475	487	962	161	245	405	1 368	9 548
55–59	48	5	53	480	26	506	1 423	723	2 145	94	153	247	1 628	4 579
60–64	13	1	14	128	9	138	1 855	1 048	2 902	125	211	335	1 889	5 279
65–69	0	0	0	0	0	0	1 459	591	2 050	94	181	275	1 868	4 193
70–74	0	0	0	0	0	0	1 175	319	1 495	60	119	179	1 392	3 065
75–79	0	0	0	0	0	0	984	104	1 088	52	80	132	811	2 031
80–84	0	0	0	0	0	0	519	57	575	25	48	73	406	1 054
85–89	0	0	0	0	0	0	187	57	206	12	19	31	201	438
90–94	0	0	0	0	0	0	55	5	60	3	8	10	59	128
95+	0	0	0	0	0	0	10	1	11	0	4	4	19	34
Total	4 909	1 839	6 748	52 721	9 647	62 367	8 175	3 388	11 563	1 719	2 901	4 621	14 701	100 000
Beneficiaries per 100 active contributors	—	—	—	—	—	—	16	35	19	3	30	7	24	—

[1] FNR of Senegal, 1995.

Figure 8.7 Transition from adolescence over active contributions and retirement to death

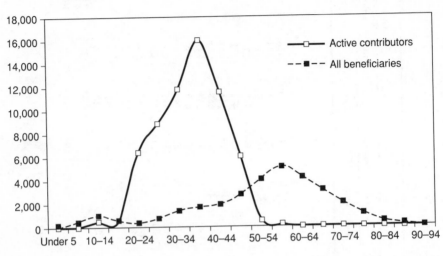

Equation 8.7 Number of active contributors (stock approach)

$$ACT_{x,s,t} = EMP_{x,s,t} * act_{x,s,t}$$

where

$act_{x,s,t+1} = ACT_{x,s,t}/EMP_{x,s,t}$ = Rate of active participation in the scheme

$ACT_{x,s,t}$ = Number of active contributors of age x and sex s in year t

$EMP_{x,s,t}$ = Number of employed of age x and sex s in year t

The number of active participants in year t is thus calculated as a factor or a ratio (here the active participation ratio) multiplied by the total number of employed persons in the country of the same age and sex cohort. This calculation provides a number which usually reflects the average stock of active participants during a year t or – synonomously – the estimated stock of active participants in the middle of that year.

The stock approach has the advantage of being simple. However, particularly with young schemes, it has substantial disadvantages. The above active participation ratio is systematically changing over time when the scheme matures. This is even more true for the pensioner ratio which, in the stock approach, accordingly could be defined as the number of scheme pensioners per age group (by sex) over the number of all elderly people of the population in that same age group (by sex). The direction of change of such ratios is difficult to predict on an aggregate basis. The exact value of the pensioner ratio, for example of age 85 and sex m in year 1999, actually depends on the observed consecutive participation ratios of the cohort born in 1904 during their active lives, between around 1919 and probably 1969 to 1974. The longitudinal participation profile of a cohort cannot easily be transformed into a single pensioner ratio for projection purposes. Most major pension projection models thus use the flow method for demographic projections.

The *flow method* interprets the number of a certain population group at a specific point in time as the respective number in that group at a point in time one period earlier plus the new entrants into the group minus the exits during the period. The equivalent equation to equation 8.7 would be:

Equation 8.8 Number of active contributors (flow approach)

$$ACT_{x,s,t+1} = ACT_{x,s,t} + NEWACT_{x,s,t+1} - ACTEXITS_{x,s,t+1}$$

where new actives ($NEWACT$) could be recruited from inactives (unemployed), the educational systems or from migration; and exits ($ACTEXIT$) could be attributed to withdrawals from the scheme or the labour force, entry into the "pensioner force" or death. In terms of calculating the flows, entries and exits, every relevant subgroup of the demographic structure of the pension scheme (the demographic matrix) is produced by transition rules used to shift the demographic matrix forward in time.

These transition rules describe the change of status within the system for each single age cohort of active or inactive members of age x and sex s, or each single age cohort of beneficiaries of age x or sex s.

Example: Out of the members of a cohort of, say, 100 active 59-year-old contributors of age x and sex s at the beginning of year t,

- 94 will stay active (stay in the scheme, keep status and turn 60),
- two will die (leave the scheme) and leave a survivor,
- one will retire early (stay in the scheme, change status and turn 60),
- one will draw an invalidity pension (stay in the scheme, change status and turn 60),
- two will become inactive (stay in the scheme, change status and turn 60).

Other groups in the demographic matrix of a pension scheme might experience other transformations. Some of the transformation rules depend on the demographic conditions in the population (for example, mortality), others on labour force participation behaviour (expressed in age- and time-dependent labour force participation rates), or economic conditions (for example, the demand for labour). Figure 8.8 provides a visual representation of the main transition processes in a fully fledged demographic projection of an actuarial pension model. Wherever lines cross, the transition can proceed in all directions at the intersections. Oval figures indicate that lines do not really cross and in a three-dimensional graph would pass under or over each other without actual intersection.

The ILO's actuarial pension model (ILO_PENS)[22] endeavours to map virtually all the above flows. Most of the other existing models take short-cuts

Figure 8.8 Demographic transformation from t to $t + 1$ in a pension scheme for all ages x and sex s

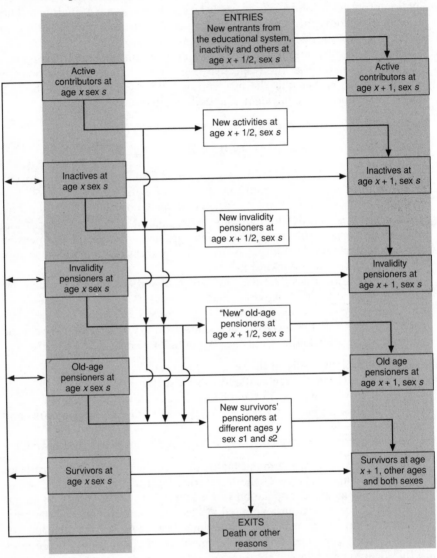

when it comes to transition flows of minor importance. The generic pension model used in the standard version of the ILO's Social Budget model is no exception. It is here described as one example for a relatively simple pension projection model. In fact, it employs a mixture of stock and flow methodologies.

From a methodological and programming point of view, the pension model is constructed as an extension of the labour force model. In general, the model calculates the number of insured persons by individual age and sex by applying population coverage rates (alternatively called insurance participation rates) to the respective cohorts of the employed labour force at the middle of the respective projection years. The coverage rate reflects both legal limitations of coverage (for example, stemming from the exclusion of certain occupational groups, such as the self-employed), as well as non-compliance and deficient management and administration.

Depending on the country-specific circumstances, it may be necessary to disaggregate the coverage rate further to permit more precise sensitivity tests. It may be necessary or desirable, for example, to distinguish between covered (insured) persons and contributors, in which case a two-stage process would have to be introduced. First the labour force would have to be multiplied by a coverage ratio. This would establish the group of registered insured persons, or all persons with an insurance record. This group might contain a number of persons who are not actively contributing for a longer period, for example drop-outs from the labour market. In a second step, the number of employed persons would be multiplied by a contributor ratio which would narrow the number of covered (insured) persons down to the number of persons who are actively contributing. This group can be defined for example as the total number of all persons who are contributing at least one monthly contribution in a given year. For simplicity, this disaggregation of the coverage ratio has not been pursued here. It is assumed that all covered persons are also contributing to some extent.

On the expenditure side, the standard ILO model first calculates the number of old-age pensions. If a single age breakdown of present pensioners is not available, then in a first step the overall number of old-age pensions is allocated to single ages based on age group information available from the pension scheme and/or with the help of the age structure of the population and observed past coverage or insurance rates. The projection method is a pragmatic combination of a stock and flow approach. For pensioners younger than the normal retirement age, the stock method is used. The numbers are projected by keeping the ratio of the number of pensioners to the total population in the single ages constant under the benchmark "normal" retirement ages, which normally differ for men and women. For example, for much of Central and Eastern Europe and the developing world this is 55 years for women and 60 for men.

For ages over 55 and 60, the flow method is used. For each year t of the projection period, the following procedure takes place: at and after the benchmark retirement age, the difference between the number of employed persons in the middle of the previous year $t - 1$ and the number still in employment in t are "pensioned off" and added to the average number of "existing and surviving" pensioners in year t. This assumes implicitly that all people retiring between the middle of t and $t + 1$ retire at the beginning of $t + 1$. On the one hand, this is a prudent assumption, as some of these workers might choose to leave the labour market for other reasons; on the other hand, there might be additional beneficiaries coming from the group of insured non-active persons who have pension entitlements but were not employed immediately before the retirement age. Here, for the sake of easy understanding, it is assumed that these two effects cancel each other out. In any case, statistical data on the group of non-active potential beneficiaries are very often not available, but the latest version of the pension module in the above ILO standard model enables the user to treat the inactive participants as a distinct group.

In some cases, especially when labour force and employment age structure data are not reliable, this procedure has produced "negative pensioners" in some age groups. This happens when the level of measured employment in a single age cohort actually increases after the normal retirement age. Then, an alternative way to project new pensioners can be found, by using retirement rates, that is, the probability of active or inactive contributors retiring between the middle of year t and $t + 1$.

Invalidity pensioners are projected as a constant proportion of the contributing population, survivors as a constant proportion of old-age pensioners and social pensioners (or persons receiving a minimum pension) as a constant relation to old-age and invalidity pensioners.

Financial projections

The financial projections of pension models consist of the calculation of total insurable earnings and the calculation of average pension benefits in each category of pensions: old-age, survivors' and invalidity pensions. Once these averages have been projected, the total amount of income and expenditure for the pension scheme can be calculated.

General principles

Generally, there is a more or less stringent link between the wages calculated in the economic module and the insurable earnings bases used for the pension model. The only principal difficulty arises if the scheme has a ceiling on insurable earnings. Then, a distribution of wages by amount is needed in order to calculate the amount of wages below the ceiling that is subject to contributions. But projecting income distributions is cumbersome, and the degree of accuracy achieved has to be traded off against the additional resources required. Normally, the ceiling effect on contribution revenue can be regarded as negligible, especially when the ceiling is fixed so that the mass of wages in the economy is covered and if it is regularly adjusted in line with general wage inflation. But many schemes fail in these respects, in which case the insurable earnings base shrinks over time. Example 8.4 shows the effect of alternative contribution ceilings on the expected contribution income of a Turkish social insurance scheme.

In actuarial models, pension benefits are calculated in a way which strongly resembles a microsimulation approach. Benefits in payment are adjusted

Example 8.4   Turkey: The effect of an increase in the contribution ceiling[1]

Figure E8.4 demonstrates the estimated effect of increasing the contribution ceiling in the main Turkish social insurance fund, the SSK. The SSK contribution income is presently subject to a very low ceiling on wages, that has not been adjusted for several years. In order to measure the effect of an adjustment of the ceiling on contribution income earnings, distribution data derived from a small sub-sample of the scheme members were used. It is estimated that an immediate fivefold increase of the ceiling would lead to an increase in the average insurable earnings of the SSK, and hence the contribution revenue, by some 35 per cent as compared with the amounts to be expected if there were no such change. Raising the ceiling to an even higher level would clearly further increase the revenue, although the marginal gain would decrease. The graph illustrates these estimates. However, the theoretical nature of this analysis should be noted, as no account is taken of offsetting effects, such as a possible reduction in compliance rates which may weaken the revenue enhancement effect. It is possible that, beyond a certain point, the marginal effect of increasing the contribution ceiling might turn negative, because of rising non-compliance – an effect similar to that known as the Laffer curve.

Figure E8.4   Turkey: Wage ceiling effect on the contribution income of the SSK

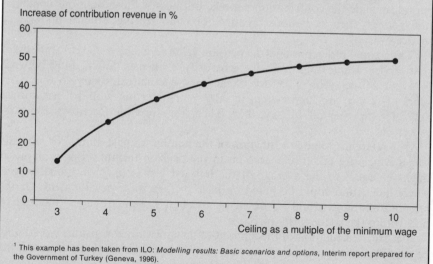

Increase of contribution revenue in %

Ceiling as a multiple of the minimum wage

[1] This example has been taken from ILO: *Modelling results: Basic scenarios and options*, Interim report prepared for the Government of Turkey (Geneva, 1996).

annually in line with the legal requirements, often according to a suitably chosen rate of change in insurable earnings or inflation. Newly awarded pensions are generally calculated by applying the actual pension formula to each age and sex cohort of new pensioners. Many pension formulae are derivatives of the generic form of an earnings-related pension formula (equation 8.9). This means that the models have to retain the average length of service and the reference wage of the members of each cohort.

Equation 8.9 A generic pension formula

$$PE_{t,x} = FR + n * ACR * RE_{x,t}$$

where the pension is calculated for an individual of age x in year t and

$PE_{t,x}$ = Individual amount of the new pension

FR = A flat-rate amount

n = Number of insurance years ("past service credits")

ACR = Accrual rate

$RE_{x,t}$ = Reference earnings

The flat-rate amount is often introduced for redistributive reasons; it might or might not be equal to the minimum pension payable to each pensioner.

Past service credits are the total number of insurance months or years which are taken into account in the specific pension formula. These insurance periods include the contribution periods, but possibly also fictitious contribution periods such as periods credited for child rearing, studies or military service.

The accrual rate represents the pension value added by each year (month) of past service. Depending on their "generosity", schemes "offer" rates between 0.75 and 2.0 per year of service. Sometimes, accrual rates vary so that early years of service are higher than in later years, starting with 1.5 per annum and later tapering off to, say, 0.75. Then, they provide incentives for early retirement.

The reference wage is a function of the number of past annual or monthly wages which are taken into account in the pension formula. For example, it might be equal to the average of the indexed last m $(m \leq n)$ annual wages, where indexation could be based on past average wage development. Or the reference earnings could be based on the best k annual wages (indexed or not) within the last m years $(m \leq n)$.

An exact calculation of the amount of newly awarded pensions would only be possible if the pension formula were applied to each individual case and if the individual scheme members' retirement pattern over the course of the year were known. Pension models try to get close to this reality by applying the individual formula to cohort-specific (average) reference wages and cohort-specific (average) service biographies. By so doing, projection errors are minimized but, of course, cannot be fully avoided. The ILO standard actuarial model establishes distributions of the duration of past service and assumes three different levels of reference earnings (as a function of the observed wage base). These two parameters are then combined in a way which reflects the observed correlation between income levels and duration of past service. Past service distributions are built up by a flow procedure. First an initial matrix of past service distribution for each sex and each individual age cohort is established from statistical observation. Then, for each year of the projection period, a certain credit is added to each past service data. For each cohort belonging to a certain cell in the past-service-reference-earnings (PSRE) matrix, this credit depends on the accrual rate of the pension formula and the measured average annual density of contribution payment, which is the proportion of the year during which the cohort paid contributions.

The ILO Social Budget model approach

The pension model within the generic version of the ILO Social Budget model again takes certain short-cuts.

First, it assigns age-specific average insurable wages to each age cohort of the insured persons. Average insurable earnings are a product of the average wage of the economy multiplied by a factor which accounts for the difference normally observed between the average wage and the statistically reported average insurable earnings in a social insurance scheme. This factor accounts for the numerous possible legal, statistical and other impacts that may be quoted in order to explain such differences, as for example:

- there might be under-reporting of wages subject to contributions by employers;
- there might be less than full insurable employment during the year;
- the respective scheme might not include the full formal sector workforce;
- there might be a ceiling on the maximum income subject to contributions;
- low incomes might be exempted from contribution payments.

It should be noted that this factor is often smaller than 1, but can also be higher, for instance, when in developing countries social security systems cover privileged parts of the labour force, or in developed countries when they focus on established middle-class workers. In practice, this factor is usually calculated by dividing the recorded average insurable income by the national average wage (for the projection base year). When a national average wage is not available, the data from the social security institution might be the only wage data available; then, the factor is set to 1. If information on age-specific wages is missing, then all age-specific wages are (technically) considered to equal the average. Based on these values (assumptions) and the projected number of contributors, the overall sum of all earnings subject to contributions (the total insurable earnings) can be established.

Average old-age pension amounts are calculated on the basis of the reference wage, past service credits and the respective national pension formula(e) similar to the ILO standard pension model. However, a storage-saving short-cut was developed here. The component calculating the amounts of newly awarded old-age pensions operates on the basis of a "condensed" 9×9 PSRE matrix. This matrix has a top row and a left-hand column (both outside the 9×9 dimension) as follows (see example 8.5). The top row contains nine classes of past service expressed as a percentage of the average past service and, similarly, the left-hand column consists of nine classes of reference wages as a percentage of the average reference wage. Thus, the top row reflects time (years of service), whereas the left-hand column reflects money (reference earnings). Each cell of the 9×9 matrix contains the relative frequency of all new pension awards which are calculated on the basis of that specific combination of reference earnings and service years. On the basis of the pension formula and the numerical values in the PSRE matrix top row and left-hand column, the value of the newly awarded pension for each of the $9 \times 9 = 81$ combinations of past service and reference wage can be calculated. By using the relative frequencies, the average newly awarded pension can then be calculated.

The bi-variant distribution described by the PSRE matrix is kept constant throughout the projection period, whereas the average number of past service years and the average reference wage is normally changing over time. These changes are especially marked when the scheme is still maturing, and each year pension entitlements increase structurally because each generation of pensioners has longer past credits than the previous one, since on average they have contributed or "served" one year longer. Their reference wage also changes structurally, as the full reference period for calculation of the reference wage gradually builds up.

The use of a discrete distribution for the calculation of pensions allows the number of minimum pensions, which in many schemes plays an important role, to be calculated each year. Especially in young schemes, the number of minimum pensions might lead to considerable expenditure which would not be captured if pensions were calculated exclusively on the basis of average pensions and average reference wages.

Keeping the relative distribution constant around an average past service and an average reference wage is obviously a simplification but justified, as a "dynamization" of the distribution would lead to exponentially increasing numbers of assumptions.

Example 8.5 demonstrates the process of calculating the average new pension on the basis of a PSRE matrix as it is included in the generic Social Budget model of the ILO, and as it was assumed – using country-specific estimates – for Ukraine.[23]

The relationship between the average reference wage and the national average wage (or, if not available, the average insurable wage) is described by a single factor which makes the reference wage a linear function of the national average wage (average insurable wage). This factor might vary over time. The factor incorporates structural features of the pension scheme,

Example 8.5   The bi-variant PSRE matrix of the ILO generic model

The generic ILO Social Budget model uses the following PSRE matrix for formerly active male new pensioners. The matrix in table E8.5a assumes a close correlation between the length of a person's career and the level of the reference wage.

Table E8.5a   PSRE matrix of formerly active male persons at retirement[1]

Reference earnings as % of average reference earnings[2]	Past service as % of average past service[2]									
	up to 20	20–40	40–60	60–80	80–100	100–120	120–140	140–160	160 and over	Total
Up to 20	0	0	0	0	0	0	0	0	0	0
20–40	0	0	0	0	0	0	0	0	0	0
40–60	0	0	0	2	4	5	0	0	0	11
60–80	0	0	0	1	5	7	0	0	0	13
80–100	0	0	0	1	10	11	1	0	0	23
100–120	0	0	0	0	12	15	0	0	0	27
20–140	0	0	0	0	10	10	0	0	0	20
40–160	0	0	0	0	2	4	0	0	0	6
60 and over	0	0	0	0	0	0	0	0	0	0
Total	0	0	0	4	43	52	1	0	0	100

[1] The cells in the white area contain relative shares (frequencies) in percentages. [2] For calculation: mid-points of classes; for lowest and highest classes pragmatically fixed.

The matrix in table E8.5b – which is not explicitly integrated in the generic model, but may be generated – provides an example of possible monthly pension amounts under different past-earnings/past-service combinations as they might result from the application of a specific pension formula. The dotted cells in table E8.5b mark the (arbitrarily assumed) part of the discrete distribution where the combination of past-service duration and earnings leads to receipt of a minimum pension only (here 113.7 currency units). By calculating the (absolute equivalent of the) sum product of the cells in matrices 1 and 2, one would estimate the volume of new male pensions to be paid in a given year of the projection period.

Table E8.5b   Matrix of new male pension amounts[1]

Reference earnings as % of average reference earnings[2]	Past service as % of average past service[2]									
	up to 20	20–40	40–60	60–80	80–100	100–120	120–140	140–160	160 and over	Total
Up to 20	113.7	113.7	113.7	113.7	113.7	113.7	113.7	113.7	113.7	–
20–40	113.7	113.7	124.7	147.6	170.2	192.9	215.6	238.2	249.6	–
40–60	113.7	124.7	207.8	245.9	283.7	321.5	359.3	397.1	416.0	–
60–80	113.7	174.6	290.9	344.3	397.2	450.1	503.0	555.9	582.4	–
80–100	113.7	224.4	374.1	442.7	510.7	578.7	646.7	714.7	748.7	–
100–120	155.9	311.7	519.5	614.9	709.3	803.8	898.2	992.7	1 039.9	–
120–140	218.2	436.4	727.3	860.8	993.0	1 125.3	1 257.5	1 389.8	1 455.9	–
140–160	280.5	561.1	935.1	1 106.7	1 276.8	1 446.8	1 616.8	1 786.8	1 871.8	–
160 and over	311.7	623.4	1 039.0	1 229.7	1 418.6	1 607.5	1 796.5	1 985.4	2 079.8	–
Total	–	–	–	–	–	–	–	–	–	–

[1] The cells in the white area contain relative shares (frequencies) in percentages. [2] For calculation: mid-points of classes; for lowest and highest classes pragmatically fixed.

such as:

- differing income biographies;
- varying efficiency of contribution collection; and
- changes in compliance.

Once the average new pension is calculated, the benefit expenditure on all new old-age pensions can be calculated by multiplying the average amount with the projected number of new pensioners. The average amount of newly awarded invalidity pensions is considered equal to the average new old-age pension. Survivors' pensions are calculated as a fixed percentage of old-age pensions. The percentage is normally stipulated by law; for example, widows' pensions are often calculated as 60 per cent of the pension entitlements of a deceased active insured person or of the old-age pension of a deceased pensioner.

Pensions in payment are adjusted over time according to the indexing provisions of the pension scheme in question, for example by ad hoc adjustments at a certain periodicity, or by annual adjustments in line with the development of wages or of the consumer price index, or by any another legally prescribed formula.

Administrative expenditure (including investments in tangible assets) is calculated as a percentage of total benefit expenditures; the percentage may be constant or change over time.

Financing calculations

Accounting for other income and using the contribution rate actually charged, the annual fiscal balance of the pension scheme throughout the projection period, as well as the development of any reserves, can be calculated. Normally, each scheme adopts a certain financial system by law. The financial system defines whether the scheme is operating on a PAYG basis, a partial funding basis, or a fully funded basis and how the respective contribution rates are set. The alternative systems are described in full in a forthcoming volume in the *Quantitative Methods in Social Protection* series.[24] Here it is assumed that most systems are adopting a scaled premium approach which keeps the charged contribution rate constant for a defined period of equilibrium. Alternatively, schemes might aim at charging a definitely constant contribution rate (the so-called general average premium – GAP). In a Social Budget environment, a certain contribution rate would generally be adopted, and the fiscal balance and the development of the reserve or debt would be calculated according to that contribution rate as a basis for policy decisions.

Example 8.6 provides the main projection results for a typical African pension scheme. The following formulae provide readers with a starting point for their own model development.

Example 8.6   A standard financial development pattern of an African pension scheme[1]

The cost development of a hypothetical pension scheme in Africa is here demonstrated using an adjusted pension model of the ILO Social Budget model. The case describes the development of a new pension scheme over its first six-and-a-half decades. The standard set of projections assumes that the scheme will start from zero, while the alternative set assumes that the scheme will replace an existing provident fund and thus commence with an inherited number of insured persons and pensioners.

Assumptions

Demography
Zimbabwe is used as a reference for the population structure. This includes the determinants of the future demographic development, i.e. mortality and fertility.[2]

Economic assumptions
The economy in question has an annual 3 per cent real GDP growth rate. The wage share of GDP is assumed to be 44 per cent. Labour force participation rates and employment rates again are those of Zimbabwe.[3]

Governance assumptions
It is assumed that the scheme has a benchmark replacement rate of 40 per cent of career average earnings which are approximated by a ten-year average of revalued earnings, subject to a minimum replacement rate of 20 per cent. The 40 per cent roughly corresponds to the requirements of the ILO Social Security (Minimum Standards) Convention, 1952 (No.102). Shorter periods of employment lead to a reduction of the pension level by about 1.33 per cent. This is a fairly conservative pension formula which does not reflect most of the more generous formulae in francophone Africa. In the base case, pensions in payment are adjusted in line with insurable wages. Invalidity pensions are paid at the benchmark rate and survivors' pensions are paid at a rate of 60 per cent of the entitlements of the deceased.

It is assumed that the population coverage rate increases from an initial value of 10 per cent to 80 per cent after 35 years and stays constant thereafter. Wage compliance increases from 50 per cent to 80 per cent after 15 years and stays constant thereafter.

Cost developments
Under these assumptions two basic cost indicators, i.e. the PAYG cost rate and the ratio of the nominal cost to nominal GDP (GDP cost ratio), develop as mirrored in figure E8.6a under a simulated new scheme, as well as under a simulated conversion option. The conversion case is calculated on the assumption that the provident fund has been in existence for about 30 years and that all new pensioners in the start year will convert 100 per cent of their balance into pensions.

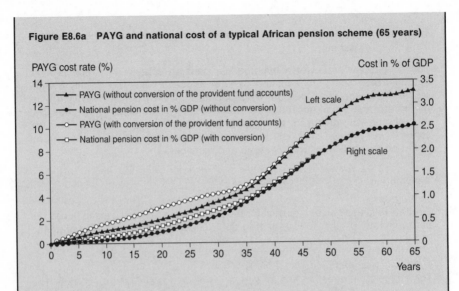

Figure E8.6a   PAYG and national cost of a typical African pension scheme (65 years)

The results show that under rather conservative assumptions on the pension formula and with a slowly ageing population, the overall cost of the pension scheme remains at a fairly low level for at least the next six-and-a-half decades, provided the scheme is managed soundly.

Figures E.8.6b and c present three financing options for the above standard case without conversion.

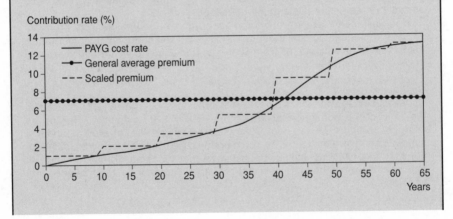

Figure E8.6b   Financing options of a typical African pension scheme (without conversion of the provident fund accounts) (65 years)

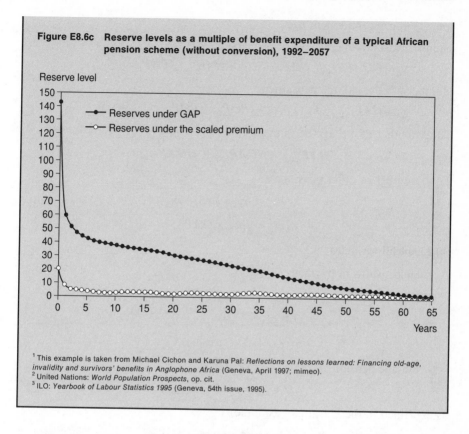

Figure E8.6c   **Reserve levels as a multiple of benefit expenditure of a typical African pension scheme (without conversion), 1992–2057**

[1] This example is taken from Michael Cichon and Karuna Pal: *Reflections on lessons learned: Financing old-age, invalidity and survivors' benefits in Anglophone Africa* (Geneva, April 1997; mimeo).
[2] United Nations: *World Population Prospects*, op. cit.
[3] ILO: *Yearbook of Labour Statistics 1995* (Geneva, 54th issue, 1995).

Equation 8.10   Pension revenue and expenditure

Revenue base

$$INS_{t,x.s} = cov_{t,x,s} * E_{t,x,s}$$

$$IE_{t,x,s} = catch_{t,x,s} * W_{t,x,s}$$

$$TIE_t = \sum_{x,s}(INS_{t,x,s} * IE_{t,x,s})$$

Expenditure

(a) Demographic variables

Number of pensioners:

for $x <$ normal retirement age

$$OAP_{t,x,s} = (OAP_{t=0,x,s}/POP_{t=0,x,s}) * POP_{t,x,s}$$

for $x \geq$ normal retirement age

Number of surviving old-age pensioners:

$$OOAP_{t,x,s} = OAP_{t-1,x-1,s} * (POP_{t,x,s}/POP_{t-1,x-1,s})$$

Number of new old-age pensioners:

$$NOAP_{t,x,s} = E_{t-1,x-1,s} * (POP_{t,x,s}/POP_{t-1,x-1,s}) - E_{t,x,s}$$

Total number of old-age pensioners:

$$OAP_{t,x,s} = NOAP_{t,x,s} + OOAP_{t,x,s}$$

Total number of other pensioners:

$$IP_{t,s} = ir_{t,s} * INS_{t,s}$$

$$SP_{t,s} = sur_{t,s} * OAP_{t,s}$$

(b) Financial variables

Average pensions in payment:

$$OA_{t+1,x+1,s} = OA_{t,x,s} * (1 + w_t/100) \quad [\text{or } (1 + p_t/100)]$$

$$I_{t,x,s} = OA_{t,x,s}$$

$$S_{t,x,s} = Sf * OA_{t,x,s}$$

New old-age pensions:

$$NOA_{t,x,s} = f(MAT_{t,s,pensf})$$

as explained in the Ukrainian example.

(c) Total expenditure, PAYG cost and reserves

$$TE_t = \left(\sum_{t,x,s}(OAP_{t,x,s} * OA_{t,x,s}) + \sum_{t,s}(IP_{t,s} * I_{t,s}) + \sum_{t,s}(SP_{t,s} * S_{t,s}) \right)$$

$$+ AE_t + OE_t$$

$$PAYG_t = (TE_t - II_t - OI_t)/TIE_t$$

$$RES_{t+1} = RES_t * (1 + i_t/100) + (TIE_t * CONR_t + OI_t - TE_t)$$

$$* (1 + 0.5 * i_t/100) \text{ (approximation)}$$

where:

w_t	= Rate of increase of wages in t
p_t	= Rate of increase of prices in t
$E_{t,x,s}$	= Employed persons in t of age x and sex s
$INS_{t,x,s}$	= Insured persons in period t of age x and sex s
$IE_{t,x,s}$	= Insured earnings in t of insured persons of age x and sex s

$cov_{t,x,s}$	$=$ Coverage rate in t for sex s and age x
$catch_{t,x,s}$	$=$ Catchment factor in t for insured earnings of a person of age x and sex s
$W_{t,x,s}$	$=$ Total wage in t of a person of age x and sex s
TIE_t	$=$ Total insurable earnings in t
$OAP_{t,x,s}$	$=$ Old-age pensioner in t of age x and sex s
$OA_{t,x,s}$	$=$ Average old-age pension in t of age x and sex s
$NOAP_{t,x,s}$	$=$ New old-age pensioner in t of age x and sex s
$NOA_{t,x,s}$	$=$ New old-age pension in t of age x and sex s
$OOAP_{t,x,s}$	$=$ Surviving old-age pensioners in t of age x and sex s
$IP_{t,s}$	$=$ Invalidity pensioner in t of sex s
$I_{t,s}$	$=$ Invalidity pension in t of sex s
$SP_{t,s}$	$=$ Survivors' pensioner in t of sex s
$S_{t,s}$	$=$ Survivors' pension in t of sex s
$PAYG_t$	$=$ Pay-as-you-go cost rate in t
RES_t	$=$ Reserves of the scheme in t
$ir_{t,s}$	$=$ Invalidity pensioner ratio for s in t
$sur_{t,s}$	$=$ Survivors' pensioner ratio for s in t
$pensf$	$=$ Pension formula
$MAT_{t,s}$	$=$ PSRE matrix in t for sex s
Sf	$=$ Survivor pension rate
TE_t	$=$ Total expenditure in t
II_t	$=$ Investment income in t
OI_t	$=$ Other income in t
OE_t	$=$ Other expenditure in t

Exogenous: All initial values for variables with fewer than four capital letters and all ratios described with letters in lower case.

8.2.4.2 The health care model

Modelling the financial structure of the health sector means dealing with the most complex part of social protection. While in pension and other cash benefits systems, the economic and demographic environment, as well as their legal rules, almost fully define their financial developments, health systems face the additional complexity of patient–provider relationships in less than perfect markets, as well as often unpredictable morbidity structures. This section describes the building of a health module only in a superficial way; more details can be found in the health care modelling volume of the *Quantitative Methods in Social Protection Series*.[25]

Just as in the case of pensions, health care projection results can either be imported from an external health care model, or obtained by operating one's own health care module integrated into the Social Budget model. The principal methods for importing results from an external model are the same as for those of the pension model. Thus, the following explanations and proposals are limited to an integrated projection and simulation model version of health care expenditure and revenues. Yet again, most of the technical reasoning reflects standard methods which are used in many health care financing models.

For modelling purposes, it may generally be assumed that:

- the government ultimately remains responsible for the financing of primary preventive measures, the education of health professionals, and the investment and maintenance of public health provider facilities;

- in addition, the government may directly provide care for the total population (as in the case of a national health service) or a part of the population (for example, the poor or civil servants, including the armed services, and other public employees);

- other parts of the population might be covered by a social insurance scheme, and yet others might not be covered by any public or parastatal third-party financing scheme and might finance their health care entirely on a private basis by direct purchase or private insurance. Direct purchase or private insurance may also complement coverage by a public third-party payer.

The specific combination of these three financing subsystems is different in each country. They may range, for example, from Central and Eastern European countries where the Soviet-type public service health care systems remained in operation during the 1990s (while reform plans are under preparation or have just been introduced, as in the cases of Bulgaria, Poland and the Ukraine) or countries with a dominant national health service (NHS), such as that in the United Kingdom, to countries with dominant Bismarckian social insurance schemes (such as France, Germany and Belgium), and also those with a prominent private financing sector (such as the United States). The specific overall health budget, which is a subsystem of the Social Budget of a country, thus has to be specifically built by acknowledging the different weights of the three basic "building-blocks". The major techniques used in the generic ILO Social Budget model for the quantitative mapping of these blocks are described in the following sections.

Before giving technical specifications, it might now be appropriate to describe in more detail some procedural aspects of health care modelling. Mutatis mutandis, the considerations in example 8.7 might also be taken as representative for other modules of the social protection model.

Government health expenditure

Government health expenditure can be projected on the basis of the following breakdown of main expenditure components:

- total administrative expenditure for health care;

- total expenditure on government outpatient care facilities (excluding administration and investments);

- expenditure on government hospitals (excluding administration and investments); and
- total health investment expenditure.

Administrative expenditure for each year of the projection period for each expenditure category is estimated as the product of last year's expenditure times the rate of increase of the total population times the rate of increase of wages in the economy times a factor describing the "usual" differential between the development of wages in government health care administration and the development of the national average wage. The values for deviation factors are observed from statistical data. Alternatively, administration cost is described simply as a constant proportion of benefit expenditure.

Expenditure on the two major categories of health care (outpatient facilities such as ambulatory, and hospitals) should be separated into staff and non-staff

---

Example 8.7 Building a health care model

Model building is a tedious exercise. Social Budget models are generally built by teams. Most of them are relatively complex, so that one person will normally not be able to build and operate an entire model. There will be economists and labour market specialists working on the economic and labour market sub-models, demographers working on the demographic projections, and public finance specialists on the government budget forecasts, as well as quantitative social protection specialists working on different modules of the social protection model. In general, different groups will be in charge of cash benefits and health benefits, and specialists might be sought for the modelling of social assistance and – most importantly – poverty. This example describes the work of the health expert(s) in the overall Social Budget task force.

The crux of modelling is data. Models can only be as good as their database. Also, every modeller knows that data are never perfect. This is one major reason why modelling has to proceed with imperfect information. Yet, imperfect information should not be an excuse for not modelling. Governments will in any case take decisions on the future of national health systems with imperfect information, driven by public opinion or fiscal necessities. If decisions have to be taken, then efforts to place them on a coherent quantitative basis – however weak this might be – is likely to improve the quality and impact of the decision.

Establishing a model of the health sector within the framework of a Social Budget alone will normally take several months and proceed in a number of steps, starting from identifying the scope and empirical and legal structure of the sector, identifying and collecting the required data, then mapping the model in its theoretical mathematical structure including its calibration (i.e. comparison with observed reality), producing results and, finally, exporting the results to other social protection modules, to the summary Social Budget or to the government accounts. This sequence is portrayed in the following flowchart (figure E8.7). Most of the time will be spent on data collection and interpretation. An extensive search of national and, in some cases,

---

international data will be necessary, often dispersed among institutions; hypotheses on future developments will have to be discussed with experts. The mathematical mapping and the linking of the module to the Social Budget model are, by contrast, tasks that can normally be accomplished relatively fast.

Figure E8.7 Building a health care (HC) module of the Social Budget model

Identifying the scope, the logical structure and the links to other modules of the HC submodel

LINKS

Importing data from the demographic, economic labour market modules or submodels

LINKS

Data collection and analysis; analysis of the legal system

Data collection on:
• health infrastructure
• health utilization in different categories of care and subsystems
• health expenditure in different categories of care and subsystems

Mathematical formulation of the model

Model calibration: adjusting to observed reality

Establish national health accounts (or budgets)

Exporting results to
• other modules
• summary accounts
• institutional accounts

LINKS   LINKS

LINKS

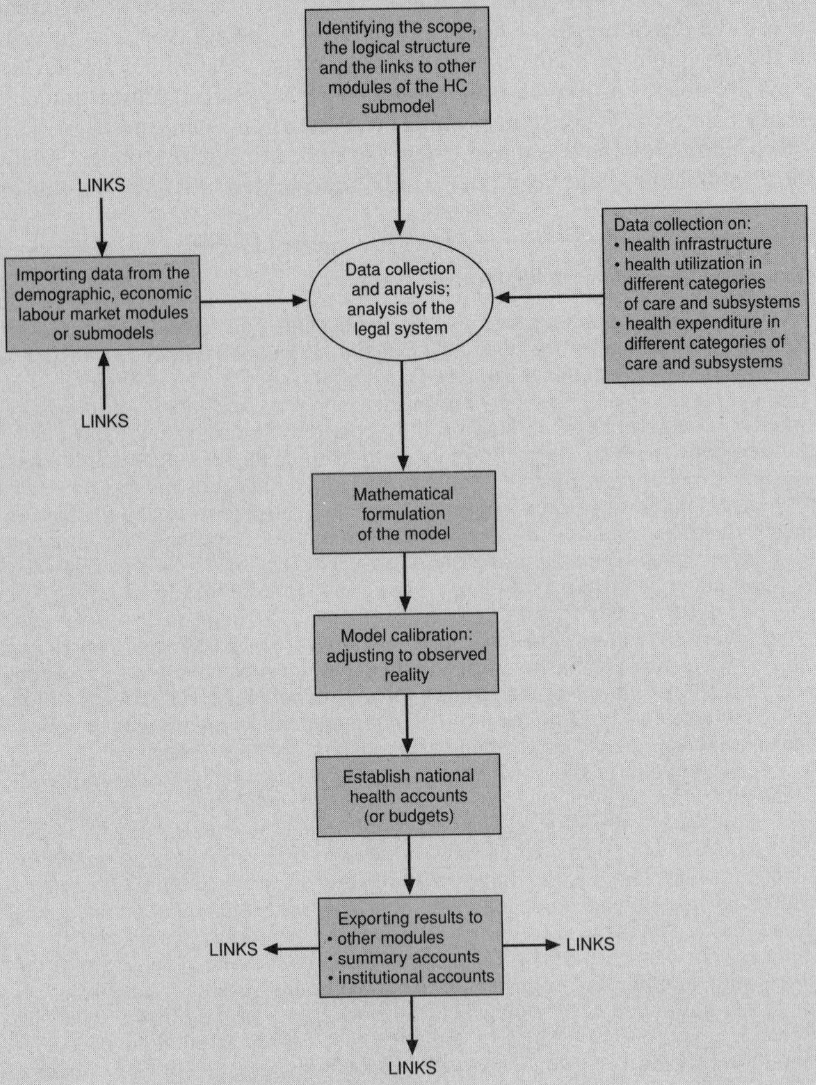

cost per ambulatory care unit and per hospital bed, and projected separately. Major variables explaining the development of these two components are:

- the number of ambulatory care units and the number of beds in hospitals;
- the level and development of the national average wage; and
- the development and structure of the total population.

In addition, the staff and non-staff components are multiplied by deviation factors which describe their historically observed deviation from the development of GDP or CPI inflation. The deviation factors are the pivotal calibration tool in the health care component; they implicitly map all the structural exogenous and endogenous influences on prices, staff cost and utilization which cannot be explicitly explained by a health care model. These deviation factors, among other things, also implicitly contain productivity increases in the health sector. Productivity increases in the sector are difficult to measure at this level of aggregation, as the contents of the package of goods and services provided by the health care delivery systems are continuously changing.

The staff cost components are furthermore multiplied by a factor which reflects the staffing trend per care unit or per hospital bed. This allows for simulations of the expenditure differentials incurred by reductions or increases in the number of care units or hospital beds. Compensatory or compounding effects of changes in the intensity of care (approximated by the factor describing the development in the staffing per care unit or per hospital bed) are thus implicitly projected.

The most important factor driving health expenditure, however, is the development of the population's health care utilization, which is usually directly affected by the population structure, since differences in age and sex have been proved to influence the per capita utilization rates significantly.

To include changing utilization patterns may still not be directly possible because, although statistics of government health services usually provide reliable financial data, they often do not disaggregate expenditure by age and sex of the users of the health facilities (the patients). Thus, even if age- and sex-specific utilization patterns were available, no corresponding expenditure amounts could be calculated. Thus, the impact of a changing demographic structure on costs can often only be reflected by a general factor which mirrors the structural demographic change from one period to the next.

Equation 8.11 A general demographic utilization indicator

$$IND_t = \frac{\sum_{x,s}(POP_{x,s,t} * UR_{x,s})/TOTPOP_t}{\sum_{x,s}(POP_{x,s,t-1} * UR_{x,s})/TOTPOP_{t-1}}$$

where $UR_{x,s}$ are observed or assumed age- and sex-specific cases of utilization per patient ("utilization rates" or weights).

If no national or scheme-based age-specific utilization rates are available, then international experience might be drawn upon, and a typical standard utilization function used in order to estimate the development of the average utilization rate over time. Since only the change of the overall utilization rate is used in the projection, rather than absolute values, the errors made by using standard age-specific profiles are probably smaller than by ignoring the impact of the age structure on the forecasted expenditure altogether. Example 8.8 provides a typical utilization function.

Health insurance scheme expenditure

Only part of the total population is assumed to be eligible for health insurance benefits. The projection of total health insurance expenditure may be based on the following aggregates:

- expenditure on hospital care;
- expenditure on ambulatory care;
- expenditure on dental care;
- expenditure on pharmaceuticals;
- expenditure on other care; and
- administrative expenditure.

If more disaggregated statistical information is available, it should of course be used.

Administrative costs may be projected as a constant percentage of total benefit expenditure without further specification.

The projections for all other expenditure categories consist of the multiplication of per capita cost items by the projected number of eligible persons. The per capita costs of hospitals are calculated as the average costs of one bed-day per person (the unit cost) multiplied by the number of hospital days utilized per capita (the frequency of utilization). The per capita cost of ambulatory care is calculated as the number of cases per capita per year times the cost per case. Cost calculations for dental care follow the same structure. The per capita amount of pharmaceuticals is not disaggregated into cases and prices; the initial per capita amount is projected into the future using the price increase and the respective deviation factor.

The average costs per one bed-day or per one case may be split further into staff and non-staff costs. Deviation factors could then be attached to both cost categories, incorporating the future deviation of staff costs from the national average wage, and of non-staff costs from the CPI or GDP deflator.

In order to enhance the explanatory power of the projections of the above categories of care, a disaggregation by age is always recommended. Such a disaggregation allows especially for a mapping of the health cost effects of a changing age structure. The standard model distinguishes six population

Example 8.8   Australia: A health care utilization function

Empirical age-specific health care utilization functions are rare. Many schemes around the world do not maintain age-specific utilization data by category of care on a routine basis. The functions or curves that do exist all have the form of a lying J – almost regardless of the specific category of care (i.e. ambulatory care, hospital care, dental care, etc.). This means that health utilization per capita is relatively high at the very young ages, drops to a low around ages 15 to 20, and then increases again until reaching several multiples of the minimum in the final age groups of life. The curve for females shows a specific peak of utilization in the fertile age groups ("fertility bump"). The usual absence of data has led the ILO to develop a proxy parabola formula for the lying J curve which can be used in countries where no data are available on age-specific utilization. Readers might refer to the health care modelling volume of the *Quantitative Methods in Social Protection Series*.[1]

The curves in figure E8.8 have been extracted from the utilization data of the Australian Health Insurance Commission's annual report for 1996/97.

Figure E8.8   Australia: Number of health services utilized per capita and year by age group and sex, 1996/97

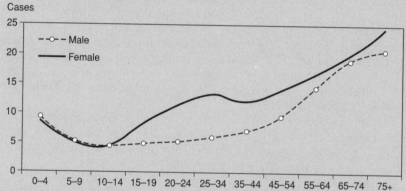

There is also statistical evidence that the utilization of health care facilities correlates positively with real GDP per capita – the richer a country, the higher the supply and utilization of health services throughout its population. Analysis of statistical data may allow for an estimation of the elasticity between health care utilization and GDP per capita. If no such observation is available, then the elasticity may best be assumed as zero; utilization rates per capita will then be exclusively driven by changes in the population structure.

Based on these explanations, the overall gross government expenditure on health care can be calculated. Net government expenditure is equal to gross expenditure minus the amount of the patients' co-payments to government facilities. Co-payments are generally projected as a constant percentage of gross government expenditure. However, depending on national circumstances, this factor might well be used as a policy variable.

[1] Cf. Cichon *et al.*, op cit.

groups: male and female children, male and female persons of working age, and male and female persons of pension age. Contrary to government health care schemes, social insurance health care schemes normally keep individual accounts of the insured persons, recording the contributions paid and the benefits received. Thus it should be possible, at least in principle, to publish age-group-related utilization data as well as age-group-related average benefit costs per hospital bed-day or ambulatory care contact. If age-specific utilization data and cost rates are not part of the standard statistical programme of the health insurance scheme, it may be necessary to organize specific surveys to obtain the required data.

The compilation of total expenditures, total insurable earnings, the PAYG cost indicator and any reserve accumulation follow the same accounting principles as in the pension insurance, and do not have to be repeated here.

Private health expenditure

If only a small portion of a country's health care system is covered by privately financed arrangements, then the projection of that private share can be kept relatively simple. The easiest way is to link the privately covered expenditure share to the respective development of the other major systems and estimate the revenues (private out-of-pocket outlays and/or private insurance premiums) as of the same amount. This would mean estimating private health expenditure as a (constant) portion of government health expenditure or social insurance health expenditure. Any private co-payments to government facilities (see above) would have to be added.

This approach tends to offer very conservative (too low) estimates of private health expenditure; notably, in many developing and Central and Eastern European transition countries, unknown but probably significant additional amounts of private monies are paid to public health facilities.

In countries with a predominantly privately financed health care sector, after some methodological adaptation the same techniques can be used as in the social insurance scheme (see the previous section). The main adaptation would be to transform the financing part of the social insurance model into one based on age-specific flat-rate premia which are not income but morbidity risk related, in other words, often age dependent. Also, individual premiums would be paid on behalf of every covered person (including dependants who are considered to be party to a normal private insurance contract) contrary to social insurance schemes where dependants are normally insured without contribution supplements.

Under this financing method, a substantial technical reserve is normally accrued. The other main difference between private insurance and social insurance is the usually much higher administrative costs in private insurance, which are caused mainly and most often by substantial promotion expenditures.

An example of a national health budget

Example 8.9 draws on a Social Budget exercise undertaken by the ILO in Turkey in 1995. The objective was to establish a health budget as a sub-budget to the overall national Social Budget, which would give health policy-makers an independent policy evaluation tool. The health module aligns the expenditure forecast to the results of a stand-alone health care model which was developed by a second team of researchers in parallel to the ILO Social Budget model.

Sample equations for a comprehensive health care system

Equation 8.12   Three-pillar health care system

First pillar: The government scheme (public health care scheme)

   Expenditure

Administrative cost

$$GAEHC_{t+1} = GAEHC_t * dtsa * AW_{t+1}/AW_t * TPOP_{t+1}/TPOP_t * dvha$$

Ambulatory care cost

$$GEAC_{t+1} = (STAC_t * dsta * dvstac * Aw_{t+1}/AW_t + NSTAC_t * dvnstac)$$
$$* ACU_t * TPOP_{t+1}/TPOP_t * IND_{t+1}$$

Hospital care cost

$$GEHC_{t+1} = (STHC_t * dsthc * dvsthc * AW_{t+1}/AW_t + NSTHC_t * dvnsthc)$$
$$* BEDS_t * TPOP_{t+1}/TPOP_t * IND_{t+1}$$

Remark: The above formulae imply double dynamics, as they increase the cost in line with the number of ambulatory care units and the population, as well as the age impact; depending on the concrete budget situation of the government and possible health institution capacity restrictions, this might be too fast an increase in some national cases.

Other care

$$OEGHC_t = oep * (GEHC_t + GEAC_t)$$

Investment expenditure

$$GINV_t = inv * (GEAC_t + GEHC_t)$$

Total gross government expenditure

$$TGHC_t = GAEHC_t + GEAC_t + GEHC_t + GINV_t$$

Total net government expenditure

$$NTGHC_t = TGHC_t - TEBHCSS_t - TCOPG_t + GCON_t$$

Exogenous: $GAEHC_{t_0}$, $STAC_{t_0}$, $NSTAC_{t_0}$, ACU_{t_0}, $STHC_{t_0}$, $NSTHC_{t_0}$, $BEDS_{t_0}$, oep, $dtsad$, $dvha$, $dsta$, $dvstac$, $dvnsthc$, $dsthc$, $dvsthc$, $dvnsthc$

Second pillar: Social insurance scheme

Expenditure

Ambulatory care

$$ACEt = \sum_{a,s} FAC_{a,s} * COV_{a,s,t} * CAC_{a,s,t} * dvuac$$

$$CAC_{a,s,t} = (STCAC_{a,s,t-1} * AW_t/AW_{t-1} * dvstac + NSTAC_{a,s,t-1} * dvnstac)$$

Hospital care

$$HCE_t = \sum_{a,s} HD_{a,s} * COV_{a,s,t} * CHD_{a,s,t} * dvuhc$$

$$CHD_{a,s,t} = (STCHD_{a,s,t-1} * AW_t/AW_{t-1} * dvsthc + NSTCHD_{a,s,t-1} * dvnsthc)$$

Dental care

$$DCE = \text{Mutatis mutandis as with ambulatory and hospital care}$$

Pharmaceuticals

$$PCE_t = pv1 * \left(\sum_{a,s} PCOV_{a,s,t} * COV_{a,s,t} \right)$$

$$PCOV_{a,s,t} = PCOV_{a,s,t-1} * dvpc$$

Other personal health care benefits

$$OCEt = \sum_{a,s} OCCOV_{a,s,t} * COV_{a,s,t}$$

$$OCCOV_t = OCCOV_{t-1} * AW_t/AW_{t-1} * dvoc$$

Total benefit expenditure

$$TEBHCSS_t = ACE_t + DCE_t + HCE_t + PCE_t + OCE_t$$

Administrative expenditure

$$AEHCSS_t = aehcss * TEBHCSS_t$$

Example 8.9   Turkey: The structure of a national health budget, 1995

Table E8.9a provides a summary of total national health expenditure and its major components, the public service health care system, the parallel system of social insurance health care (which actually combines three separate insurance schemes) and private sector health care. Tables E8.9b and c provide a summary of the main structural input data, as well as the vast number of adjustment variables and deviation factors which are necessary to calibrate the model. For a better understanding of the explosive development of projected expenditure and revenue figures, it should be noted that Turkey at the time of the study (1996) was a country running at a persistent annual inflation rate of around 100 per cent.

Table E8.9a   Turkey: Health care expenditure and financing, 1995–2000 (million Turkish lira)

Institution breakdown	1995	1996	1997	1998	1999	2000
Total health care expenditure	**333 328**	**611 792**	**980 211**	**1 263 927**	**1 490 805**	**1 682 215**
in % of GDP	*4.2*	*4.3*	*4.3*	*4.3*	*4.3*	*4.3*
Expenditure in government facilities	137 941	248 663	390 092	492 534	568 776	628 392
Social insurance expenditure	77 665	147 063	243 939	325 012	395 522	459 715
Private expenditure	117 721	216 066	346 181	446 380	526 507	594 107
Total income	**333 328**	**611 792**	**980 211**	**1 263 927**	**1 490 805**	**1 682 215**
Government financing	172 271	313 710	496 701	631 868	735 877	819 433
Social security contributions	43 335	82 015	137 329	185 678	228 421	268 675
Private financing	117 721	216 066	346 181	446 380	526 507	594 107
Fiscal balance	**0**	**0**	**0**	**0**	**0**	**0**
1. Government health care system						
1.1. Expenditure	**137 941**	**248 663**	**390 092**	**492 534**	**568 776**	**628 392**
Administrative expenditure	3 299	6 070	9 897	13 042	15 654	17 981
Investment expenditure	0	0	0	0	0	0
Care in ambulatory facilities	42 735	76 998	120 673	152 189	175 559	193 743
Care in hospitals	39 399	70 987	111 253	140 309	161 855	178 619
Other care	52 508	94 607	148 270	186 994	215 709	238 051
1.2. Income	**137 941**	**248 663**	**390 092**	**492 534**	**568 776**	**628 392**
1.3. Fiscal balance	**0**	**0**	**0**	**0**	**0**	**0**
2. Social insurance health care system						
2.1. Expenditure	**77 665**	**147 063**	**243 939**	**325 012**	**395 522**	**459 715**
Ambulatory care expenditure	24 224	45 749	76 335	102 401	125 427	146 778
Hospital care expenditure	22 191	42 328	70 627	94 744	116 048	135 803
Dental care expenditure	0	0	0	0	0	0
Pharmaceutical expenditure	19 972	37 656	61 331	79 798	95 035	107 883
Other care expenditure	9 570	18 095	30 278	40 917	50 309	59 135
Administrative cost	1 709	3 236	5 368	7 152	8 703	10 116
PAYG cost rate	*13.0*	*13.0*	*12.9*	*12.7*	*12.6*	*12.4*
2.2. Income	**77 665**	**147 063**	**243 939**	**325 012**	**395 522**	**459 715**
Contribution income	43 335	82 015	137 329	185 678	228 421	268 675
Government deficit coverage	34 330	65 048	106 609	139 334	167 100	191 040
Investment income	0	0	0	0	0	0
Other income	0	0	0	0	0	0
2.3. Fiscal balance	**0**	**0**	**0**	**0**	**0**	**0**
3. Private sector health care (HC)						
3.1. Expenditure	**117 721**	**216 066**	**346 181**	**446 380**	**526 507**	**594 107**
Private insurance	2 156	3 957	6 340	8 175	9 643	10 881
Employer-based HC	0	0	0	0	0	0
Other producers of HC	0	0	0	0	0	0
Private HC provided by government and social security	115 565	212 109	339 840	438 205	516 864	583 226
3.2. Income	**117 721**	**216 066**	**346 181**	**446 380**	**526 507**	**594 107**
Co-payments to government HC	41 629	78 826	130 751	174 206	212 000	246 407
Co-payments to social security	73 937	133 283	209 089	263 998	304 864	336 818
Purchases	2 156	3 957	6 340	8 175	9 643	10 881
3.3. Fiscal balance	**0**	**0**	**0**	**0**	**0**	**0**

Table E8.9b   Main financial variables of the Turkish health budget, 1995–2000

	Case	Unit	1995	1996	1997	1998	1999	2000
1. Government health care delivery system								
Ambulatory care	Units	No.	61050	61050	61050	61050	61050	61050
Staff cost	Per unit	Million TL	0.35	0.63	1.02	1.32	1.56	1.76
Non-staff cost	''	''	0.35	0.61	0.93	1.14	1.28	1.37
Beds	Units	No.	113870	113870	113870	113870	113870	113870
Staff cost	Per bed	Million TL	0.17	0.31	0.50	0.65	0.77	0.87
Non-staff cost	''	''	0.17	0.30	0.46	0.56	0.63	0.68
2. Social insurance schemes								
Covered persons	–	No.	13869	14785	15739	16730	17759	18823
Children, male	–	''	2292	2446	2605	2771	2943	3121
Children, female	–	''	2191	2337	2490	2648	2812	2983
Workers, male	–	''	4425	4722	5030	5349	5681	6026
Workers, female	–	''	4311	4600	4900	5212	5535	5871
Pensioners, male	–	''	297	310	326	343	360	378
Pensioners, female	–	''	353	370	388	408	427	445
Ambulatory care	Per	''						
Staff cost per case	Child, m	Million TL	0.36	0.64	1.03	1.34	1.58	1.78
Non-staff cost per case	''	''	0.36	0.62	0.94	1.15	1.29	1.39
Staff cost per case	Child, f	''	0.36	0.64	1.03	1.34	1.58	1.78
Non-staff cost per case	''	''	0.36	0.62	0.94	1.15	1.29	1.39
Staff cost per case	Worker, m	''	0.36	0.64	1.03	1.34	1.58	1.78
Non-staff cost per case	''	''	0.36	0.62	0.94	1.15	1.29	1.39
Staff cost per case	Worker, f	''	0.36	0.64	1.03	1.34	1.58	1.78
Non-staff cost per case	''	''	0.36	0.62	0.94	1.15	1.29	1.39
Staff cost per case	Pensioner, m	''	0.36	0.64	1.03	1.34	1.58	1.78
Non-staff cost per case	''	''	0.36	0.62	0.94	1.15	1.29	1.39
Staff cost per case	Pensioner, f	''	0.36	0.64	1.03	1.34	1.58	1.78
Non-staff cost per case	''	''	0.36	0.62	0.94	1.15	1.29	1.39
Hospital care	Per							
Staff cost per case	Child, m	Million TL	2.00	3.62	5.80	7.52	8.89	10.05
Non-staff cost per case	''	''	2.00	3.47	5.31	6.49	7.29	7.80
Staff cost per case	Child, f	''	2.00	3.62	5.80	7.52	8.89	10.05
Non-staff cost per case	''	''	2.00	3.47	5.31	6.49	7.29	7.80
Staff cost per case	Worker, m	''	2.00	3.62	5.80	7.52	8.89	10.05
Non-staff cost per case	''	''	2.00	3.47	5.31	6.49	7.29	7.80
Staff cost per case	Worker, f	''	2.00	3.62	5.80	7.52	8.89	10.05
Non-staff cost per case	''	''	2.00	3.47	5.31	6.49	7.29	7.80
Staff cost per case	Pensioner, m	''	2.00	3.62	5.80	7.52	8.89	10.05
Non-staff cost per case	''	''	2.00	3.47	5.31	6.49	7.29	7.80
Staff cost per case	Pensioner, f	''	2.00	3.62	5.80	7.52	8.89	10.05
Non-staff cost per case	''	''	2.00	3.47	5.31	6.49	7.29	7.80
Pharmaceutical expenditure	Per							
Staff and non-staff cost per case	Child, m	Million TL	1.44	2.50	3.82	4.68	5.25	5.62
Staff and non-staff cost per case	Child, f	''	1.44	2.50	3.82	4.68	5.25	5.62
Staff and non-staff cost per case	Worker, m	''	1.44	2.50	3.82	4.68	5.25	5.62
Staff and non-staff cost per case	Worker, f	''	1.44	2.50	3.82	4.68	5.25	5.62
Staff and non-staff cost per case	Pensioner, m		1.44	2.50	3.82	4.68	5.25	5.62

Table E8.9b   (Continued)

	Case	Unit	1995	1996	1997	1998	1999	2000
Staff and non-staff cost per case	Pensioner, *f* ''		1.44	2.50	3.82	4.68	5.25	5.62
Other care	Per							
Staff and non-staff cost per case	Child, *m*	Million TL	0.69	1.22	1.92	2.45	2.83	3.14
Staff and non-staff cost per case	Child, *f*	''	0.69	1.22	1.92	2.45	2.83	3.14
Staff and non-staff cost per case	Worker, *m*	''	0.69	1.22	1.92	2.45	2.83	3.14
Staff and non-staff cost per case	Worker, *f*	''	0.69	1.22	1.92	2.45	2.83	3.14
Staff and non-staff cost per case	Pensioner, *m* ''		0.69	1.22	1.92	2.45	2.83	3.14
Staff and non-staff cost per case	Pensioner, *f* ''		0.69	1.22	1.92	2.45	2.83	3.14
Income subject to contributions	–	Million TL	597 727	1 131 248	1 894 198	2 561 077	3 150 639	3 705 865
Legal contribution rate	–	%	7.5	7.5	7.5	7.5	7.5	7.5

Table E8.9c   Other initial inputs and start values of the Turkish health budget, 1995

Item	Input	Unit	Value
1. **Government health care delivery system**	Government investments in health facilities	Million TL	0.00
	Deviation factor for health investments	–	1.00
	Annual staff cost per ambulatory care unit	Million TL	0.35
	Non-staff cost per ambulatory care unit	''	0.35
	Deviation factor for non-staff cost per ambulatory	–	1.02
	Deviation factor for number of staff per ambulatory care unit	–	1.00
	Deviation factor for health care staff salaries	–	1.02
	Annual staff cost per bed	Million TL	0.17
	Deviation factor for number of staff in in-patient care	–	1.00
	Deviation factor for staff cost in hospitals	–	1.02
	Annual non-staff cost per hospital bed	–	0.17
	Deviation factor for non-staff cost	–	1.02
2. **Social insurance schemes** **Initial coverage ratios**	Children, male	–	0.23
	Children, female	–	0.23
	Workers, male	–	0.23
	Workers, female	–	0.23
	Pensioners, male	–	0.23
	Pensioners, female	–	0.23
Annual frequency of ambulatory care utilization	Children, male	Cases	2.46
	Children, female	''	2.46
	Workers, male	''	2.46
	Workers, female	''	2.46
	Pensioners, male	''	2.46
	Pensioners, female	''	2.46

Table E8.9c (Continued)

Item	Input	Unit	Value
Initial cost per ambulatory care case	Children, male	Million TL	0.71
	Children, female	''	0.71
	Workers, male	''	0.71
	Workers, female	''	0.71
	Pensioners, male	''	0.71
	Pensioners, female	''	0.71
	Deviation factor for ambulatory care utilization	''	1.00
	Cost share of health insurance	%	1.00
Frequency of hospital care per capita	Children, male	Days	0.40
	Children, female	''	0.40
	Workers, male	''	0.40
	Workers, female	''	0.40
	Pensioners, male	''	0.40
	Pensioners, female	''	0.40
Cost per hospital day	Children, male	Million TL	4.00
	Children, female	''	4.00
	Workers, male	''	4.00
	Workers, female	''	4.00
	Pensioners, male	''	4.00
	Pensioners, female	''	4.00
	Volume adjustment factor	–	1.00
	Deviation factor of hospital care utilization	–	1.01
	Cost share of health insurance	%	1.00
Frequency of dental care utilization	Children, male	Number	0.00
	Children, female	''	0.00
	Workers, male	''	0.00
	Workers, female	''	0.00
	Pensioners, male	''	0.00
	Pensioners, female	''	0.00
Cost per dental care case	Children, male	Million TL	0.00
	Children, female	''	0.00
	Workers, male	''	0.00
	Workers, female	''	0.00
	Pensioners, male	''	0.00
	Pensioners, female	''	0.00
	Deviation factor of dental care	–	1.00
	Cost share of dental care	%	1.00
Pharmaceutical expenditure per capita	Children, male	Million TL	1.44
	Children, female	''	1.44
	Workers, male	''	1.44
	Workers, female	''	1.44
	Pensioners, male	''	1.44
	Pensioners, female	''	1.44
	Deviation of pharmaceutical expenditure	–	1.02
	Policy variable for pharmaceutical expenditure	–	1.00
Per capita expenditure for other care	Children, male	Million TL	0.69
	Children, female	''	0.69
	Workers, male	''	0.69
	Workers, female	''	0.69
	Pensioners, male	''	0.69

Table E8.9c (Continued)

Item	Input	Unit	Value
	Pensioners, female	''	0.69
	Deviation of other care	–	1.00
	Share of administrative cost	%	2.00
Real interest rate		%	3.00
Minimum wage		Million TL	32.32
Reduction factor for government participation		–	0.10
Transfer rate from health care scheme to other schemes		Million TL	0.00
Initial reserves		Million TL	0.00

'' = ditto; – = no units.

Total expenditure

$$TEHCSS_t = (1 + aehcss) * TEBHCSS_t$$

Remark: a denotes age group breakdown of least age groups (0–5), (16–64), (65+); a breakdown into single age x would be ideal, but the data situation in most countries will not permit it.

Income

Contribution income, investment income, other income mutatis mutandis, as in the case of pensions with **CRHC** instead of **CONR**.

Reserves

Mutatis mutandis, as with the pension scheme.

Patient co-payments

$$TCOP_t = ACE_t/sac * (1 - sac) + HCE_t/shc * (1 - shc) + DCE_t/stc$$

$$* (1 - stc) + PCE_t/(pv1 * spc) * (1 - pv1 * spc)$$

Exogenous: $STAC_{t=0}$, $NSTAC_{t=0}$, $STCHD_{t=0}$, $NSTHD_{t=0}$, $PECOV_{t=0}$, $OCCOV_{t=0}$, aehcss, dvstac, dvnstac, dvsthac, dvntshc, dvpc, dvoc, pv1, pv2, dvpc, sac, shc, spc

where:

Government scheme

ACU	Number of ambulatory care facilities
AW	Average wage in the economy
BEDS	Number of beds
dsta	Staffing trend per ambulatory care facility
dsthc	Staffing trend per hospital bed

dtsa	Development of administrative staffing
dvha	Deviation of wages of administration staff from average wage
dvnstac	Deviation of average non-staff cost from inflation
dvnsthc	Deviation of average non-staff cost per bed from inflation
dvstac	Deviation of wages of ambulatory care staff from average wage
dvsthc	Deviation of wages of hospital staff from average wage
GAEHC	Government administrative cost
GCON	Government contribution to social insurance scheme
GEAC	Expenditure for government ambulatory care facilities
GEHC	Expenditure for government hospitals
GINV	Government investment expenditure in health facilities
IND	Indicator for the demographic impact on utilization
inv	Investment ratio
NSTAC	Average non-staff cost per ambulatory care facility
NSTHC	Average non-staff cost per hospital bed
NTGHC	Total net government health care expenditure
OEGHC$_t$	Other expenditure in government health care
oep	Other expenditure ratio
STAC	Average staff cost in government per ambulatory care facility
STHC	Average staff cost in government hospitals per bed
TCOPG	Total amount of patients' co-payments
TGHC	Total gross government health expenditure
TPOP	Number of total population

Social insurance scheme

ACE	Ambulatory cost expenditure
AEHCSS	Administrative expenditure of the social security system
aehcss	Administrative expenditure rate
CAC	Average cost per ambulatory care case
CHD	Cost per hospital day
COV	Covered persons in defined age group
DCE	Dental care expenditure
dvnstac	Deviation of non-staff cost increase in ambulatory care from inflation
dvnsthc	Deviation of non-staff cost increase in hospital care from inflation
dvoc	Deviation factor of increase of other care cost from inflation
dvpc	Deviation factor of increase of pharmaceutical cost from inflation
dvstac	Deviation of staff cost increase in ambulatory care from average wage
dvsthc	Deviation of staff cost increase in hospital care from average wage
dvuac	General utilization trend factor for ambulatory care
dvuhc	General utilization trend factor for utilization of hospital care
FAC	Annual number of cases per covered person

HCE	Hospital care expenditure
HD	Annual hospital days per covered person
NSTAC	Non-staff cost per ambulatory care case
OCCOV	Other care expenditure per covered persons
OCE	Expenditure on other care
PCE	Pharmaceutical expenditure
PCOV	Pharmaceutical expenditure per covered person
pv1	Policy variable for pharmaceutical expenditure
RESIC	Initial reserve in health care scheme
sac	Share of ambulatory cost borne by scheme
sdc	Share of dental care borne by the scheme
shc	Share of ambulatory cost borne by scheme
spc	Share of pharmaceutical cost borne by scheme
STAC	Staff cost per ambulatory care case
TEBHCSS	Total personal health care expenditure of the social security system
TEHCSS	Contribution rate of the social security health care system

8.2.4.3 The poverty, social assistance and housing complex model

Contrary to social insurance benefits and benefits delivered by the national health service, there are social protection benefits in many countries which are granted only in case of need. In general, these benefits are called means-tested benefits. The pros and cons of means testing are not discussed in this book. We simply model the financial structure of these benefits. In order to do so, we have to instrumentalize the concept of need. We approximate need here by poverty, and assume that some benefits are paid only to poor people. The two most important benefits in this category are normally cash and benefits in kind, paid under social assistance provisions and housing benefits. In some national social protection systems, there might be other benefits which fall into the means-tested category. We limit our analysis here to social assistance and housing, assuming that methods developed could ceteris paribus be applied to other types of benefits (such as means-tested family benefits).

Social assistance and housing benefits are generally both anti-poverty benefits which follow a household-based means testing procedure. A household may consist of one person only, or of several persons living together who organize their day-to-day expenses on a common economic basis. Theoretically, the projection of the benefit amounts due requires forecasting the expected number of poor households and their individual poverty gaps; the amounts to be paid to all households with a positive gap would be summed up, resulting in the expected total budget expense. For an individual household, the poverty gap is defined as the difference between the household's income, and that level of income which constitutes the borderline between a household living in poverty or not. This borderline income is often called the poverty line.

In principle, there are as many poverty lines as households. Each of them lives under different circumstances – the required minimum means for a life without poverty is affected, for example, by regional factors or by the household's sociological composition. Persons living in a rural area might have access to in-kind income, whereas those living in urban regions normally depend on cash income. The cost of living is higher in high-income regions than in medium- or low-income regions. It makes a vast difference in individual households' poverty lines whether the household members are young or old, or whether they are healthy or depend on medical care. The ideal approach to projecting social assistance expenses is therefore a microsimulation model which is capable of taking into account many of the described characteristics of individual households. In fact, a number of governments have made successful efforts to establish such models. If such a model exists, its results can be exported to the Social Budget model, just as in the case of stand-alone pension and health care models.

Mainly because of the enormous data requirements, maintenance cost and size, a microsimulation social assistance model has not yet been developed by the ILO. This is why we here describe a different pragmatic method for the projection of expenditure for means-tested benefits, integrated into the Social Budget model framework, and based on averages, not on individual household data. Basically this method avoids the individual household approach but, instead, uses a generally defined poverty line, and calculates the average income of the poor and, thus, an average poverty gap. By referring to the population's income distribution, the number of poor households can be estimated, the total benefits due projected by relating benefit amounts to the product of the average poverty gap and the number of poor households. Housing benefits play a major role in poverty alleviation; this is why they are considered to be closely linked to social assistance.

In the ILO model, the projection of social assistance and housing benefits is technically in three different modules, a "household/poverty" module, a "social assistance" module and a "housing" module. The main features of these modules are briefly described in the following sections.

The household/poverty module

Measurement of poverty is one of the most difficult undertakings in social policy analysis. Projecting it meets with even more conceptual difficulties. The methodological difficulties are explicitly acknowledged, but in the interest of providing some benchmark estimate on poverty, a simple robust methodology is necessary and is described here. The methodologies that have been applied in different country cases vary to a considerable extent, since they are highly dependent on national situations. The following paragraphs thus describe the general reasoning pursued by different applied versions of the ILO model. The country example provided at the end of the section complements the general "philosophy" of poverty projections by a concrete case.

The initial poverty line is taken from government estimates, or from the estimates of other institutions. It might be an absolute poverty line, a poverty line which is calculated on the basis of the pricing of a basket of goods and services which is regarded essential for the physical survival of an average adult person. Children's needs are normally defined as a fraction of an adult person's needs, in "adult equivalents". In other cases, average "minimum consumption baskets" are calculated uniformly for the whole population. By contrast, a relative poverty concept could be chosen which would place the poverty line at a certain fraction of the average income or the average wage of the economy. This concept is pursued, for example, by the United Nations Children's Fund (UNICEF) in some of its literature, and is often used in international comparisons of poverty. The fraction of the average wage used varies between 35 and 50 per cent.[26]

As officially or implicitly acknowledged levels of poverty depend on political decisions, the ILO model permits the optional use of exogenously determined poverty-line levels on the absolute or the relative concept. The absolute line is simply projected by annually adjusting its previous year's value in line with the movement of the CPI, and the relative line is calculated as a constant percentage of the national average wage.

Once the line is established, the number of households with incomes below the line is calculated. Housing and social assistance benefits are usually being paid only if the income of a household is less than the amount determined by the poverty line. The household income comprises labour and capital income, transfers from institutions paying non-means-tested social benefits (these may be pensions, unemployment benefits, sickness and maternity benefits, or others), withdrawals from private savings and private donations. Thus, before calculating the number of eligible households, the number of households with pre-means-tested income below the poverty line has to be estimated.

One of the preconditions of any such calculation is data availability. Some recent estimates of the household income distribution should at least be available in order to pursue the steps described below. Ideally, there should be a database with a representative sample of individual household data, including data on different types of income received by households.

In order to calculate the number of households with pre-means-tested income below the poverty line, the households have to be classified by income brackets defined as multiples of the national average wage (starting, for example, at 10 per cent of the average wage and ending at 500 per cent or more). For each income bracket, an average income per capita has to be found and calculated as a percentage of the national average wage. These calculations have to be based on existing statistics or assumptions derived from other information. Furthermore, they must be calibrated to match the statistically observed average per capita incomes.

For each income bracket, average per capita income has to be split into its components:

- income from labour, property and profits;
- income from pensions and other non-means-tested social benefits (social insurance and universal benefits); and
- income from means-tested social benefits.

Now a *pre-means-test transfer income distribution* (the distribution *before* any social assistance and/or housing benefits are paid) can be calculated. The average pre-transfer incomes in the different classes are projected by increasing the components of the total income in each income bracket by the projected increases in the respective types of income.

If the poverty line is constant, then any increase in pre-transfer incomes will result in a reduction in the number of eligible households and a reduction in the poverty gap of these households, and thus to a reduction in the volume of social assistance payments. If the poverty line is dynamized, then any effect of pre-transfer income increases on the number of eligible households and the average poverty gap depends on the relative speed of income versus poverty line adjustments.

It is acknowledged that, especially, the assumption of a constant income distribution over time is a crude simplification. While this assumption might be valid, *cum grano salis*, over the medium term for established OECD market economies, it is definitely critical in many other countries. For example, independently of their stage of economic development, the income distribution has widened in practically all Central and Eastern European transition countries, as well as in many others, and poverty levels have increased at the same time.[27] However, projecting such changes in the shape of the income distribution is one of the most difficult tasks in socio-economic modelling and is, if tried, not often successful. In some countries, information might be available allowing educated assessments of future trends in the shape of the income distribution. But most often the household/poverty module would be used only to simulate the effects of possible changes of the income distribution on social expenditure. Such sensitivity analyses could contribute to the formulation of objectives of national income policies.

Depending on the actual benefit provisions of means-tested benefits, the total number of households might be split into certain categories, grouped, for example by the number of dependent children or the labour market status of the main breadwinner. These could again be split into poor and non-poor households. It is obvious that continued disaggregation, although desirable, will inevitably meet with statistical limitations in each and every country. Many Social Budget models will thus have to confine them-selves to the described establishment of a poverty head-count index and a poverty gap.

Equation 8.13   Poverty indices

Poverty head-count index I (absolute poverty line)

$$POOR(I)_t = \sum_i (HOUSP_{i,t} * HSIZE_{i,t})$$

for all $HOUS_{i,t} = HOUSP_{i,t}$ with $E_{i,t} \leq PL(I)_t$ and $PL(I)_t = PL(I)_{t-1} * (1 + p_t)$

Poverty head-count index II (relative poverty line)

$$POOR(II)_t = \sum_i (HOUSP_{i,t} * HSIZE_{i,t})$$

for all $HOUS_{i,t} = HOUSP_{i,t}$ with $E_{i,t} \leq PL(II)_t$ and $PL(II)_t = rpl * AW_t$

Remark: Since income distributions normally are organized in the form of income classes, the number of households under the poverty line in the "last" class in which the poverty line lies is estimated as follows:

If $PL(I, II)_t < UPIC_{i,t}$ then

$$HOUSP_{i,t} = (PL(I, II)_t - LOIC_{i,t})/(UPIC_{i,t} - LOIC_{i,t}) * HOUS_{i,t}$$

Poverty gap

$$Pg_t = \sum_i (HOUSP_{i,t} * HSIZE_{i,t} * (PL_t - E_{i,t}))$$

for all $HOUS_{i,t} = HOUSP_{i,t}$ with $E_{i,t} \leq PL_t$

Remark: Where the "last" class is treated in the same way as mentioned above, with the earnings in the class being the average between the *PL* and the *LOIC*.

where:

$E_{i,t}$ = Average individual earnings in class I at t

PL = Poverty line

PG = Poverty gap

$HOUS_{i,t}$ = Number of households in income class i

$HOUSP_{i,t}$ = Number of poor households in income class i

$HSIZE_{i,t}$ = Average household size in class i

$UPIC_{i,t}$ = Upper income limit of class i

$LOIC_{i,t}$ = Lower income limit of class i

pt = Rate of increase of CPI

rpl = Ratio of poverty line to average wage (in the case of a relative poverty line)

AW_t = Average wage

Exogenous: All except *PL* and *PG*.

Example 8.10 describes and demonstrates the estimated development of the poverty indicators for Poland. The methodology was applied by a Polish task force which established a Polish Social Budget model (on the basis of the general ILO approach) in 1998–99.

The social assistance and housing modules

Social assistance

Social assistance generally provides benefits both in cash and in kind. Together, they are designed to close the gap between the actual cash income of a household and the poverty line. A "social assistance intervention line" (SAIL) may be defined as a fixed percentage share of the poverty line. SAIL determines the borderline up to which social assistance would top up an eligible household's income in cash. This might mean that – depending on the fiscal constraints of the government – the poverty gap couldn't be fully closed by social assistance payments.

Once the income distribution for each of the projection years, as well as SAIL, has been established, it would theoretically be possible to calculate the number of poor pre-transfer households, the income gap to SAIL, the in-kind component and thus, finally, the total social assistance benefits. But the reality is more complicated: social assistance schemes in general face two problems which are difficult to incorporate adequately. One problem is the development of the benefit take-up rate, and the other is the efficiency of benefit delivery through the administration. The take-up of benefits may be far less or even higher than 100 per cent of the theoretically eligible number of persons; the actual take-up depends on the population's awareness of benefit entitlement, the rigorousness of the means test, the social stigma possibly attached to the benefit, and other social values. The efficiency of benefit delivery may be far from socially optimal, as when social assistance administrators fail to identify all those in need, or if budget shortages force them to deliver less than full benefits, or no benefits at all, to some of the eligible persons.

In order to avoid substantial errors in benefit expenditure projections, the well-known "anchoring" technique may be resorted to by multiplying last year's total amount of social assistance benefits by the annual change in the total amount of resources representing the poverty gap. It could thus be ascertained that the total amount of social assistance expenditure follows the projected trend of need, without being forced to make explicit assumptions about the benefit take-up rate or the administration's delivery efficiency. This procedure assumes implicitly that the beneficiaries' behaviour, as well as that of the benefit administration, does not change during the projection period – which is reasonable over the short and medium term. If, in the long term, behavioural changes are to be expected, then the inclusion of factors reflecting changes in the take-up rate or changes in delivery efficiency is advised.

In the ILO social assistance module it is assumed that benefits are generally financed from municipalities' coffers. Being a classical PAYG system, the

Example 8.10   Poland: Projections of poverty indices

The approach used in this example requires the initial income distribution data for four classes of households:

- households with employed breadwinners (employees or self-employed) and non-agricultural income as a main source of income;
- households with breadwinners with income from a farm as a main source of income;
- households with breadwinners with pensions (old-age, disability, survivors') as a main source of income;
- households with inactive non-pensioners having other main sources of income.

The input income distribution for the initial year (1996) was derived from a household budget survey. All the households within the above four types are ranked by their *average monthly per capita income* (excluding social assistance and other means-tested benefits) and grouped into income brackets defined as percentages of the national average wage. In the current model version, there are 22 income brackets. The lowest is the zero income group, the highest a group with average per capita income higher than 100 per cent of the national average wage.

For each household type and income bracket, the following data are required:

- number of households;
- average number of persons per household (average household size); and
- average number of equivalent units per household.

For each income bracket, data on average monthly household incomes from different income sources are required. The current model version distinguishes between the following sources of income:

- income from employment, self-employment, agriculture, property or profits;
- income from pensions;
- income from unemployment benefits;
- income from family benefits;
- income from social assistance;
- income from other social benefits not listed separately.

Based on the overall number of households and household members, aggregate (macro) income amounts are calculated for the initial (survey) year. These aggregates are compared with respective aggregate income amounts derived from other parts of the model (income from labour and profits, pensions, unemployment benefits, family benefits, short-term social insurance benefits). As they usually differ (incomes in the household budget survey are normally under-reported), correction coefficients are calculated and then used for the projection of the income distribution.

Based on the demographic projections, as well as the projections of the labour force, employed persons, inactives, unemployed and pensioners, the total number of households and the number of households in the four categories are projected. The proportions of different types of households within the total are assumed to change in line with changes in the size of the respective population groups with different labour market statuses (employed in and outside agriculture, pensioners, unemployed).

The projection of the overall household income distribution is made in two steps. The first step assumes that the initial income distributions for the different household types remain unchanged during the projection period. The overall household income distribution will then change as a result of projected changes in the weights of the different types of households within the overall structure. These weights are changing in time in line with changes in the labour market situation and numbers of pensioners. For example, an increase in unemployment will increase the share of households headed by "inactive non-pensioners" and then will change the overall income distribution through an increased percentage of households in lower income brackets.

The second step calculates the allocation of the total household income (excluding social assistance and other means-tested benefits) to the different income brackets. This allocation is then used to calculate the number of households below the social assistance poverty line (or any other poverty line defined) and to calculate a poverty gap. It is assumed that the distribution of the amounts of the different types of income between income brackets stays constant throughout the projection period. Next it calculates the distribution of total income as a weighted average of the above distributions, where the weights are the shares of the different types of income in the total

Figure E8.10a   Poland: Poverty criterion and number of households below the poverty line, 1996–2020 (two alternatives)

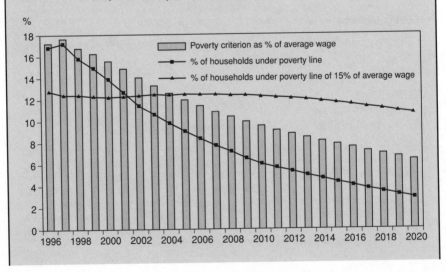

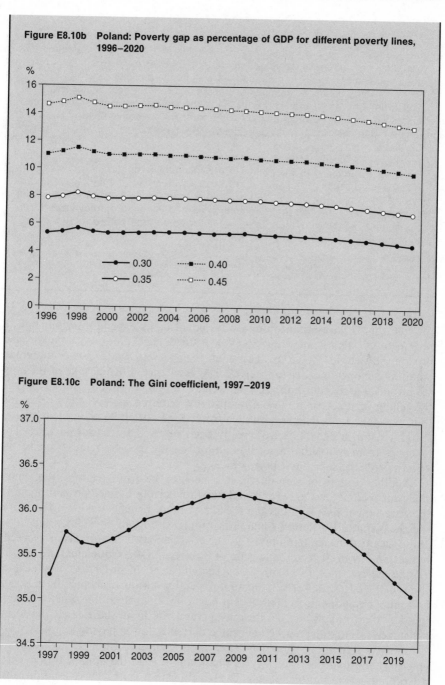

Figure E8.10b   Poland: Poverty gap as percentage of GDP for different poverty lines, 1996–2020

Figure E8.10c   Poland: The Gini coefficient, 1997–2019

pre-social-assistance income. Finally, the average future income for each income bracket, with distribution of households and persons projected in the first step, can be calculated together with the number of households and persons below any poverty line defined, as well as the poverty gap.

Under fairly optimistic assumptions about longer-term economic growth, the Polish poverty model predicts reduction of the poverty head-count index, both under the present absolute poverty line and under a relative poverty line. The poverty gap will also gradually close. The results are shown in figures E8.10a–c.

Figure E8.10c shows the estimated development of the Gini coefficient, which is a measure of inequality in the income distribution.[1] It shows that inequality increases for some years before it decreases again towards the end of the projection period. The reverse U-shape of the Gini curve here is a consequence of the fact that unemployment and low-paid employment in the agricultural sector is thought to increase for some time before it falls, owing to rising employment levels.

[1] The Gini coefficient is the ratio of two integrals. The numerator is the integral of the difference between the curve which describes a cumulative perfect equal income distribution (i.e. a 45-degree diagonal) and the actual Lorenz curve of a country's cumulative income distribution. The denominator is the integral under the 45-degree diagonal.

revenues of social assistance are always equal to its expenditure, but not all revenue must stem from public sources. Instead, legislation may stipulate that private households have to liquidate their assets (with some minimum amounts exempt) in order to receive social assistance. For the sake of the individual social assistance applicant, as well as the general public (the taxpayer), the selling of assets is by law normally not required at any (low) price and thus may take time. This is why such income may often be realized only after social assistance benefits have already been received for a certain time. The revenues from individual asset liquidation would then be reimbursed to the government (the social assistance office).

Another source of non-public income may be from relatives who have sufficient income and/or wealth and are thus legally obliged to reimburse to the government part or all of the social assistance benefits paid. Furthermore, social assistance legislation sometimes stipulates that any benefits received by an applicant must be reimbursed to the government if the applicant succeeds in escaping from the economic state of poverty.[28] Often municipalities receive earmarked transfers from other government levels in order to cover part of the social assistance costs. Sometimes social insurance schemes have social assistance components in their benefit portfolio, as for example social pensions in many Central and Eastern European countries. In all these cases, the social assistance revenues have to be allocated correctly to the paying sectors.

Finally, something should be said about administration. If high-delivery efficiency is pursued – socially and financially – then the administrative costs are probably comparatively high. The reason is that beneficiaries (and possibly their relatives) have to be identified, their means have to be tested, their income and wealth status has to be established, and measures have to be taken to minimize the time they depend on benefits. Measures to prevent misuse of the legal provisions have to be implemented and maintained. All this is time-consuming and requires a large number of staff. For example, in Germany the administrative cost is estimated to be in the order of 10 per cent of total social assistance expenditure – a rate which is about five times as high as that for public pension insurance.

Housing

Housing benefits are generally calculated as the product of a number of households and the average amount of benefits. The number of households in poverty is a proxy for the eligible households. The number of recipient households should again be anchored to the number of recipient households in the previous year. The average amount of benefits may be indexed in line with consumer price inflation, but a specific housing index (comprising rent, energy, etc.) may be available, and should then be used. The administrative costs are normally estimated as a fixed percentage of the benefit expenditure. The financing of the benefits is normally shared between the central and local governments.

Equation 8.14 Social assistance and housing expenditure

$$TSAE_t = TCBE_t + TBKI_t + AE_t$$

$$TCBE_t = TCBE_{t-1} * (PGAP_t / PGAP_{t-1})$$

$$TBKI_t = tk * TCBE_t$$

$$AE_t = ae * TCBE_t$$

$$THBE_t = TPH_t * Ab_{t-1} * (1 + p_t)$$

where:

TSAE	Total amount of social assistance expenditure
TCBE	Total amount of cash benefit expenditure under social assistance
TBKI	Total amount of benefits in kind under social assistance
AE	Administrative expenditure
tk	Benefit-in-kind ratio
ae	Administrative cost ratio
THBE	Total amount of housing benefits
TPH	Total number of poor households
PGAP	Amount of poverty gap
AB	Average amount of housing benefit
p	Annual increase of CPI

Exogenous: *tk*, *ae* and the initial values for *TSAE* and *TCBE*.

8.2.4.4 The sickness and maternity benefit model

The projection of sickness in the ILO Social Budget model is based on the last available benefit data, the average number of benefit days per insured person, and the average replacement rate for the daily sickness benefit. Accordingly, projections of maternity benefits are based on the number of maternity days per woman of "reproductive" age (for example, 18 to 45 years) and the average daily maternity benefit. Benefits of minor importance might be included in this module, for example, funeral lump-sum payments, and calculated on basically the same method. For status quo projections, the number of sickness days per head, the average replacement rate for sickness benefits, and the number of maternity benefits per woman in the reproductive age group are kept constant; they may be varied in simulations.

Other expenditure and administrative costs can be calculated as percentages of the sickness and maternity benefit expenditure. Contribution income, PAYG costs and reserve development are calculated mutatis mutandis as in the pension schemes if the benefits are provided by an independent branch of social security. Should these benefits be provided by other institutions, then the benefit expenditure equations are introduced on the expenditure side of the respective institutions. Sometimes such expenditures are financed directly by employers; in that case, revenues would automatically equal expenditure and be considered as imputed contributions by employers. A country example is provided in the next section, as well as an unemployment benefit example.

Equation 8.15 Sickness and maternity (short-term) benefits

$$TSBE_t = \sum_{x,s}(MAXS_t/MAXS_{t-1} * ARSB_{t,x,s} * (LRS_t/LRS_{t-1}) * sd_{t,x,s}$$

$$* IE(t,x,s * INS_{t,x,s})\text{ for all } x \text{ in active age groups}$$

$$TMBE + t = \sum_{x,s}(MAXM_t/MAXM_{t-1} * ARMB_{t,x} * (LRM_t/LRM_{t-1}) * md_{t,x}$$

$$* IE_{t,x} * INS_{t,x,s})\text{ for } x = 15\text{ to }45$$

where:

TSBE	Total sickness benefit expenditure
TMBE	Total maternity benefit expenditure
sd	Sickness days per employed worker
md	Maternity days per insured woman aged 15 to 45
MAXS	Legal maximum duration of sickness benefits
MAXM	Legal maximum duration of maternity benefits
ARSB	Average (statistical) replacement rate for sickness benefits
ARMB	Average replacement rate for maternity benefits

LRS   Legal replacement-rate sickness benefits
LRM   Legal replacement-rate maternity benefits
INS   Insured and contributing persons
IE   Insurable earnings

Exogenous: All initial values for *sd, md, ARSB, ARMB* and constant values for
  LRS, LRM, MAXS, MAXM.

8.2.4.5   The unemployment benefit model

The ILO model assumes that unemployment benefits are paid by a social insurance type of scheme, which also provides active labour market services (placement, training, etc). If benefits are provided by way of a different institutional arrangement, then the income side of the unemployment scheme would have to be modified accordingly. The projection of benefit expenditure should not be affected.

For a mature scheme, aggregate unemployment benefits are calculated as the product of the number of registered unemployed, the average wage, the ratio of beneficiaries receiving benefits and the replacement rate (ratio of the average benefit over the average wage or the average insurable earnings).

The ratio of beneficiaries to the total number of unemployed is called the beneficiary rate. It reflects the take-up of benefits, but also reflects non-receipt of benefits for a variety of other reasons, ranging from administrative failures in identifying all eligible persons, the "nature" of unemployment – seasonal, cyclical, structural – to the expiration of benefits. In times of persistently high and long-term unemployment, due to relatively encrusted labour markets, the beneficiary rate tends to drop, since more and more persons exhaust their benefits but remain registered and possibly "move on" to social assistance benefits. With a sudden upsurge of unemployment, the beneficiary rate normally increases significantly, as almost all of the additional unemployed are eligible for benefits. If it is assumed that a high level of unemployment were to prevail for a number of years, then – if proved by past experience – a declining beneficiary rate could be assumed. However, if such experience is not available, the order of magnitude of such a decline will be difficult to establish, and it might be prudent to maintain an initially observed (relatively high) beneficiary rate throughout the protection period.

The observed beneficiary rate is implicitly a function of the maximum duration of benefits. The most frequently simulated policy alternatives in unemployment benefit systems are changes in the maximum duration of benefit receipt. In order to assess the effects of such variations, distributions of unemployed persons by duration are needed. A simple case is demonstrated in the following example, which uses structural data from the Department of Social Welfare in Ireland.

However, such distributions are not always available. The simplest way to model the change in a maximum duration of benefits is to adjust the beneficiary

Example 8.11   Ireland: Simulation of alternative benefit duration[1]

On 18 October 1996 the Irish unemployment live register counted a total of 269,030 unemployed in the country, of which 168,501 were male and 100,529 female. By duration of unemployment, they were distributed as shown in table E8.11.

Table E8.11   Ireland: Distribution of the unemployed by duration of unemployment, October 1996

Duration in months	Males No.	%	Females No.	%	Total No.	%
Under 3	33 165	19.7	29 468	29.3	62 633	23.3
3–6	19 385	11.5	14 342	14.3	33 727	12.5
6–12	22 542	13.4	15 804	15.7	38 346	14.3
12–24	25 005	14.8	15 282	15.2	40 287	15.0
24–36	17 059	10.1	8 655	8.6	25 714	9.6
Over 36	51 345	30.5	16 978	16.9	68 323	25.4
Total	168 501	100.0	100 529	100.0	269 030	100.0
Beneficiary rates (%)						
Up to 6 months	31.2	–	43.6	–	35.8	–
Up to 12 months	44.6	–	59.3	–	50.1	–

Figure E8.11 is a visual reflection of this distribution for males and females:

Figure E8.11   Ireland: Distribution of the unemployed by duration of unemployment, October 1996

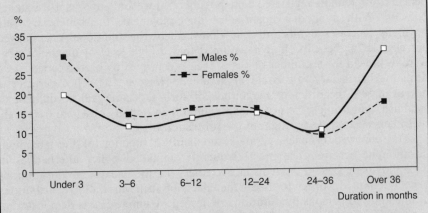

The graph shows a double clustering of the unemployed around a short duration (under three months) and a very long duration (over three years). Let us now look at the theoretical case that there were no unemployment benefit and the Government considered the introduction of unemployment benefit to be paid to all unemployed persons for a maximum of six months. A critical parameter of the cost to be expected would then be the (unknown) beneficiary rate – how many out of all registered unemployed would on average per year receive the benefit. In order to establish an estimate, it could be assumed that the distribution of the duration of unemployment on 18 October is representative of the whole year. From the information in table E8.10 a beneficiary ratio could be calculated, at about 36 per cent. Multiplying that rate by the average number of unemployed, and the envisaged average benefit would yield the total annual benefit expenditure. If the Government had to choose whether to double the maximum duration of benefits or to double the benefit rate, it would probably opt for the first. Doubling the benefit rate would double the cost in any case. Because of the distribution of the duration of unemployment, the doubling of the maximum duration would raise the beneficiary ratio only to about 50 per cent, which would lead to a cost increase of about 40 per cent. It is obvious that these calculations hold true only if the distribution of unemployment by duration does not react to changes in the legally defined maximum period, which is probably valid in the short term, but critical in the longer term.

[1] Cf. Government of Ireland: *1996 – Statistical information on social welfare services* (Dublin, 1996).

rate linearly, which means that it is assumed implicitly that the behaviour of the unemployed with respect to the "exhaustion" of the benefits is independent of its duration; that is, that people would exhaust a relatively long duration of unemployment benefits to the same (relative) extent as a comparatively short maximum duration. This simple assumption is not endorsed here as a behavioural model, but is regarded as a pragmatic possibility in order to model the impact of changes in the maximum benefit durations. It can be regarded as a rather optimistic assumption when simulating a shorter duration. If there is an extension of the maximum benefit duration it might be considered a conservative assumption. In the case of a shorter average duration, "benefit exhaustion" might be higher, and when there is an extended duration, the opposite might be true.[29]

The average replacement rate is a statistically observed value, even if the replacement rate of unemployment benefits, as for other short-term benefits, is usually stipulated by law. An initially observed replacement rate might, for example, deteriorate in individual cases because of inflation and non-adjustment, which would lead to a statistically observed lower average replacement rate than the legally prescribed rate. This is a standard phenomenon. However, the statistically observed average replacement rate (calculated as the average benefit over the national average wage) might vary over time through changes in the structure of the (new) unemployed, for example if the unemployed represented the low-wage-level sector of the labour market only. Changes in the legal replacement rate are again easiest modelled by a linear modification of the average replacement rate.

Beneficiary rates, as well as replacement rates, ideally should be calculated separately by age and sex, but this is often impossible, because of poor data situations. Projections have thus to be limited to disaggregation by sex.

Expenditure on active labour market policies may be calculated as fixed proportions of the expenditure on unemployment allowances, which makes sense as long as unemployment is primarily regarded as a cyclical phenomenon. It might then be correctly assumed that labour market measures are positively correlated with unemployment, because such measures might be understood as tools against excessive unemployment growth, the resources being reduced during periods of lower unemployment. In other words, the measures would follow a pro-cyclical trend. By contrast, labour market conditions might exist where a low level of unemployment would be the result of high compensatory active labour market measures and vice versa; labour market measures would thus predominantly be understood as an anti-cyclical instrument. Therefore, labour market measures would then be high when unemployment is low, and vice versa. Reality normally shows an overlapping of both policies. When applied to concrete country cases, such principal differences in modelling active labour market policies would have to be taken into account. The administrative costs of the employment service can be calculated as a constant percentage share of total expenditure on benefits and measures.

Income, PAYG costs and reserve development are calculated mutatis mutandis, as in the pension module.

In the ILO standard modelling approach, it is assumed that insurable earnings are the same as in the pension scheme. This might not always be the case, as the schemes often operate separate collection systems of differing efficiency or any ceilings on insurable earnings may vary in different social insurance branches. Then, a specific formula has to be introduced which establishes a link between the insurable earnings in the unemployment benefit schemes (which also serve as the reference income for the calculation of contributions) and the national average wage.

Example 8.12 shows the unemployment benefit module of the Social Budget model version which was used by the ILO in 1996 to assess the financial situation of the Unemployment Insurance Fund (UIF) in South Africa.

In formal terms, the above explanations can be summarized in the following two equations.

Equation 8.16 Unemployment benefits

$$TUBE_t = \sum_{x,s} (U_{t,x,s} * br_{t,x,s} * MAX_t / MAX_{t-1} * ars_{t,x,s} * (Lr_t / Lr_{t-1}) * IE_{t,x,s})$$

$$ACTE_t = TUBE_t * ale_t$$

Example 8.12   South Africa: Assessing the financial development of the Unemployment Insurance Fund (UIF)[1]

Table E8.12a summarizes the key economic assumptions for the valuation of the UIF in 1996. The UIF is an unemployment scheme that also provides other short-term cash benefits (sickness and maternity). This is due to the fact that no short-term benefit social insurance scheme yet exists in South Africa.

Table E8.12a   South Africa: Economic assumptions for the projections of the UIF, base case, 1994–2000

	Year						
	1994	1995	1996	1997	1998	1999	2000
Real growth rate (%)	n.a.	3.30	3.30	2.00	2.50	2.90	3.30
Inflation rate (CPI)	n.a.	8.70	8.40	10.90	9.60	9.30	9.10
Interest rates (%)							
Real bank rate	n.a.	n.a.	7.00	6.00	5.00	4.50	3.70
Long-term government stock rate	n.a.	16.00	15.40	16.90	14.60	13.80	12.80
Total employment, in 1 000[1]	9 641	9 742	9 839	9 940	10 023	10 127	10 261
Growth (%)	n.a.	1.05	1.00	1.03	0.84	1.04	1.32
Average real wage growth (in %)							
Private sector	n.a.	n.a.	0.80	1.50	1.70	1.30	1.40
Government sector	n.a.	n.a.	4.80	0.40	0.40	0.30	0.00
Total unemployment – Expanded definition	4 659	4 916	5 185	5 450	5 732	5 994	6 226
Unemployment rate (%)	32.58	33.54	34.51	35.41	36.38	37.18	37.76
Total unemployment – Strict definition	2 453	2 588	2 730	2 869	3 018	3 156	3 278
Unemployment rate	20.28	20.87	21.48	22.04	22.64	23.14	23.50

[1] Estimated on the basis of UIF statistics and special benefit survey.
Source: Department of Finance: *Growth, employment and redistribution: A macroeconomic strategy* (Pretoria, 1996).

Tables E8.12b and c summarize the benefit experience data for 1995.

Table E8.12b   South Africa: Frequency and duration of benefits, UIF, 1993–95

Type of benefit	Claims per 1 000 insured persons					Average benefit duration (in months)		
	1993	1994	1995			1995		
	Total	Total	Total	Male	Female	Male	Female	Total
Unemployment	134	117	121	121	120	3.5	3.6	3.53
Sickness	9	7	7	6	8	4.1	4.2	4.14
Maternity[1]	45	42	42	0	42	0	3.5	n.a
Death[2]	4	3	3	n.a	n.a	n.a	n.a	3.4

[1] The total for this benefit applies only to insured females. [2] Duration here means the number of months used to calculate the lump-sum benefit.

Table E8.12c   South Africa: Average monthly benefit amounts and replacement rates, UIF, 1995 [1]

Type of benefit	Average monthly benefit amount (R)			Average replacement rate (as % of average insurable earnings)		
	Male	Female	Total	Male	Female	Total
Unemployment	736.34	617.29	699.72	41.74	43.92	42.16
Sickness	910.65	720.65	842.80	51.61	51.27	51.57
Maternity	0.00	831.50	n.a.	0.00	59.16	n.a.
Death[2]	n.a.	n.a.	4 243.20	n.a.	n.a.	n.a.

[1] Estimated on the basis of UIF statistics and special benefit survey. [2] Average benefit per case.

For the purpose of the projections, it was assumed that:

- the frequencies, average benefit durations and the average replacement rates remain constant at the 1995 level for sickness and maternity benefits; the frequency of unemployment benefit cases follows a double dynamic:

  - it is assumed to increase by a total of 10 per cent until the end of the projection period; and

  - it is further modified by the estimates of absolute numbers of unemployed persons in the economy;

- the actual relation between insured wages to total wages in the economy (the catchment rate) will not change;

- the death rate among insured persons remains approximately constant.

Based on the above assumptions, the income and expenditure of the UIF were projected over a period of five years. Table E8.12d provides the most important fiscal results of the projection.

The key financial indicators, that is, the overall PAYG contribution rate (total expenditure divided by total income subject to contribution) and the funding ratio of the scheme for the future financial status have also been calculated.

According to the projections, the PAYG cost rate of the scheme will already exceed the presently levied rate in 1996. As a consequence, the funding ratio of the scheme (which is equivalent to the accumulated debt of the scheme during the years with negative current balances) will decrease sharply, to become negative in 1998. In 2000 the funding ratio will amount to about 56 per cent of the annual benefit expenditure. The PAYG cost rate in 2000 will amount to 2.7 per cent.

Figures E8.12a and b map out the development of the key financial indicators for, alternatively, a base case and a low-growth scenario.

Table E8.12d   South Africa: Summary of projection results of the UIF, 1990–2000 (millions of rand)

	1990	1991	1992	1993	1994	1995	1995	1995	1996	1997	1998	1999	2000
Income													
Contribution income	1 015.60	1 179.70	1 258.10	1 447.40	1 765.20	1 958.80	1 958.80	1 950.22	2 168.48	2 459.11	2 756.05	3 080.01	3 457.04
Investment income	169.20	182.80	157.80	91.40	38.60	43.50	43.50	80.79	74.76	82.68	47.71	−3.16	−84.15
State contribution	7.00	7.00	7.00	7.00	7.00	7.00	7.00	7.00	7.00	7.00	7.00	7.00	7.00
Other income	24.20	20.70	52.60	37.60	30.90	47.70	47.70	47.39	52.69	59.76	66.97	74.84	84.01
Total	1 216.00	1 390.20	1 475.50	1 583.40	1 841.70	2 057.00	2 057.00	2 085.40	2 302.94	2 608.54	2 877.73	3 158.70	3 463.90
Expenditure													
Benefit expenditure	812.23	1 236.85	1 620.40	2 078.40	1 817.90	1 871.40	1 871.40	1 871.97	2 206.05	2 646.21	3 141.18	3 702.08	4 359.72
Unemployment	556.70	930.60	1 263.00	1 665.40	1 446.10	1 495.00	1 495.00	1 495.55	1 787.51	2 171.58	2 609.23	3 107.60	3 692.47
Sickness	80.90	102.80	122.20	153.50	128.60	117.20	117.20	117.12	130.23	147.68	165.51	184.97	207.61
Maternity	135.50	155.90	177.00	184.90	174.80	190.00	190.00	190.09	211.37	239.69	268.64	300.22	336.96
Adoption	0.23	0.25	0.20	0.20	0.20	0.40	0.40	0.40	0.44	0.50	0.56	0.63	0.71
Death	38.90	47.30	58.00	74.40	68.20	68.80	68.80	68.81	76.51	86.76	97.24	108.67	121.97
Other expenditure	10.40	10.40	12.10	20.80	9.20	45.20	45.20	44.87	53.63	65.15	78.28	93.23	110.77
Transfers to former independent state[3]	48.20	51.50	0.00	0.00	0.00	0.00	0.00	0.00	0.00	0.00	0.00	0.00	0.00
Administrative expenditure	42.70	55.10	74.50	89.20	116.50	104.60	104.60	93.60	110.30	132.31	157.06	185.10	217.99
Total	913.53	1 353.85	1 707.00	2 188.40	1 943.60	2 021.20	2 021.20	2 010.43	2 369.98	2 843.67	3 376.51	3 980.41	4 688.48
Current surplus/deficit	302.47	36.35	−231.50	−605.00	−101.90	35.80	35.80	74.97	−67.04	−235.13	−498.78	−821.71	−1 224.59
Reserves at 1 January[1]	916.20	1 218.67	1 377.02	1 145.52	540.52	438.62	438.62	474.42	549.39	482.34	247.22	−251.57	−1 073.28
Reserves at 31 December	1 218.67	1 255.02	1 145.52	540.52	438.62	474.42	474.42	549.39	482.34	247.22	−251.57	−1 073.28	−2 297.86
Reserves at 31 December as multiples of benefit expenditure (funding ratio)	1.50	1.01	0.71	0.26	0.24	0.25	0.25	0.29	0.22	0.09	−0.08	−0.29	−0.53
PAYG cost rate (%)	1.62	2.07	2.44	2.80	2.20	2.06	2.06	2.06	2.19	2.31	2.45	2.58	2.71
Total benefit cost (% of earnings)	1.44	1.89	2.32	2.66	2.06	1.91	1.91	1.92	2.03	2.15	2.28	2.40	2.52
Unemployment	0.99	1.42	1.81	2.13	1.64	1.53	1.53	1.53	1.65	1.77	1.89	2.02	2.14
Sickness	0.14	0.16	0.17	0.20	0.15	0.12	0.12	0.12	0.12	0.12	0.12	0.12	0.12
Maternity	0.24	0.24	0.25	0.24	0.20	0.19	0.19	0.19	0.19	0.19	0.19	0.19	0.19
Death	0.07	0.07	0.08	0.10	0.08	0.07	0.07	0.07	0.07	0.07	0.07	0.07	0.07
Cost as % of GDP								0.41	0.45	0.49	0.53	0.57	0.62

[1] Special adjustment of reserves in 1992 by 122 million rand. [2] Some negligible deviations from annual records are due, inter alia, to retroactive account adjustments. [3] Net transfers to former independent states as of 1992 included in other income.

Source: Income and expenditure accounts of UIF, 1990–95.

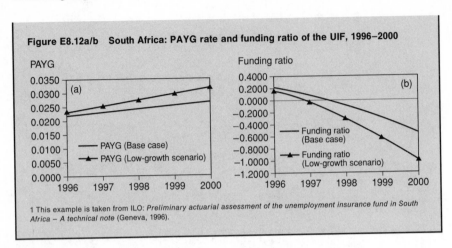

Figure E8.12a/b   South Africa: PAYG rate and funding ratio of the UIF, 1996–2000

1 This example is taken from ILO: *Preliminary actuarial assessment of the unemployment insurance fund in South Africa – A technical note* (Geneva, 1996).

where:

TUBE	Total unemployment benefit expenditure
ACTE	Active labour market expenditure
ale	Ratio of active labour market expenses to benefit expenditure
U	Number of unemployed persons
br	Beneficiary rate
MAX	Legal maximum duration of benefits
ars	Average (statistical) replacement rate
LR	Legal replacement rate
IE	Insurable earnings

Exogenous: *ale, br, MAX, ars, LR*

8.2.4.6   *Further social protection components*

Family benefits

Family benefits are generally tax financed (with some exception in francophone countries, where certain family benefits are financed by social insurance). Typically, these benefits include parental leave, child benefits, benefits for large families, benefits for caring for children or adults with disabilities, and so on. Administrative expenditure is again assumed to amount to a certain percentage of total benefit expenditure. The benefits can be calculated as the product of the estimated number of recipient families multiplied by the average amount of annual benefits. The number of beneficiaries is supplied by the household module. The average annual benefit amounts are anchored to the initial observed or estimated amounts and indexed to inflation. The equations are straightforward and need no special display.

Other benefits

These consist of benefits which do not fall under any of the other categories. Because of its heterogeneity, this residual position of national social expenditure is difficult to project. As it is supposed to be of only minor importance fiscally, an ad hoc projection method is suggested. The expenditure levels are anchored to the values in the last observation year and can then be indexed according to their trend, or in correlation with a suitably chosen indicator, such as inflation or nominal GDP.

When estimates are available, tax exemptions with social purposes ("social tax benefits") could also be included in this module. The estimation of the induced losses of tax revenue (regarded as equivalent to the benefit) is complicated and controversial, as it depends on numerous empirical and legislative conditions, as well as assumptions of behavioural changes and tax compliance of households, if such legislation does not exist. The applied estimation method would also more or less determine the projection method. In countries where such estimations and projections do exist, this work is normally left to specialists of the ministries of finance who run short- to medium-term simulation models in order to assess "winners" and "losers" in changes in tax legislation. Within the ILO Social Budget model context, only a method based on reasonable trend assumptions can be applied.

8.2.4.7 The Social Budget summary accounts

The Social Budget is the crucial summary of all expenditure and revenue results of the individual components of the social protection submodel. Ideally, the results should be presented in the same classifications (table structures) as in Part I of this book. In practice, higher or lower levels of aggregation will often be used. Institutions and functions, and types of expenditure and revenue might be more "close" to, or more distant from, the formal frame of Part I. However, the summary account should at least display all major expenditure and income items in absolute and in relative terms (in relation to nominal GDP and as a share of total expenditure/revenue) on the basis of a clear institutional breakdown. A functional breakdown should be pursued. This displays, for example, how much the country spends on pensions, health or unemployment. It thus permits at least crude international comparisons of the overall level of national social expenditure, as well as the expenditure levels of its individual components. This would supply policy-makers with some indicators as to where the overall portfolio of income and expenditure might require further exploration or adjustments. It is the point of departure for an analysis of the cost efficiency of the national social protection system.

Example 8.13 Turkey: A Social Budget

This example provides a summary of one scenario projection of a Social Budget which the ILO undertook in Turkey in 1995–96. The results presented were obtained under fairly optimistic average annual growth assumptions (i.e. 5.9 per cent per year), under an assumed annual productivity growth of 2.3 per cent and a declining unemployment rate. The resulting Social Budget summary (see table E8.13 below) shows an increasing social expenditure ratio, driven primarily by fast-growing expenditure on old-age pensions. Since contribution income of the pension schemes does not keep pace with expenditure, the increasing government deficit coverage results in a fairly steep increase of the financing share in the Social Budget, which will have to come from general revenues within the next five years. Simulations like these have triggered government plans to develop social sector reform plans.

Table E8.13 Turkey: A Social Budget projection, 1995–2000

Item	1995	1996	1997	1998	1999	2000
	% of nominal GDP					
Expenditure						
1. Pensions (three institutions aggregated)	3.4	3.6	3.7	3.9	4.1	4.3
1.1. Pension insurance benefits	3.3	3.5	3.6	3.8	4.0	4.2
1.1.1. Old-age pensions	2.6	2.8	2.9	3.0	3.2	3.4
1.1.2. Invalidity pensions	0.1	0.1	0.1	0.1	0.1	0.1
1.1.3. Survivors' pensions	0.4	0.4	0.4	0.5	0.5	0.5
1.1.4 Orphans' pensions	0.2	0.2	0.2	0.2	0.2	0.2
1.1.5 Grants	0.0	0.0	0.0	0.0	0.0	0.0
1.2. Administrative expenditure	0.1	0.1	0.1	0.1	0.1	0.1
2. Unemployment benefits	0.0	0.0	0.1	0.1	0.1	0.1
3. Short-term benefits	0.2	0.2	0.2	0.2	0.2	0.2
4. Social assistance	0.3	0.2	0.2	0.2	0.2	0.2
5. Health	4.2	4.3	4.3	4.4	4.5	4.6
6. Military Personnel Scheme	0.8	0.7	0.7	0.7	0.7	0.7
7. Private banks' schemes	0.4	0.4	0.4	0.4	0.4	0.4
8. Employers' social benefits	0.8	0.7	0.7	0.8	0.8	0.8
Total	**10.0**	**10.2**	**10.3**	**10.7**	**11.0**	**11.3**
Revenue						
1. Social insurance contributions	2.5	2.8	2.8	2.9	2.9	3.0
1.1 Pension scheme	2.0	2.0	1.9	2.0	2.0	2.0
1.2 Health insurance scheme	0.6	0.6	0.6	0.6	0.7	0.7
1.3 Unemployment Fund	0.0	0.3	0.3	0.3	0.3	0.3
2. Other income (incl. of imputed contributions)	2.8	2.7	2.7	2.8	2.8	2.9
3. Investment income	0.0	0.1	0.3	0.4	0.2	0.2
3.1. Pension scheme	0.0	0.0	0.0	0.0	0.0	0.0
3.2. Health scheme	0.0	0.0	0.0	0.0	0.0	0.0
3.3. Short-term benefit scheme	0.0	0.0	0.0	0.0	0.0	0.0
3.4. Unemployment fund	0.0	0.1	0.3	0.4	0.2	0.2
4. Income from general revenues	4.7	4.9	5.0	5.2	5.4	5.6
Total	**10.0**	**10.6**	**10.8**	**11.3**	**11.4**	**11.6**

8.2.5 The government model

The government model, describing the revenues and expenditures of central, state and local governments, has been introduced in order to assess the fiscal effects of the projected financial development of the national social protection system on the general government net lending/net borrowing position. This is one of the central indicators for the assessment of the long-term financial viability of the overall national social protection system under a given tax revenue and government expenditure structure. The model, in its construction, excludes the government social protection schemes, which are dealt with in other components of the overall model family.

Compared to the degree of sophistication of the other submodels, the government model can only be of a rudimentary character. The purpose of the Social Budget model is to focus on the social sector of countries, not on the wide sphere of taxation policies, nor on the multiple different types of government expenditures such as personnel expenses, investments in infrastructure, education, subsidies to private and public enterprises or military expenses. Of course, if sufficient statistical material and other substantial information are provided,[30] all such expenditures are covered by the model in reasonable detail, but when it comes to the social expenditures of the different government levels, more sophistication is introduced. The main components of such social expenditures directly paid out of the governments' budgets, for example public health care, social assistance, housing benefits, family/child benefits and others, will be explained in subsequent sections. In this section we focus on the revenues and the non-social security expenses of the government sector. We further limit our description to what we call "the government sector" without specifying different administrative and/or political levels (states, municipalities, public enterprises) which exist in many countries. This does not restrict the basic explanatory contents of this section; in a concrete country application such specificities would, of course, be taken into account and explicitly modelled.

The main links of the government model to other model components are reflected in figure 8.9.

The main components of government revenue are normally income tax and turnover tax.[31] Many other types of taxes may exist in addition, but they tend to be of minor importance. Government revenues also arise from fees or from privatization (selling of assets). The modelling of such revenue items is usually extremely country specific and, thus, is of no further interest in the context of this section.

With respect to income tax, the model distinguishes between taxes on profits and on wages; analysis of historical data usually provides for past average tax rates, calculated as the respective government tax income, either over total profits (primary capital income), or over total labour income. If these rates are kept constant, future (projected) tax revenue depends on the development of nominal capital and labour income. The projected development of the tax

Figure 8.9 The government model: Inputs from other model components

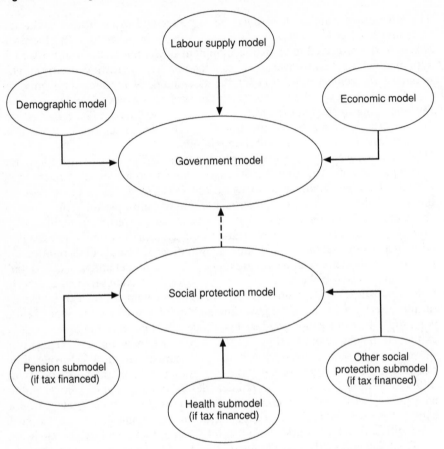

rates is, of course, crucial to the revenue projection. In principle, we distinguish the different sets of combinations of the following indicators when projecting the future development of income tax rates:

- The projection horizon: is it short, medium or long term?
- The level of economic and social development: where does the country at present stand in an international comparison and to where, in this respect, does the GDP projection carry it?
- The prevailing philosophy of tax legislation (tax system): is it proportional, progressive or regressive?

For short-term projections, those over the next one or two years, it would be assumed that the prevailing income tax system continues to exert its (regressive, proportional, progressive) impact, irrespective of whether the growth target is low, medium or high.

In medium-term projections, the intended policies as announced by the government would be analysed. If there is no explicit announcement, the continuation of the prevailing measured impact would be assumed – just as over the recent past years. Again, any tax reform measures would be modelled separately and exogenously introduced.

In long-term (and very long-term) projections, it can reasonably be assumed that regressive and progressive tax systems converge to proportional systems. Convergence will be triggered off by the taxpayers; if, for example, a progressive tax system were kept unchanged over longer periods of economic (income) growth, then average taxation rates would increase proportionally, and thus provoke counter-balancing reactions of taxpayers, especially in the upper income brackets. The same line of argument would hold true in a continued regressive system; then, pressure would grow, especially from those taxpayers in the lower income groups.

The fact that we consider all tax systems to converge over the long term to "proportionality" does not imply, however, that the now observed average income tax rates would remain (more or less) stable over time. We assume that the faster an economy is growing **over the long term** the higher the (target) average tax rate can (and will) be, because tax resistance will be weaker and the demand for public infrastructure higher. The concrete fixing of the target value will depend on the last statistically observed value, the assumed long-term economic growth rate, and possibly the development differentials to a suitably chosen set of comparator countries.

In formal terms, the (labour) income tax projection is based on the following equation:

Equation 8.17

$$TAX_{LI,t} = R_{TAXLI,t} * LI_t$$

where:

$$R_{TAXLI,t} = f(R_{TAXLI,t_0}, R_{TAXLI,t_0+N}, GDP_t, GDPt - GDP_{INT,t})$$

R_{TAXLI,t_0} = Last observed labour income tax rate

R_{TAXLI,t_0+N} = Target rate in the final projection year

f = Functional relationship *between* $R_{TAXLI,t_0}, GDP_t, R_{TAXLI,t_0+N}$, and $GDP_{INT,t}$

$GDP_{INT,t}$ = Economic development of comparator country

The same argument and equation hold true, mutatis mutandis, with respect to income tax on profits.

Turnover tax depends on the average turnover tax rate and the level and development of the tax basis. For political reasons, there is usually a bundle of different rates, for example in order to subsidize certain types of consumer goods for the poor, or to skim off resources from high income earners by applying high rates to luxury goods. Therefore, it is advisable to construct an index reflecting changes in any of the different turnover tax rates.

In restricting ourselves to private households' purchases of consumer goods, omitting any taxable purchases of investment goods by enterprises or taxation of imports, this index could be designed as follows:

Equation 8.18

$$I_{TO,t} = g_1 * R_{TO1,t} + g_2 * R_{TO2,t} + \cdots + g_n * R_{TOn,t}$$

where:

$C_t = \sum_i C_{i,t}$, total consumption of consumer goods with the same turnover tax rate $R_{TOi,t}$

$g_i = C_{i,t}/C_t$, weight of expenditures on good C_i in total purchases C

$R_{TOi,t} =$ Turnover tax rate for good C_i in year t

$$1 = \sum_{i=1}^{n}(g_i)$$

Over a short- to medium-term period, this index might be valid as the weights will probably not change very much. Over longer projection periods, however, it will lead to biased results, because the share of expenditure on goods with the specific turnover tax rates applied will change over time, through changes in the shape of the income distribution, especially under sustained long-term economic growth assumptions. In order to cover such developments, it is necessary to construct a special household spending model, with private households' income distribution linked to general economic growth, their spending disaggregated by types of goods purchased and, finally, the weights of the turnover tax index linked to that changing spending pattern over time. Such an approach would afford quite sophisticated interdependent modelling techniques and is clearly beyond the scope of this book. Thus, this approach – although mentioned – is not pursued further here.

The choice of the tax basis to which to apply the turnover tax rates depends on the underlying regulations in detail. In general, turnover tax rates are usually applied to the purchase of consumer goods, to the purchase of investment goods, and to imports. Export taxes are usually of a negligible amount.

Therefore, a classical way of projecting government turnover tax revenues is to link revenues by means of using the above-mentioned index joined to a suitably chosen aggregation of single expenditure side components of (projected) nominal GDP; for example, the sum of private consumption plus investments plus imports. Under this assumption, the equation for projecting turnover tax revenue would read as follows:

Equation 8.19

$$TO_t = TO_{t-1} * I_{TO,t}/I_{TO,t-1} * D_t/D_{t-1}$$

where:

TO_t = Total amount of turnover tax in year t

I_{TO} = Index turnover tax

D_t = Total demand (basis for turnover tax) in t

As in the revenue side of the government budget, the future development of its expenditure components depends heavily on policy formulation and execution. Policy-induced variations in expenditures can only be exogenously introduced into the model. The model structure itself offers a "standard basis" as a platform for simulation calculations.

The main components of government expenditures as distinguished in this section, excluding social expenditure paid directly out of the government budget, are:

- consumption (personnel, purchases of military equipment, others);
- current transfers;
- investments (in infrastructure, etc.); and
- interest payments on public debt.

Social expenditure is omitted, as this category will be treated separately.

Government consumption depends primarily on the development of the number of public employees (and military personnel) and their average wages. When the pensions to former public employees (and/or military personnel) are paid directly out of taxation, these might be a component of government consumption, or be a separate item under government social expenditures. In both cases, expenditure would be projected with the help of the pension projection tool, which will be described separately.

Purchases of military equipment, expenses for military manoeuvres and similar expenses are normally treated under special security regulations. The respective projections might therefore be delivered on an anonymous basis by the ministry of defence. For long-term projections, reasonable assumptions about the share of military expenditure in GDP will have to be made.

In formal terms, government consumption may be expressed as follows:

Equation 8.20

$$CG_t = WAGEG_t * EMPLG_t + MIL_t + COTHG_t$$

where:

$$CG_t = \text{Government consumption in year } t$$

$$WAGEG_t = \text{Average wage in the public sector in } t$$

$$EMPLG_t = \text{Number of public employees in } t$$

$$MIL_t = \text{Military expenses in } t$$

$$COTHG_t = \text{Other government consumption expenses in } t$$

The number of public employees would be taken from the labour market balance and average wages from the wage model. Military expenses would have to be designed along the lines described, and the other government expenses could, for example, be calculated as a constant share of GDP.

Current transfers would, for example, include expenses on education, subsidies to enterprises and other transfers, thus in formal terms:

Equation 8.21

$$TRANG_t = EDUCG_t + SUBSG_t + OTRANG_t$$

where:

$$TRANG_t = \text{Current government transfers in year } t$$

$$EDUCG_t = \text{Government education expenses in } t$$

$$SUBSG_t = \text{Government subsidies in } t$$

$$OTRANG_t = \text{Other current government transfers in } t$$

Unless specific expert knowledge is available on how to model future development of subsidies and other current transfers, both might be kept in a constant relation to GDP. Often, explicitly formulated government policies concerning these two items may give rise either to increasing or decreasing their GDP share accordingly. There is no way of designing more sophisticated modelling approaches on this general level.

Education (excluding education-related investments as, for example, school buildings, universities) usually comprises a conglomeration of expenses at different levels, such as primary and secondary education, different types of higher university education and so on. Here, we describe only one way of solving the modelling problem – again, more detailed methods may be used in concrete country applications.

Current education expenses depend on the number of students[32] and the costs per student. Under stable government education policy, the development of the number of students depends on population development by single age groups and the number of students per age group, the "take-up rate". The take-up rate will normally be high in the younger ages, for example between 5 and, say, 14 and lower in the higher ages, say, between 18 and 24, later tapering off fast. The costs per student are equivalent to the costs per "service unit". The costs per service unit might or might not actually include the costs of the personnel employed in the education sector. If the education personnel is included in government consumption (see above), then these costs cannot be included here again, in order to avoid double counting. But even if excluded, it is rational to assume that the remaining costs per service unit are linked to the development of wages of the personnel working in the education sector. Thus, the formal approach to estimating the expenditures on education would be as follows:

Equation 8.22

$$EDUCG_t = EDUCG_{t-1} * (STUD_t/STUD_{t-1}) * (WAGEG_t/WAGEG_{t-1})$$
$$STUD_t = TU_t * POP_{xSTUD,t}$$

where:

$STUD_t$ = Number of students in year t

$POP_{xSTUD,t}$ = Population in the education age group in t

TU_t = Percentage of students in $POP_{xSTUD,t}$ in t (take-up rate)

For each year t, the population in the education age group could, for example, be defined as between 0 and 25. The take-up rate may be positively correlated with the *level* of real GDP, but, of course, may not exceed a reasonably chosen threshold below 100 per cent. A prerequisite for a more disaggregate model of education expenses, by expenses on single age groups, is statistical information structured accordingly. In applied country cases statistical inference and legislation will provide information as to whether the projection of per capita service costs on the basis of wages is appropriate, or whether a different approach, for example on the basis of price developments, would be more suitable.

The short- and medium-term modelling of government investments in tangible assets clearly has to be based on intended policies. In the long term, estimations will refer to a specified share in GDP or similar approaches. If the overall number of the population is changing significantly, then a long-term investment function based, among other things, on a fixed amount of real investment per capita of the population might be suitable, assuming that major government investments go into the infrastructure, and that this, in turn, needs reinvestments and/or additional investments according to population density.

If government investments contain components which are social policy related, for instance investments in health infrastructure (hospitals, etc.), then a per-capita-of-the-population approach is suitable for any projection horizon, but may also be tested (for this part of total investments) in case of short- and medium-term projections.

Usually governments have built up public debt, and thus pay interest on the aggregate liabilities. If governments run current surpluses in their budgets, they are being discharged of these liabilities; if they run deficits – which is usually the case – the government adds the respective amount to the existing debt.

A simple formula used for the calculation of the interest on public debt is included in the government model as follows:

Equation 8.23

$$INTG_t = DEBTG_{t-1} * R_{INTG,t}$$

where:

$INTG_t$ = Government interest payment in year t on debt in $t - 1$

$DEBTG_t$ = Government debt at the end of t

$R_{INTG,t}$ = Interest rate on government debt in t

This formula is appropriate and convenient for long-term projections, because it avoids circular model relations that can only be solved by numerical iterations. As long as governments also use short-term money market instruments in order to finance their debt, equation 8.12 is inappropriate under short- and medium-term projections. Then a more appropriate formula would have to be designed, according to the following reasoning:

Equation 8.24

$$INTG_t = DEBTG_{t-1} * R^L_{INTG,t} + (DEBTG_t - DEBTG_{t-1})/2 * R^S_{INTG,t}$$

It is assumed that $DEBTG_t > DEBTG_{t-1}$, that is, the balance of the government budget, is negative. The long-term interest rate $R^L_{INTG,t}$ is applied to the debt stock which exists at the end of the year; the short-term interest rate $R^S_{INTG,t}$ is applied to that part of the debt stock which is built up during the year t. A disadvantage of this formula is that it needs iteration because the actual value of the term $DEBTG_t - DEBTG_{t-1}$ depends on $INTG_t$, that is, on the calculation result of equation 8.13. Iterations are not a principal problem of modelling, but do require suitably chosen start values because otherwise the programme might not find a solution. Also, if the model has a complicated structure of mutual interrelationships (requiring iterations to several variables), then a sequence of iterations might not provide identical results.

8.2.6 Methodological extension: Feedback between social protection and the economy

The nature and size of possible feedback between the social protection system and the economy are the subject of controversial academic debate. The outcome of the debate is inconclusive, as no effort to isolate the effects statistically or econometrically has yet met with methodological consensus. However, the topic is of considerable interest for many governments which plan to design new elements of their social protection systems or explore major reforms. Therefore, the ILO modelling team has developed a pragmatic extension to its standard Social Budget approach which will provide interested governments with some tentative information on the subject. However, this extension has not been used in all Social Budget exercises. Particularly in exercises with a relatively short time horizon, the feedback are not assumed to have more than a marginal impact, as many economic agents will react to changing social security parameters with a considerable time lag.

Because of inconclusive factual information about the nature and dimension of the impact of social protection systems on the performance of the economy, in this respect national debates are generally based on theoretical hypotheses rather than analytical facts. As is often the case in social policy-making – responding to fiscal, financial or political necessities – policy decisions have to be made even in the absence of full information. Then the task of the modeller is to offer information which limits the range of possible outcomes of policy decisions, using a series of scenario analyses assuming alternative assumptions about the theoretical relationships between the performance of the social protection systems and the economy. This type of analysis will still help to assess the potential risk involved in particular policy conditions.

First, the most relevant feedback types have to be identified. Four basic types of feedback between the social security systems and the economy are often quoted in the debate:

1. The incentive effect, which assumes that the payment of transfer incomes to non-employed persons (almost regardless of whether they are unemployment benefits, social assistance payments or pension payments) is in fact discouraging people from staying in the workforce or seeking re-employment.

2. The interest/deficit rate effect, which assumes that high social expenditure might lead to government deficits that push up national interest rates, which in turn will compress investments and hence hamper economic growth.

3. The labour-cost effect, which assumes that high labour costs due, among other things, to high contribution rates suppress the demand for labour, can have two effects:
   - it reduces growth owing to reduced employment of labour at constant productivity rates;
   - it increases productivity, produces higher unemployment (and social protection costs), but does not affect growth.

4. The productivity effect, which assumes that increased social protection, notably good health care and income security, enhances the productivity of the individual worker without increasing the labour or the capital costs of production, and thus positively affects economic growth.

Because of the general absence of any statistical information about the extent of the effects, these have been analytically parameterized. This means that the modeller is given the option to undertake economic experiments by making assumptions on the different sizes of the feedback, and can isolate the overall effects of these assumptions on growth, and government and institutional budgets, by comparing the outcomes of the experiments with a baseline scenario without feedback.

In view of the present low level of social protection benefits and the substantial underemployment of the workforce in many countries, the first effect is probably neglected in those countries. In addition, any model starts from observed relationships between the level of benefits and utilization behaviour. Under status quo conditions, as long as no major legal changes are planned for the entitlement conditions, and no abrupt change in economic conditions is taking place, no dramatic alteration in utilization behaviour should normally be expected. Should the effect be modelled, for example when major modifications of benefit levels are contemplated, then time-lagged elasticities could be constructed which establish the link between the rates of change in payment durations of unemployment benefits and other short-term benefits, as well as the rates of change in early retirement rates and in benefit levels.

The three remaining feedback are technically defined in the shape of the following elasticities:

1. The interest rate/deficit effect assumes an almost linear relationship between the increase in the deficit and the increase in the interest rate to bring the demand for investment resources and savings into equilibrium. It is then assumed that the reduction in investment leads to a lagged effect on growth. This effect is expressed in the elasticity of economic growth to the growth of the government deficit.

2. The labour-cost effect is mapped through elasticity of labour productivity growth to the share of labour cost in GDP. The reasoning behind this is simple. If labour costs increase, the economy will react, after a time lag, by substituting capital for labour and hence increase labour productivity. This in turn will automatically reduce the demand for labour.

3. The productivity effect is mapped in the form of an assumed elasticity of productivity growth to social spending. This effect thus assumes increased social spending in certain social protection branches, whose benefits can be assumed to increase productivity, for example through the provision of health care, rehabilitation services or simply by providing income security. This social spending impact has two aspects: firstly, better health care, for example a reduced number of days lost due to sickness; and second, increased social transfers to the "non-fit for work", which permits this group to withdraw from the labour market with a positive effect on the average productivity of those remaining in the labour force. This productivity effect should have no immediate effect on wages, that is, on labour costs, and thus should have a direct positive effect on economic growth.

All these elasticities are assumed to be lagged by one year – for example, the increasing labour costs in year t do not affect the growth rate in year t but in year $t+1$. This simplifies the modelling, as no iterations to a new equilibrium are necessary in year t, and also reflects the fact that an economic production process does not react instantaneously to changing exogenous conditions.

An example of the use of the above elasticities in exploring the potential effects of feedback between social expenditure and economic growth is given in the Ukraine example in Part IV.

8.3 THE TIME HORIZON

It is often claimed that complex socio-economic systems cannot be projected over more than a few years. Thereafter, the number of endogenous and exogenous variables, and the complex multiplication of their potential error margins, may make any form of projection highly uncertain and hence questionable.

Indeed, modellers and social protection policy planners face a dilemma. On the one hand, the above argument obviously has some truth in it but, on the other hand, social security systems often provide benefits that create long-term liabilities. Thus, every social protection planner has to develop a view about the systemic behaviour of the national social protection system under a given set of assumptions, even if one can never be certain about the accuracy and probability of their occurrence. Projections are not prophecies; they simply try to map out systemic behaviour under plausible assumptions. In addition, for the generic use of a model as a governance instrument, it would be far too complicated to try to assess the probability of a certain set of assumptions, or of a defined subset of all theoretically possible subsets of assumptions in the form of stochastic models, which take into account the probability of occurrence of individual model assumptions and outputs.

In its present form, the ILO's Social Budget modelling approach is deterministic, recursive and designed to run over short-, medium- and long-term periods. The stochastic nature of many of the model variables can be taken into account by undertaking sensitivity analysis and risk assessments of the financial results. A concrete projection period of 20 years might be chosen, since in this time frame the majority of all beneficiaries receiving benefits at the last historical observation point can be assumed to have "grown out" of the system (for example, present pensioners, recipients of family benefits or social assistance, etc.). Most present old-age and invalidity pensioners would probably have died before the end of the second decade, and certainly most other beneficiaries would have left the system. Of course, the projection period is open to adjustments and the model has, in fact, been used for short-term projections of up to three years,[33] as well as for very long-term projections of up to 50 years and more.[34]

Sometimes even longer time frames might be considered appropriate. For example, pensions influence the entire life of workers, through survivors' pensions during their early years, through contribution payments during their active years, and through pensions during the inactive phases. In theory, Social Budget models should thus have at least an 80-year projection period. While this would be technically possible, projecting a host of demographic, economic and governance variables for 80 years, affecting at least ten different benefit categories, does not seem to make much sense. However, for systems which are most profoundly influenced by demographic developments, such as pension systems, the projection range might be extended exclusively, and separate long-term projections be undertaken. In pension systems, this is the usual measure to determine the future financial affordability in a stationary demographic and legal state, when the scheme has reached demographic maturity and all the legal provisions have become fully effective for all contributors and beneficiaries. For example, if it were found that under a normal demographic development, which had been observed in a variety of typical countries, the actual pension formula would lead to contribution rates of more than 30 per cent of insurable wages, it could safely be concluded that most likely the scheme would at some point meet with political rejection. It would thus be wiser to start with less generous pension formulae in order to avoid future financial and political difficulties.

Notes

[1] It should be noted that this approach – despite its advantages – has been fundamentally criticized; one result of this criticism was the development of microsimulation models.

[2] Initially the reader might try Damodar N. Gujarati: *Basic econometrics* (New York, McGraw-Hill, 2nd ed., 1988) and the quoted literature.

[3] Concerning issues as to how the design of (privately and/or state-defined) institutionalized data collection programmes ("statistics") influences our perception and interpretation of reality, see, for example, Wolfgang Bonß: *Die Einübung des Tatsachenblicks. Zur Struktur und Veränderung empirischer Sozialforschung* [Exercising our views on reality: About the structure of and changes in empirical social research] (Frankfurt am Main, Suhrkamp, 1982).

[4] The term "social accounting" as used in this book should not be confused with the term "social accounting matrix" as used in *SNA 1993* (see section 6.4).

[5] There are a number of countries running econometric social protection models. For example, the German Federal Ministry of Labour and Social Affairs, Bonn, uses a large econometric model for the purposes of its revolving short- and medium-term forecasts of the social security system's revenues and expenditures, including the repercussive price and real effects on the "rest" of the economy.

[6] ILO: *The ILO Social Budget Model, version 6* (Geneva, 1999).

[7] Biometric parameters (life expectancy, fertility parameters) were obtained from United Nations: *World Population Prospects, 1996 Revision* (New York, 1996).

[8] For further information, see ILO: *The ILO Population Projection Model – A technical guide* (Geneva, 1998). For further information or software transfer, contact the International Labour Office, Financial, Actuarial and Statistical Branch, Social Security Department, 4 route des Morillons, CH-1211 Geneva 22, Switzerland.

[9] Applied demographic mathematics have developed a detailed nomenclature for variables used. Here we use the notion "rate" without further specification, as follows: fertility rate = number of live

births in t over the average number of population in t; mortality rate = number of deaths in t over the average number of population in t; emigration/immigration rate = number of emigrants/immigrants in t over the average number of population in t.

[10] The ILO has transferred the standard United Nations methodology into a spreadsheet-based model which can be obtained from the Financial, Actuarial and Statistical Branch of the ILO's Social Security Department.

[11] The chart was developed by K. Hirose and has been taken from ILO: *The ILO Population Projection Model – A technical guide*, op. cit.

[12] United Nations: *World Population Prospects*, op. cit.

[13] Here, "consistently" simply means that all numbers add up.

[14] See the ILO Minimum Age Convention (No. 138), and Recommendation (No. 146), 1973.

[15] For a detailed definition of unemployment, aiming at statistically consistent measurement, see, for example: ILO: *Yearbook of Labour Statistics 1997* (Geneva, 56th issue, 1997), p. 427.

[16] Theoretically, this argument could be pushed to the extreme and could assume a separate model for each single social protection institution. Under this condition, a Social Budget model's role would be transformed into one of a (mere) "clearing house" which would, under the guise of improving governance, still have its merits but lose practically all its value as regards simulations.

[17] The World Bank pension model is called PROST.

[18] The stand-alone ILO pension model is described in full detail in ILO: *The ILO pension model: Draft technical guide* (Geneva, 1997).

[19] Subramaniam Iyer: *Actuarial mathematics of social security pensions* (Geneva, ILO/ISSA, 1999); Anne Drouin et al.: *Actuarial practice in social security* (Geneva, ILO/ISSA, forthcoming).

[20] These two populations are not necessarily fully disjunct, as some recipients of benefits might be at the same time registered as active members. In some schemes recipients of partial or full old-age pensions might be active contributors at the same time. In other schemes, simultaneous receipt of survivors' pensions or partial invalidity pensions and employment are permitted.

[21] The number of beneficiaries in figure 8.7 is also positive in the younger ages because we have included survivors (orphans and widows/widowers).

[22] See ILO: *The ILO pension model*, op. cit.

[23] See ILO: *Social budgeting in Ukraine* (Budapest, 1998) and section 9.2.5.3, "Pensions and other benefits".

[24] cf. Anne Drouin et al., op. cit.

[25] cf. Michael Cichon et al.: *Modelling in health care finance – A compendium of quantitative techniques for health care financing* (Geneva, ILO/ISSA, 1999).

[26] See UNICEF: *Central and Eastern Europe in transition: Public policy and social contributions*, Regional Monitoring Report, No. 1 (New York, Nov. 1993), pp. 8, 9.

[27] See ILO: *World Employment Report 1998–99: Employability in the global economy. How training matters* (Geneva, 1998), p. 48 ff.

[28] To what extent such provisions are being enforced in individual cases is often a difficult question to answer.

[29] The standard argument of "prudence" of cost estimates must not be taken to the extreme. For example, if cost estimates of changes in legislation unduly overestimate the cost effects, then any legislative changes might overreact.

[30] It is not self-evident to expect free access to such information; for example, military expenses – although included and published in the budget – are in many countries treated under state security regulations. Many governments also tend to rely on off-budget accounts for certain political purposes; even if these are published, it is often difficult to draw a clear picture of their interrelation with the official budget.

[31] Note that taxes are usually levied on production and imports, on income and wealth, and so on. For a full taxation nomenclature see, for example, *SNA 1993*, pp. 169–173 and 191–193. The *SNA* approach to taxation coincides fully with the definitions used in the IMF publication *A manual on government finance statistics (GFS)*, 1986, or as developed in the OECD publication *Revenue statistics of OECD member countries* – except that the *SNA* does not classify social security contributions under the heading of taxes (and some other minor exceptions).

[32] The notion "student" is here used in a comprehensive way, including the whole range from young children attending kindergartens to postgraduate students at universities.

[33] See ILO/UNDP: *Bulgaria – Short-term budget projections for the National Social Security Institute*, Report to the Government (Geneva, Sofia, 1998).

[34] See ILO: *Panama*, op. cit., and idem: *Saint Lucia Report to the Government on the Sixth Actuarial Review of the National Insurance Board as of 30 June 1996* and *Supplement on the Study of Reform Measures Concerning Old-age Pensions* (Geneva, 1999).

TWO CASE STUDIES

CASE STUDIES OF PANAMA AND UKRAINE

9

Part IV demonstrates the applications of the Social Budgeting concept in two concrete cases. Both are countries in which ILO teams introduced the Social Budget concept as a factual basis for the exploration of major social protection reforms. The first case is Panama, where an ILO team was operating in 1997 and 1998, and the second is Ukraine, where a Social Budget model was developed in collaboration with a national interministerial task force in 1997.

Both projects were carried out by different teams and had different purposes. The Panama project focused mainly on an evaluation of the long-term financial viability of the country's existing formal sector pension system with a view to enhancing its revenue–expenditure structure in a gradually changing demographic and economic environment. The Ukraine project was oriented more towards medium-term poverty assessment, and the possibilities of reforming the existing system under conditions of an economic shock situation, in order to improve its social relevance and robustness for an extended period of only gradually decreasing economic hardship. Not surprisingly, the results of both exercises are quite different.

Panama grew slowly during the 1980s and the 1990s, but in future will have to grow considerably faster in order to solve its forthcoming labour market problems, which are a result of the young broad basis of its population pyramid. The country is divided into a relatively well-developed formal sector and a possibly growing informal sector. The statistical database is satisfying; the idea of a Social Budget is not completely new, as parts of the fiscal statistics have long since been based on a tradition of presenting results on a functional breakdown. Panama is a country that currently seems to be developing precariously: if pushed forward by supportive political decisions, it has the possibility of joining the club of developed countries within the next 10 to 20 years or, if incorrect political decisions are taken, it will fall behind present development levels and lose contact with the "developed world".

Ukraine represents an economy that is still suffering from the traumatic effects of a difficult economic transition, and has to adapt its traditional social security systems to increasing fiscal pressures. Unlike Panama, it has a typical European "matured" population pyramid structure, reflecting the two world wars, the economic crises of the 1920s and 1930s, periods of famine and a rapidly declining birth rate. Like Panama, it will also need high economic growth rates in future – but for different reasons, so as to overcome its continued pressing poverty problems.

This part reports only on the factual findings of the case studies. Policy recommendations, which were also made to the two governments, have been excluded.

9.1 PANAMA

9.1.1 A young population ageing

In 1997 Panama had a population of around 2.7 million inhabitants, and of those, approximately 1 million were aged 14 and younger. The measured labour force was in the order of 1.05 million persons, representing a labour market participation rate of 61.6 per cent. The population and labour force have been growing relatively fast in recent years. The total population grew from 1991 to 1997 by an annual average rate of 1.8 per cent, whereas the labour force grew by 3.2 per cent, thus significantly faster. The average age of the population is low. It was just below 26 years in 1990 and has grown to around 27 years in 1997.

Under standard assumptions on future fertility decline and mortality improvement, the number and structure of Panama's population will significantly change in the future. Projections were carried out making use of the ILO's population model, which resulted in the expectation of the following population developments.

Annual population growth will significantly decline to an average rate of 0.9 per cent over the period 1997 to 2050; by the end of the projection period, it will almost come to a halt. Still, the total population will increase by 60 per cent in comparison with 1997, and will reach a level of about 4.3 million. During this process, the average age of the population will increase from its present level of around 27 years to 40 years. Figure 9.1 provides a graphical presentation of the expected population development, showing the population pyramids for 1997, 2025 and 2050.

Under the technical assumption of constant age-specific labour market participation rates, the total labour force will grow over the same period by 90 per cent, much faster than the population – and will almost double from its present level of slightly over 1 million to nearly 2 million. The constant participation rate assumption is very conservative, as it implies that, because of changes in the population composition, the overall participation rate declines continuously from its present level to 58.5 per cent, thus clearly reversing the trend that was observed during the 1990s.

The related labour market pressure, that is, the increasing labour supply (even under conservative assumptions), is one of the main factors adding to the need to pursue an explicitly growth-oriented economic policy in order to avoid unsustainable levels of unemployment. Past policies based on absorbing the growing labour force mainly by real-wage reductions will no longer be appreciated by a labour force ageing at basically the same pace as the overall population. A policy of permanent real-wage reductions might be feasible concerning a young and inexperienced labour force, but probably is not sustainable over longer periods when applied to employees and the self-employed in their prime ages, who have accepted social and individual responsibilities.

9.1.2 Economic development and employment: The labour market balance

Panama's growth performance was mixed over the observed past and heavily influenced by political events. On average, it grew over the period 1980 to 1996 at an annual rate of just over 2.5 per cent. After a few years of growth during the 1980s, the economy slumped during 1987 to 1989; the temporary strong recovery, resulting mainly from a construction boom, brought it to an average growth level of about 5.5 per cent over the period 1989 to 1996. Since the boom came to a halt in 1994, the country's intrinsic growth path may only at present be in the order of 2.5 to 3.5 per cent annually.

Total employment grew by an impressive annual rate of 3.5 per cent from 1989 to 1996, not only – as was to be expected – during the employment recovery period from 1990 to 1995 (+4 per cent per annum), but also since 1995, when employment still grew at an annual rate of around 2.5 per cent.[1] Total employment grew from a level of 686,000 in 1989 to well over 900,000 in 1997, thus by 33 per cent. From these developments some preliminary estimates were derived with respect to labour productivity (equals real GDP per employed); it may have grown by almost 15 per cent from 1989 to 1996, that is, by an annual average rate of 1.9 per cent.

Over the same period, the real national average wage declined significantly. If set in 1989 = 100, it reached a level of only 81 in 1996, reflecting an *annual average reduction* in its purchasing power of almost 3 per cent, which may be contrasted by the *annual average growth* of real GDP of 5.4 per cent over the same period. Interestingly enough, however, real average wages in the public sector, representing around 25 per cent of all dependent employees, declined only by an annual rate of 1 per cent; in the private sector (representing 45 per cent of all employees) they increased by an annual rate of 1.5 per cent, and in a separate high-productivity area (representing 3 per cent of employees) by 2 per cent annually. In other words, around one-fourth of the dependent employed labour force (the remaining part) had to bear the main weight of the real-wage reduction. For this group, the annual average reduction was in the order of 15 per cent.

Figure 9.1 Panama: Population pyramids, 1997, 2025 and 2050

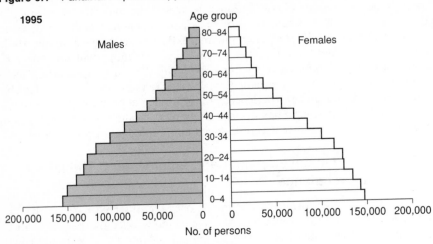

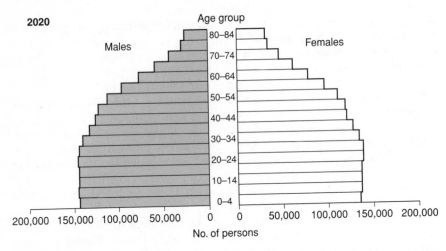

At the same time, it was not the group with the highest real-wage reductions that gained highest employment growth. Employment grew in that group from 1989 to 1996 by a total of about 40 per cent, which is impressive when compared to the public sector employment growth of only 3 per cent, and the separate high-productivity area employment growth of 5 per cent over the same seven-year period. But it was still less than employment growth in the private enterprise sector, where over the same period dependent employment grew by 70 per cent.

As a result of these developments, Panama managed to keep absolute un-employment figures at a level of around 130,000 to 140,000 – the unemployment rate declining from over 16 per cent in 1989 to slightly over 13 per cent in 1997.

Figure 9.1 (Continued)

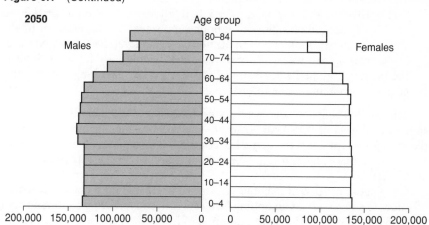

Based on this information, a strategic scenario decision was taken about the future economic, labour market and wage developments. In a condensed form, the information was as follows:

- Future labour supply pressure will grow because of population development.
- Declining real-wage development has so far contributed to the past increase in employment.
- Real average-wage growth and high-employment growth were possible, especially in the private sector of the economy.

The political conclusions to be drawn were as follows:

- Labour supply pressure is unavoidable.
- It is not the sectors with the steepest decline in real wages that create most employment, but rather the competitive productive sectors. The private sector will have to be fostered in future.
- Declining real-wage development has so far contributed to the past increase in employment (stabilization of employment in the public sector), but cannot be sustained over the long term, especially if the real adjustment burden is borne by a specific group of "non-protected" employees.

The conclusions drawn for the economic projection scenario were as follows:

- Annual GDP growth was to be based on the assumption that measures would be taken to lift Panama's growth to a level approximately twice as high as observed in the past. Overall labour productivity growth should increase to rates only slightly higher than over past observed trends – reflecting the efficiency effects of the assumed growth-related economic policy.

- The number of actual workplaces provided by the economy (equals employed) would grow at a speed that allowed the labour market to absorb the additional inflow of labour supply (equals stabilization of the absolute number of unemployed at the mid-1990s level) *and* to pay continuously growing real wages. Price development would lose its past volatility, the projected annual rates being close to observed past long-term trends, gradually declining in the future.

The main results of the projections based on these considerations are summarized in table 9.1. Apart from the macroeconomic income variables (in the lower part of the table), it also contains information on major labour market variables. The more detailed labour market balance was documented in Part III.

Clearly, on the basis of Panama's described past experience, the projected set of values has to be seen as an optimistic target scenario reflecting continued high non-inflationary growth, solid labour productivity increases, employment growth and diminishing unemployment. Nominal wages increase moderately; the labour income share in domestic income increases only gradually, thus allowing for sufficient profits as a basis for sustained investment. However, real wages increase considerably over time.

At the time of the project, this scenario was an outcome of the discussions between the project team and Panama's counterparts, and was regarded as an upper scenario. Alternative scenarios were postulated as well. The intrinsic value of the upper scenario was that it confirmed the need to start social security system reform in the near future. Even under optimistic future economic and labour market developments, the legal regulations of social protection seem no longer sustainable over the long term, but must be reformed – although more moderately than under less optimistic assumptions.

9.1.3 The consolidated public sector budget

The consolidated budget of the public sector comprises the budgets of the central government and the municipalities, public enterprises, and social security and other parastatal institutions. The projection results for Panama are presented in table 9.2.

The table contains very detailed information in a highly condensed format. Here, we would like to direct the readers' attention to the two main long-term results:

- The expenditure structure will change significantly over time.
- The country's public debt increases with the continuation of its present spending and revenue programmes.

Both results can best be shown by figures 9.2 and 9.3.

Figure 9.2 simply shows that the relative weights of public expenditure will be altered in favour of "social expenses", whereas "economic expenses" will lose their share. We would like to stress that this result, as such, was no reason for the ILO to recommend social security reform. The ageing of a population inevitably needs support by relatively increasing transfers, and the relative lowering of economic expenses can possibly be compensated by the enhanced efficiency of their use.

Figure 9.3 reflects the development of total debt as a percentage of GDP. At first, there is a significant tendency of a declining debt–GDP ratio – which is not surprising because of the assumed high economic growth and moderate wage development in the public sector combined with a continued consolidation strategy. Furthermore, during that period the social security system is expected still to have reserves. Only later, these reserves will be eaten up relatively quickly, and the build-up of the social security debt will start to counterbalance and even outpace the projected relative public debt reduction taking place in the "pure" government sector. Nevertheless, under this optimistic growth scenario, the total public debt burden would remain within reasonable limits.

9.1.4   The Social Budget and its components

A number of different scenarios were calculated for the Social Budget of Panama. The economic elements of one of these scenarios has just been described. In section 9.1.4.1 we describe the effects of this scenario on the country's total Social Budget and some of its components. For illustration purposes, the results that would be expected under an alternative economic scenario are presented in section 9.1.4.2. This scenario was actually a low-growth scenario with all the typical implications that are not described here in any detail as, for example, lower employment, higher unemployment, and lower wages in an almost unchanged price development structure.

Both scenarios were calculated under a legislative status quo assumption, that is, no legislative changes were anticipated. However, for the target scenario, we introduced exogenously the assumption that pensions in payment were regularly adjusted to average wage increases, on an annual basis, which is not explicitly foreseen in Panama's pension legislation. In the alternative scenario, we dropped this assumption, resulting – not surprisingly – in significantly different developments of the Social Budget to GDP ratio ("social expenditure ratio") over time (see below).

In both scenarios, it is furthermore assumed that Panama's future governments will be successful in managing the declared health cost containment policy. If not, this will add to expenditure dynamics.

For a proper interpretation, it should also be noted that, according to all our assumptions, after 25 to 30 years Panama would reach social expenditure ratios comparable to present spending ratios in the Organisation for Economic Co-operation and Development (OECD) countries – in the target scenario, close

Table 9.1 Panama: Demographic and economic frame, 1997–2050

Item	Unit	1997	1998	1999	2000	2010[1]	2020[1]	2030[1]	2040[1]	2050[1]
Population	1 000 pers.	2 719	2 764	2 809	2 856	3 266	3 620	3 939	4 160	4 288
Change over previous period	%	1.7	1.7	1.7	1.7	1.4	1.0	0.8	0.5	0.3
Population ≥15 years of age	1 000 pers.	1 716	1 755	1 796	1 838	2 254	2 630	2 973	3 211	3 350
Change over previous period	%	2.7	2.3	2.3	2.3	2.1	1.6	1.2	0.8	0.4
Share in population	%	63.1	63.5	63.9	64.4	69.0	72.7	75.5	77.2	78.1
Labour force	1 000 pers.	1 060	1 085	1 110	1 136	1 381	1 574	1 716	1 803	1 835
Change over previous period	%	2.4	2.4	2.3	2.4	2.0	1.3	0.9	0.5	0.2
Share in population ≥15	%	61.8	61.8	61.8	61.8	61.2	59.9	57.7	56.1	54.8
Number of employed	1 000 pers.	901	936	977	1 021	1 176	1 493	1 693	1 805	1 901
Change over previous period	%	3.4	3.9	4.4	4.5	1.4	2.4	1.3	0.6	0.5
Share in labour force	%	85.0	86.3	88.0	89.9	85.2	94.8	98.7	100.1	103.6
of which:										
Dependent employees	1 000 pers.	608	634	664	696	825	1 077	1 255	1 374	1 485
Change over previous period	%	3.4	4.3	4.7	4.8	1.7	2.7	1.5	0.9	0.8
Salaried employees	1 000 pers.	439	458	479	503	596	778	907	993	1073
Change over previous period	%	3.4	4.3	4.7	4.8	1.7	2.7	1.5	0.9	0.8
Share in dependent employees	%	72.2	72.2	72.2	72.2	72.2	72.2	72.2	72.2	72.2
Self-employed, owners and family workers	1 000 pers.	292	302	313	326	351	416	438	431	416
Change over previous period	%	3.4	3.3	3.7	3.9	0.8	1.7	0.5	-0.2	-0.4
Unemployment rate	%	15.0	13.7	12.0	10.1	14.8	5.2	1.3	-0.1	-3.6

GDP (in constant prices)	Million balboa	6 736	7 140	7 568	8 022	14 367	24 890	39 966	59 659	87 780
Change over previous period	%	6.0	6.0	6.0	6.0	6.0	5.6	4.8	4.1	3.9
GDP deflator	Index	129.5	131.4	133.2	135.1	153.5	171.8	190.0	208.0	225.9
Change over previous period	%	1.5	1.4	1.4	1.4	1.3	1.1	1.0	0.9	0.8
Domestic income	Million balboa	7 240	7 785	8 368	8 993	18 303	35 488	63 008	102 983	164 566
Change over previous period	%	7.5	7.5	7.5	7.5	7.4	6.8	5.9	5.0	4.8
Labour factor income	Million balboa	4 159	4 475	4 815	5 179	10 628	20 778	37 196	61 292	98 740
Share in domestic income	%	57.4	57.5	57.5	57.6	58.1	58.6	59.0	59.5	60.0
Sum of wages	Million balboa	3 794	4 082	4 392	4 724	9 695	18 954	33 930	55 910	90 070
Change over previous period	%	7.6	7.6	7.6	7.6	7.5	6.9	6.0	5.1	4.9
Wages per capita (National Accounts)	Balboa per month	520	537	551	566	980	1 467	2 253	3 391	5 054
Change over previous period	%	4.0	3.2	2.8	2.6	5.6	4.1	4.4	4.2	4.1
Nominal rate of return	%	6.6	6.5	6.4	6.3	5.5	5.0	5.0	5.0	5.0
Labour unit costs	%^{2}	1.5	1.2	1.2	1.2	1.1	0.9	0.8	0.7	0.6
Labour productivity	%^{2}	2.5	2.0	1.5	1.4	4.5	3.2	3.5	3.4	3.4

Notes: [1] Percentage change = ten-year average rate. [2] Change over previous period.

Table 9.2 Panama: Consolidated public sector account, 1997–2050 (thousands of balboas)

Item	1997	1998	1999	2000	2010	2020	2030	2040	2050
Total revenue	**4 554 838**	**4 799 075**	**5 054 624**	**5 335 630**	**9 184 316**	**14 657 303**	**23 197 277**	**33 584 127**	**4 809 210**
Current revenue	**4 330 824**	**4 574 358**	**4 822 550**	**5 094 702**	**8 878 915**	**14 405 087**	**22 816 407**	**33 049 649**	**4 734 047**
Taxes	1 663 390	1 758 795	1 855 169	1 960 371	3 426 902	5 565 906	8 816 032	12 785 999	1 836 290
Non-tax revenue	2 650 988	2 798 111	2 948 980	3 114 910	5 417 834	8 782 701	13 910 139	20 132 026	2 878 949
Other current revenue	16 447	17 452	18 401	19 421	34 179	56 481	90 236	131 624	188 068
Cash in till (carried over)	17 972	17 972	17 972	17 972	17 972	17 972	17 972	17 972	17 972
Capital revenue	206 041	206 745	214 102	222 956	287 430	234 244	362 898	516 506	733 665
Total expenditure	**4 927 360**	**5 100 884**	**5 368 100**	**5 519 231**	**9 398 575**	**15 750 688**	**25 777 612**	**38 665 668**	**5 503 741**
General services	906 992	837 957	878 843	878 318	1 414 251	2 152 915	3 171 243	4 307 489	566 426
Social expenditure	1 367 599	1 471 203	1 557 426	1 617 808	3 168 193	6 121 368	10 885 208	16 753 210	2 333 250
Local services	155 665	166 667	178 139	180 990	346 460	612 614	1 028 343	1 537 646	215 526
Economic expenses	1 745 149	1 839 219	1 935 119	1 988 908	3 290 092	5 239 597	8 321 334	12 329 118	1 780 275
Debt service	751 956	785 837	818 572	853 572	1 179 579	1 624 176	2 371 484	3 738 205	608 262
Balance	**−372 522**	**−301 809**	**−313 476**	**−183 601**	**−214 258**	**−1 093 384**	**−2 580 335**	**−5 081 541**	**−649 530**

Figure 9.2 Panama: Public expenditure structure, 1997–2050

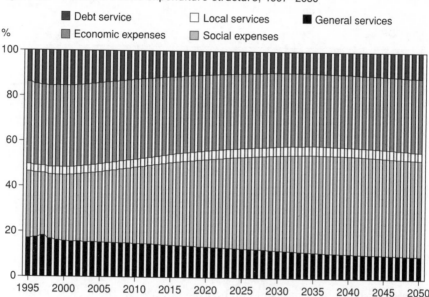

to the observed "top" OECD rates, in the alternative scenario, close to the respective "bottom" rates, in both cases having introduced neither an unemployment insurance scheme nor a sound social assistance scheme. If the target economic scenario actually materializes, Panama's population may regard itself as lucky, as under this scenario (almost) everybody works and no unemployment insurance or major social assistance scheme would seem

Figure 9.3 Panama: Public debt as a percentage of GDP, 1997–2050

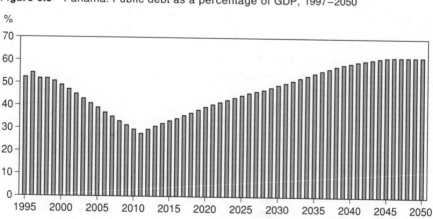

Figure 9.4   Panama: Social Budget as a percentage of GDP, 1991–2050: Economic target scenario

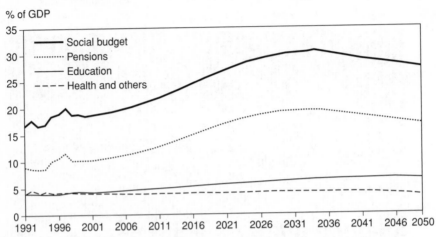

% of GDP

necessary to support significant numbers of poor people. But if these favourable conditions fail to appear, the redistributive strain on the country's GDP would dramatically increase in future. Under such conditions, a major social policy reform would be overdue.

These comments should be kept in mind when reading the following explanations.

9.1.4.1   The target case

In the late 1990s, Panama spent just below 20 per cent of its nominal GDP on social expenditure (figure 9.4). Social expenditure comprises expenses on pensions, health, education and some other financially minor items. Under the given assumptions, the ageing process, in combination with relatively favourable pension regulations, will be the main driving force of social expenditure. In relation to GDP, this expenditure will double within the next 30 years and peak at 20 per cent of GDP, thereafter declining. The other main component is education, which has to be expanded if the country wishes to achieve the targeted economic growth in future. The Social Budget concept comprises only current expenditure going directly to beneficiaries. This is why expenditure going into investments in real assets is not recorded here, but has to be taken into account when interpreting the development of health expenditure. Under the given legislative and institutional arrangements, Panama's current health expenditure is predominantly influenced by the labour costs of those employed by the public health sector. Thus, under the moderate wage growth assumption and continued cost containment policies in the public

Figure 9.5 Panama: Social Budget as a percentage of GDP, 1991–2050: Alternative economic scenario

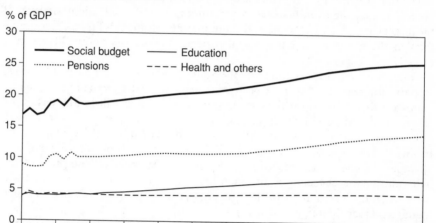

sector, no major health expenditure to GDP increases are to be expected. However, Panama's health infrastructure – hospitals, ambulances, and so on – definitely needs significant improvement in terms of health equipment per capita of the population.

All in all, the Social Budget will peak at a social expenditure rate of just over 30 per cent of GDP in the 2030s, and will decline slightly later (figure 9.4).

9.1.4.2   An alternative result

It should be recalled that the alternative scenario has been calculated under the same legislative status quo assumptions in order to assess the variability of the country's social protection system if the economy does not develop as favourably as assumed in the target case. Furthermore, the benefit indexation assumption was abolished. The model reacts correctly. The dynamic development pattern of the Social Budget is the same as before, but now the spending ratio is significantly lower, this effect being a net result of two dynamic forces pushing the system's finances in opposite directions.

First, there is the development that would occur if the indexation of benefits assumption were to be maintained. Then, the expenditure ratio would peak at over 34 per cent of GDP in the 2030s, which is considerably higher than in the target case. This is a result which would be expected, because once a social protection system is in operation on a set of legally given parameters, the intensity of its redistributive function should be higher under more strained economic conditions than in an economy developing on a high target growth path.

The second force, working in the opposite direction, is the abolition of the indexation assumption. It reduces the dynamism of the system's expenditure growth so that the overall social expenditure ratio falls well below the level of the target case, *although* the general economic environment is far less favourable than in the target case. Now, social expenditure reaches about 20 per cent of GDP.

Health expenditure remains at the same moderate levels as in the target scenario for reasons that have been explained. Education expenditure, again, increases; this is based on the assumption that Panama will in any case need a significant expansion of its education efforts to bolster its future growth performance, whatever the actual long-term growth rate will be. One should be aware that the *absolute* value of real GDP in the final projection year, and all other income values accordingly, is only in the order of one-third of the values in the target scenario, although the assumed long-term average growth rate is slightly higher than in the observed past (but, of course, not as much higher as under the target scenario).

Here, it is of special concern that the (overdue) introduction of an unemployment insurance scheme and a sound social assistance scheme were excluded from the scenario calculations. Persistently high unemployment (with significant impacts on poverty rates) is part of this scenario, the results of the long-term financial projections probably giving even more cause for concern (figure 9.5).

9.2 UKRAINE

Ukraine is a transition country whose economy has operated for seven decades under planned economy conditions. It is now slowly emerging from a period of shrinking GDP, while the economy and the political decision-making processes adjust to new rules of market economy and democracy. Sections 9.2.1 to 9.2.4 first describe the demographic situation, the economic context, the social reality and the present social protection system. Section 9.2.5 then projects the future financial development of the Social Budget under alternative scenarios. It goes on to discuss the sensitivity testing of the model, the analysis of the potential impact of social expenditure on the economy, and the analysis of some policy experiments which simulate the impact of alternative policy options on social expenditure.

9.2.1 Demographic development

The total population of Ukraine numbered 51 million in 1996. Population growth between 1980 and 1990 amounted to 3 per cent, as births exceeded deaths throughout the period. This trend has been reversed since independence in 1991, reflecting the deterioration in economic and social conditions in the wake of recession. Health care, nursery provision and standards of nutrition have all decreased, with the combined result that life expectancy and fertility have also declined, while infant mortality has increased. The deterioration of living standards for the majority of Ukraine's population, together with uncertainty regarding the future, has caused a steady decrease in fertility. While in the middle of the 1980s the fertility rate amounted to 15 births per 1,000 persons, this dropped to only 9.6 in 1995. In 1996, the fertility rate was 9.2 per 1,000, which indicates a decrease of 5.1 per cent compared to the same period in 1995. In fact, the current fertility level does not even ensure simple reproduction of Ukraine's population. Life expectancy for men declined from 66 years in 1991 to just under 63.7 years in 1995, and for women from 75 years to just over 73.8 years. Meanwhile, infant mortality increased from 12.8 per 1,000 live births in 1990 to 14.7 in 1995.

These developments have resulted in a decreased dependency ratio, that is, an increase in the proportion of the total population of working age. However, the decline in population between 1991 and 1993 caused by the higher death rate relative to the birth rate was offset by substantial net immigration from other countries. Since 1995, the trend has been towards net emigration. This has resulted in a small decline in population (94,500 net emigration in 1995; around 120,000 in 1996). Ukrainians have also begun to migrate as guest workers to other countries, where average wages are higher.

9.2.2 The economic context

As a part of a centralized trading bloc, Ukraine's economy was to a great extent intertwined with other economies. This situation inevitably led to a heavy reliance on external resources and markets, above all on Russia. Around 40 per cent of production went into the military-industrial complex. Apart from heavy industry (machine-building, shipyards, aluminium plants), agriculture plays an important role in the economy, with some 25 per cent of the labour force employed in the agricultural sector in 1995.

Economic decline had already begun several years before Ukraine's independence in 1991, but the situation worsened markedly with the break-up of the Soviet Union and the COMECON trading bloc. This disruption resulted in a dramatic decrease in output in all sectors of both industrial and consumer goods production, which was aggravated by a shrinking demand for military goods. Total production in the state sector fell by more than 50 per cent in the five years up to 1995, manufacturing production by slightly less than 50 per cent, agricultural production by 35 per cent, and consumer goods production by 56 per cent. Official data show that in 1996 real GDP was just 43 per cent of the level reached in 1990. As concerns industry, the recession has been felt more severely in sectors that produce more sophisticated products, as these have faced strong competition from imported goods of better quality. Together with shrinking output, capacity utilization has also fallen dramatically.

According to ILO estimates, the size of the informal sector could be up to 30 to 40 per cent of GDP. Notwithstanding the obviously high level of uncertainty in these estimates, it is clear that this development has had negative effects on economic growth, the state budget and the trade balance. The non-collection of taxes and social contributions has led to public budget crises and aggravated the problem of wage and pension arrears.

Although Ukraine's GDP has fallen sharply since independence, its official rate of unemployment during 1992–95 remained rather low, but started to grow later. At the beginning of 1998 there were around 680,000 inactive citizens registered at the Employment Service, including 637,000 who had the status of unemployed, which was 1.8 times more than in 1996. The fact that not all unemployed are being registered in employment centres can be explained – at least to some extent – by the fact that there is little incentive to register as unemployed, owing to low levels of unemployment benefits and long delays in benefit payments. Furthermore, enterprises have tried to respond to shrinking demand by inducing their employees to accept part-time work or take unpaid leave. Workers often decide to accept unpaid leave or work shorter hours in order to retain eligibility for other benefits, including health care and housing assistance. Consequently, hidden unemployment is thought to be much higher than the official figures indicate. According to some official estimates, actual unemployment may have reached 3.5 million (approximately 12 per cent of the labour force) by the end of 1996.

As in other countries in a similar political and economic situation, Ukraine went through a period of hyperinflation at the beginning of transition. The inflation rate reached its high point in 1993, at more than 10,000 per cent. Indeed, one of the major achievements of Ukraine's Government was the 1994–95 stabilization of the currency and reduced inflation. This was sustained by tight monetary policies.

The Government also succeeded in stabilizing the (non social insurance) budget deficit. However, to a great extent this was achieved by delaying the payment of current liabilities, mainly public sector wages, social benefits and pensions. This created huge inter-enterprise and wage arrears, as well as benefit and pension arrears, all of which hampered necessary enterprise restructuring and economic recovery.

Privatization is at the heart of the Government's reform programme. The process was officially launched in 1992 with a set of laws stipulating the various conditions for privatizing small, medium-sized and large state enterprises. However, the established targets were not reached. For example, only 25 per cent of the targeted industrial enterprises have been privatized.

9.2.3 The social reality

The social reality in Ukraine is grim. Economic recession and hyperinflation have had a severe impact on incomes and living standards for the vast majority of Ukraine's population. Through inflation, workers' earning capacity was undermined and cash assets lost their value. The purchasing power of various social benefits (including pensions) was drastically eroded, because unsystematic increases in these benefits could not keep up with inflation. Moreover, the social security system inherited from the planned economy era was inadequate to cope with the new situation.

Since 1990 wages have been constantly falling behind the CPI. The biggest fall in real wages was observed in 1993 (−63.2 per cent). In 1997 the average wage level was equal to 34.2 per cent of the 1990 level. However, income from informal sector activities is not included in the estimates of income and wages, and the growing private sector typically under-reports wages and salaries. Thus, official statistics may underestimate income levels in Ukraine.

Income disparities have grown dramatically. In 1994, the average incomes of the highest-paid decile of the population exceeded the average incomes of the lowest-paid decile by a factor of 9. In 1995, this had increased to a factor of 12, and in 1997 to 14.

Income developments have had an extremely negative effect on living standards, and on the provision of basic food products and other staples, and have pushed a considerable portion of the population beyond the limits of physical survival – especially pensioners, families with many children, and people of restricted employability. In 1997, approximately 27.6 million people (53.9 per cent of the population) had an average aggregate income that was considered under the low-income level.

The social price of economic reforms has proved to be exorbitant for many. The economic crisis and the budget deficit have made the system of social protection inefficient. The majority of families, especially those with many children and young, lone-parent families, today are socially unprotected and are not provided with the minimum resources for their existence. Social tensions run high because of the unsatisfactory financing of wages and social allowances.

9.2.4 The social protection system

The present social protection system in Ukraine is still dominated by planned economy characteristics, as well as by the more general idiosyncrasies of socialist social protection programmes as in other countries. The socialist welfare state consisted of explicit formal social protection schemes ("visible" social transfer systems), together with a variety of implicit social protection mechanisms such as subsidies for food and other goods and services (such as housing) and most notably "social employment".

It is the "formal" social protection system which is now called upon to deal with the negative side effects of transition, especially the dual problem of rapidly increasing open and hidden unemployment and poverty. The formal system is supposed to replace the former "social security" provided by the guarantee of full employment under the planned economy.

Additions have been made to the formal social protection system during the last three years (such as unemployment, social assistance and housing schemes), but elements inherited from the system of the former Soviet Union are still dominant. At present, the social protection system consists of:

- employment-related social security schemes financed through contributions (pensions, short-term cash benefits, and unemployment benefits);
- universal benefit systems, providing benefits for the entire population (the family benefit system and the National Public Service Health Care System);
- a fledgling social assistance scheme;
- a special fund, which aims to alleviate the effects of natural and technological disasters.

9.2.4.1 Contribution-financed systems

The pension system

As in other countries, the pension system in Ukraine has two main objectives: (a) to provide a minimum level of protection for all pensioners, and (b) to reflect variations in individual workers' contributions to their pension entitlements. The economic difficulties associated with a transition to market-oriented democracy resulted in priority being given to the first of these objectives. To preserve a minimum living standard for low-income pensioners, a compression in the range between minimum and maximum pensions was inevitable. In the course of time, individual earning histories came to play a smaller role in determining the amount of pensions. An increasing number of pensioners reached the maximum level, and the importance of compensation payments, which were provided to adjust pensions to inflation and protect the most vulnerable, has increased in the total pension package. The average pension is rather low, at less than 40 per cent of average earnings.

Despite efforts to keep pensions at a manageable level, the Pension Fund faces problems in maintaining adequate revenues. The main reason for this uncertainty stems from the fact that a declining share of wages is subject to social taxes or payroll contributions. The increasing number of workers either officially unemployed or on unpaid leave, but not officially declared as unemployed, reduces the contribution base considerably. Again, wage arrears – most prominent in the mining and agricultural sectors – are not taxed, which means a shortfall in revenues due.

Although the term "social insurance" is used to describe the present pension system in Ukraine, in practice the system displays many elements of a means of administrative distribution. Social pensions are assigned from the Pension Fund regardless of whether their recipients make any contributions, and certain other types of allowances unrelated to labour activity are also financed from insurance contributions.

Steps were taken to bring minimum pensions up to the minimum income level. However, the complex demographic situation, with a growing proportion of pensioners in the population, and a declining number in the productive workforce, made it impossible to fix pensions at that level. The Government also failed to meet its obligations to lift restrictions on the maximum amount of pensions.

Short-term benefits provided by the social insurance fund

The social insurance fund provides short-term benefits for temporary disability, pregnancy while employed, maternity benefits and funeral expenses, and for stays in sanatoriums or certain other types of health-related measures. Benefit payments for temporary disability amount to approximately 50 per cent of all expenses of the social insurance fund.

Maternity benefits are paid as a lump sum of four monthly minimum wages. Mothers who register at the proper medical institution in the early stages of pregnancy, regularly visit doctors, and carry out the doctor's recommendations, are entitled to an additional benefit of two monthly minimum wages.

Employment injury benefits

Damage to an employee's health is compensated as follows:

- replacement of lost earnings, depending on the level of loss of work ability;
- payment of a lump sum to the victim in certain cases (or to the family, or to persons supported by the victim);
- compensation of expenses through medical and social assistance (special foods, prosthetics, care by specialists, etc.).

Unemployment benefits

A system of unemployment insurance in Ukraine was introduced in 1991. To ensure the financing of unemployment benefits and of other measures to promote the placing of the unemployed in jobs, an Employment Fund was created as part of the state budget. Until 1997, the Fund was financed mainly through contributions made by enterprises, institutions, and organizations of all types of ownership that perform a productive economic activity. Legislative changes have occurred throughout the period of the Employment Fund's existence, concerning both the status of the Fund and its financing. Parliament reviewed allocations to the Fund several times. For a considerable period, contributions to the Fund were set at 3 per cent of the fund used for remuneration by the enterprises. In July 1997, the contribution rate was changed for enterprises, institutions, and organizations of any ownership to 1.5 per cent of the total wages paid, plus a 0.5 per cent employee contribution paid from the individual employee's wages.

Because of low unemployment between 1991 and 1995, contributions to the Employment Fund exceeded expenditures. Therefore, much of the Fund was used for other state budget measures not related to unemployment, and the contributions were eventually reduced. After unemployment began to accelerate in 1996–97, problems arose in the timely payment of unemployment benefits and other measures of social protection for inactive citizens; these problems were exacerbated by the reduced contribution rate.

In general, unemployment benefits are not paid for more than 360 calendar days during a two-year period. For persons approaching retirement age, up to 720 days may be paid. However, this figure is only 180 days for those attempting to re-enter working activity after a break of over six months and for those entering the workforce for the first time. In the first three months, the employment service pays 75 per cent of average wages as unemployment benefits. After three months, the benefit is reduced to 50 per cent of average wages, paid for 210 calendar days. From 1 January 1999, during the first 60 days of unemployment, the Employment Service will pay benefits at a level of 100 per cent of average wages at the previous workplace. This change will require significant additional financial resources; in the absence of extra allocations, the solvency of the Employment Fund may be threatened.

The Fund for Natural and Technological Disasters

This fund (referred to as the Disaster Fund) was introduced to finance compensation and continuing clean-up activities connected with a nuclear disaster in 1986. The Disaster Fund is financed through a 12 per cent payroll surcharge, borne by employers. It uses the pension scheme as a "handling agent" for some of its benefits.

There is evidence that eligibility conditions for benefits (notably old-age pension supplements) are liberal. It is also not certain that all those in need of and entitled to these benefits have applied for them. It appears that within a review of special protection benefits, their adequacy, allocation and delivery deserve special attention.

9.2.4.2 Tax-financed systems

The public service health care scheme

The health system in Ukraine is basically of the same type as the classical public systems still prevailing in most former planned-economy countries, although these are undergoing reforms in virtually all countries of the region. The public system – the backbone of health care delivery – is a branch of the civil service, financed from the state budget. The Ministry of Health operates tertiary care hospitals, research centres and medical schools. From 1992, the county delivery systems have been financed from the county budgets, while national institutions have been financed directly from the state budget through the Ministry of Health. The facilities are now preparing their own budgets and will submit them either to the county government or the Ministry.

As in most other countries of the region, the health care infrastructure appears extensive by European standards. In 1993, the country had 4.4

physicians per 1,000 persons (compared to 2.8 in the former Federal Republic of Germany and 1.4 in the United Kingdom in the late 1980s) and 13.5 hospital beds per 1,000 persons (compared to 11.0 in Germany, 6.8 in the United Kingdom, and 5.3 in the United States in the late 1980s). Ambulatory care is provided by about 6,500 polyclinics and similar outpatient care units, and in-patient care by a network of 3,800 hospitals. Utilization data indicate extensive use of facilities (for example, 4.0 hospital days per person per year). Performance indicators also suggest that delivery is less than efficient – an average length of stay is 16.5 days.

In addition, larger enterprises and agencies still operate their own facilities, polyclinics, and even hospitals. The quality of care in these facilities is reported to be superior to that provided in public facilities. Private dental care has always existed in a limited form, involving about 5 per cent of all dentists. Other types of private health care facilities are developing, albeit slowly, because of the lack of affluent patients.

The breaks in economic relations following independence led to almost complete cessation in the delivery of drugs and medical equipment from abroad (from the Russian Federation, Poland, Bulgaria, Hungary, the Czech Republic, Slovakia, Germany and Yugoslavia). This is why real access to qualified medical care is declining, although an estimate of this decline is not possible. The difficulties the country faces in obtaining inexpensive pharmaceuticals have led to strict rationing of the drug supply. The main previous supply channels from abroad have virtually evaporated, since these countries trade their goods overwhelmingly for hard currency. Drugs are free today only for infants less than 1 year old and for certain categories of seriously or chronically ill persons. For other groups, the purchase of drugs has become a predominantly private affair, even for persons with low incomes. Hospital patients are often forced to supply medicines themselves. The choice of providers was previously strictly limited, through the administrative allocation of patients to local providers. Only now is the range of choice in medical care slowly widening.

Public expenditure on health care was about 4 per cent of GDP in 1996 and 1997. However, if private outlays for the purchase of drugs, so-called gratitude payments by patients to health professionals, incomes from the Social Insurance Fund (through sanatorium treatment), and the Disaster Fund are taken into account, the outlay for health care was more in the order of 5 per cent of GDP.

The social assistance scheme

So far, social assistance benefits have played only a minor role, as the former full employment policy did not allow a sizeable number of persons to become dependent on social assistance. The main "social assistance benefit" for persons who could not earn a living was the social pension for defined categories of "non-employable" persons – for example, persons with severe physical or mental handicaps. Benefits for the "employable" poor were not necessary.

A limited general cash income-support system was introduced in December 1992 and complemented in 1993 by an income-support scheme for pensioners and low-income persons.[2] Data on the benefit experience are not yet available.[3] There are anecdotal reports that local welfare offices are increasingly paying benefits to persons in hidden unemployment (those on unpaid leave for several months).

The income support system has deficiencies. It excludes recipients of social security benefits (other than pensions). The limitation of benefits to some persons does not seem sensible (for example, to those with personal incomes under the social assistance intervention line – or SAIL – in a low-income family with average income under the SAIL). The SAIL does not seem to be differentiated by age or region. The definition of income to be used when calculating average per capita income is not clear, and no procedure for means testing is elaborated. The scheme also leaves gaps in coverage. For example, no matter how low their benefits, unemployed persons are excluded from additional income support.

Housing

The housing problem in Ukraine is acute. Housing construction activity does not reflect its social importance, since there is no hope for larger centralized capital investments in this sector. By early 1996, residential housing facilities amounted to 978.3 million square metres, or 19 square metres per resident. A total of 6.5 million square metres of residential housing was commissioned from all sources of financing in 1996, or 37 per cent of the 1990 level and 75 per cent of the 1995 level. Only 0.5 million square metres of residential housing, or 7.7 per cent of the total amount, was built with centralized state capital investments.

9.2.4.3 *Present social expenditure and fiscal and para-fiscal pressures*

Table 9.3 summarizes the present structure of social protection expenditure in Ukraine.

The 1995 and 1996 levels of social expenditure as a percentage of GDP are in the middle range of social expenditure levels found in OECD countries. The estimated total expenditure thus might not be excessive for an economy in distress. Overall social protection expenditure still does not include indirect expenses, such as productivity losses due to remnants of "social employment", although most workers so "employed" are probably now on unpaid leave and hence incur only minor expenses for their enterprises. It also fails to include other types of subsidies, such as those for housing, the real accounting costs of which are difficult to determine. The order of magnitude varies with the assumptions on the depreciation of the existing housing stock, but according to one estimate the housing subsidy could cost the country as much as 10 per cent of GDP.[4]

Table 9.3 Ukraine: Estimated social expenditure and financing, 1995–96

Item	Estimated cost (per cent of GDP)	
	1995	1996
Expenditure		
Pensions	9.0	9.6
Short-term cash benefits	1.1	1.2
Unemployment benefits	0.1	0.2
Family benefits	1.1	1.2
Health	4.9	4.1
Disaster benefits	1.7	1.9
Social assistance	0.1	0.1
Housing	0.1	0.5
Other expenditure	0.4	0.7
Total expenditure	**18.5**	**19.5**
Financing		
Social security contributions	7.7	9.1
Contributions to Employment Fund	0.3	0.3
Contributions to Disaster Fund	1.9	1.9
Financing from general tax revenue	8.4	8.5
Total financing	**18.3**	**19.8**

Source: Estimates based on data and Social Budget model calculations. For 1996, some data are preliminary.

While overall social expenditure has dropped in relative terms compared with 1994 (when it was estimated at 21.4 per cent of GDP), the tax share in overall social protection financing has increased. From the point of view of fiscal policy, this outcome is clearly undesirable. It means that while social expenditure has been cut (at substantial social cost), the budget has not benefited from the operation and – what is worse – budget financing has had to be increased to alleviate some of the social cost. A growing fiscal imbalance of the overall social protection system was largely due to a large increase in subsidies and a deteriorating balance of the pension fund. The latter has been apparently caused by a dramatic decline in the collection of contributions. There is at present a considerable "contribution gap" (non-collection of contributions, for various reasons). In financial terms, we see that the country's Social Budget has been kept under control, but at the price of increasing poverty, a sharply declining standard of living and probably also a deterioration in health status.

The country's estimated Social Budget also indicates some structural deficiencies. Expenditure on the inefficient health system and on pensions accounts for more than half of the overall total, while expenditure on social assistance – even in these times of dramatically rising poverty – remains below 1 per cent of GDP. Even if the "social assistance expenditure" hidden in the social pension scheme were added, the resources allocated to anti-poverty mechanisms are still disproportionately small.

The present level of expenditure on unemployment benefits reflects administrative inefficiencies and still-existing barriers to open unemployment, rather than the real employment situation in the country. Labour force survey results show the unemployment rate reaching over 5 per cent in 1995 and nearly 7.5 per cent in 1996, while the rate of registered unemployment was still only slightly higher than 1 per cent in the latter year, with less than one-third of those registered actually receiving benefits. Benefit expenditure should be substantially higher than the observed 0.2 per cent of GDP, in order to cushion the level of actual unemployment. A significant increase in the unemployment rate can be expected as unregistered and hidden unemployment gradually comes into the open.

Recent developments and the government budget projected for 1998 show increasing fiscal deficits and public debt. Between 1995/96 and 1997/98 the deficit of the consolidated budget doubled from 5 per cent to 10 per cent of GDP. The consolidated budget includes the social insurance schemes. The dramatically increasing deficit of the pension fund (expenditure increased from about 9.5 per cent of GDP in 1996 to about 12.4 per cent in 1997), combined with stagnation of tax and social security revenues, explain most of the deficit increase. It is obvious that the Government will not be able to support the increasing burdens of the social sector.

9.2.5   Simulating and projecting the Social Budget

9.2.5.1   Methodology

The methodology used in this case study is very similar to the general procedure described in Part III; thus no specific explanations are required here. The only departure from the normal procedure is that the modelling of the pension system uses a link to the World Bank pensions model PROST, which is used by the Bank's social protection network in their country analyses. Methodologically, this model is slightly simpler than the general ILO pension model described previously.

9.2.5.2   Scenario assumptions

The simulations performed using the Social Budget model require a set of demographic, economic and policy assumptions. Economic scenarios represent assumed future paths of development of basic economic variables; policy scenarios include assumed future developments in some selected parameters of the existing social protection schemes, such as changes in the retirement age, take-up rates, or replacement rates for various benefits, new indexation formulas, and other policy changes.

Table 9.4 Ukraine: Assumed labour force participation rates (percentages)

Age group	Male	Female	Total
15–19	18.6	22.7	20.6
20–24	70.7	69.2	70.0
25–29	88.0	81.5	84.8
30–34	87.5	83.0	85.2
35–39	88.5	89.2	88.9
40–49	95.2	96.1	95.7
50–54	95.1	88.5	91.5
55–59	82.0	45.4	61.6
60–70	33.9	22.3	26.9
15–70	**72.9**	**64.9**	**68.7**

Demography

The results concerning demographic assumptions presented in the following sections of the case study are based on the official population projections for Ukraine.

Labour force participation

Age- and sex-specific labour force participation rates (table 9.4) are taken from the 1995 and 1996 national labour force surveys. For all simulations, these rates are held constant at 1996 levels over the projection period 1998–2015. Since it is obvious that significant changes in future labour force participation rates are to be expected, the model should also be run with a variety of labour force participation assumptions, in order to check their impact on the system.

Basic macroeconomic variables

The basic economic scenario used (table 9.5) is based on consultations with a national working group. Some of the indicators for the period 1998–2001 were based on macroeconomic assumptions developed by the Ministry of Economy (and used in preparing the 1998 state budget). However, many other indicators (as well as all assumptions about the period after 2001) had to be developed independently, owing to the lack of supporting information. The basic scenario and all other scenarios presented here are of a purely indicative nature. Analysis based on these scenarios should be treated entirely as a "what if" exercise to demonstrate the impact of alternative economic developments on the country's Social Budget.

Assumed values for 1998 are the same for all three scenarios and are based on the assumptions used for the preparation of the state budget. The first scenario (basic) (which will be referred to throughout the remainder of this

Table 9.5   Ukraine: Economic scenarios (annual growth rates as percentages)

	1998	1999	2000	2001	2002	2003	2004	2005	2006–15
Scenario 1 (basic)									
GDP	0.5	2.0	4.0	5.0	5.0	5.0	5.0	5.0	4.0
Productivity	1.4	2.4	4.2	5.2	6.0	6.0	6.0	6.0	4.0
Real wages	−1.0	−0.6	0.0	0.5	4.0	5.0	5.0	5.0	4.0
Scenario 2 (stagnation)									
GDP	0.5	0.0	0.0	0.0	0.0	0.0	0.0	0.0	0.0
Productivity	1.4	0.5	0.5	0.5	0.5	0.5	0.5	0.5	0.5
Real wages	−1.0	0.5	0.5	0.5	0.5	0.5	0.5	0.5	0.5
Scenario 3 (optimistic)									
GDP	0.5	2.0	4.0	5.0	5.0	5.0	5.0	5.0	4.0
Productivity	1.4	3.0	6.0	7.0	6.0	5.0	5.0	4.0	3.0
Real wages	−1.0	3.0	6.0	7.0	6.0	5.0	5.0	4.0	3.0

section) assumes that recovery will start in 1999 and that GDP growth will then accelerate to 5 per cent per year during the period 2001–2005, declining thereafter to 4 per cent per year until 2016. Productivity growth assumptions for the period 1998–2000 are consistent with the assumptions made by the

Figure 9.6   Ukraine: Employment growth for alternative scenarios

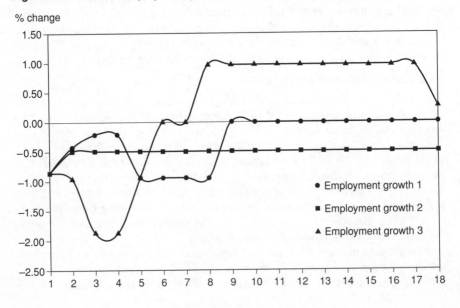

Ministry of Economy about future changes in employment. Productivity grows only slightly more than GDP, which means that employment also decreases at a rather slow rate. Only during the period 2002–05 will productivity grow by one percentage point faster than GDP, resulting in a reduction of employment by 1 per cent per year (figure 9.6). After 2006, GDP and productivity growth rates are assumed to be equal, which would result in stabilization of employment. Real wages, according to the assumptions of the basic scenario, will decrease slightly in 1998 and 1999, level out in 2000 and start to grow by 4 per cent in 2002. Thereafter, wages will grow at a rate equal to GDP growth.

The *second scenario* (*stagnation*) involves zero GDP growth, accompanied by slowly growing average productivity. This would result in permanently – but slowly – falling employment and rising unemployment. Wages would grow at the same pace as productivity. This scenario is used to show what would happen if expected growth does not materialize, and unemployment reaches high levels.

The *third scenario* (*optimistic*) is a variation of the basic scenario, with the same GDP growth rates but with much higher labour productivity growth in the period 1999–2001. Employment thus falls more sharply during the first three years, but rises thereafter, beginning in 2005. Figure 9.6 shows the employment growth rates in all three scenarios, while figure 9.7 shows corresponding unemployment rates.[5]

Figure 9.7   Ukraine: Unemployment rates for alternative scenarios

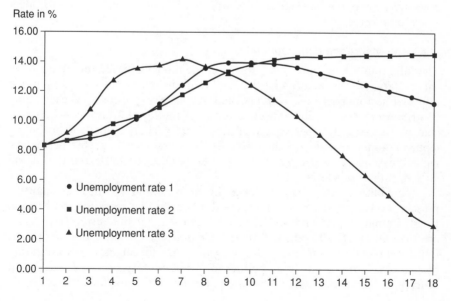

9.2.5.3   Other main assumptions

Consolidated public budget

The model provides results for the revenue and expenditure sides of the consolidated public budget only for items that are specifically part of social protection finances (social insurance contribution revenue and expenditure on social benefits and services). In order to obtain a full picture of public revenue and expenditure, it is necessary to assume some key parameters. On the revenue side, it is assumed that tax revenue will stay at the level of 24 per cent of GDP, and non-tax revenue at the level of 10 per cent of GDP (approximately the levels achieved in 1995). It is thus assumed that all public revenue other than that from social security contributions will remain at the level of 34 per cent of GDP throughout the projection period. On the expenditure side, besides the social protection expenditure calculated by the various parts of the model, only expenditure on education is projected separately. It is assumed that educational expenditure will grow at a rate equal to the growth of the population of school age (up to age 24) times GDP growth times the elasticity of education expenditure growth to GDP growth. This elasticity figure is set at 1.1 for the purposes of the status quo projections. It is also assumed that expenditure on consumer price subsidies will remain at the level of 1 per cent of GDP throughout the projection period. All other categories of government expenditure (apart from social protection, education and consumer subsidies) are assumed to have a constant share of GDP, which for the status quo projections is assumed to be 17 per cent.

The user can change the values of the above parameters to reflect alternative objectives. Changing these parameters will have an impact on the overall budget deficit or surplus.

Social insurance contribution revenue

The total number of employed persons in the model is based on labour force survey data. It thus includes all the employed, including those working in the informal sector, part-time workers, and so on. For purposes of calculating contribution revenue and some expenditure of the social insurance schemes, it is assumed that only a percentage of those employed are actually contributing (contributions are paid on their behalf). It is assumed that this percentage will increase from 69 per cent in 1995 to 80 per cent in 2001, and that it will later remain at this level.

Contribution rates for the Social Insurance Fund are held constant at present levels over the projection period. Contribution rates for the Pension Fund, Employment Fund and Disaster Fund start at the current levels, but are then automatically adjusted to levels required to balance the funds. The adjustment is not complete, and is lagged – the current period contribution rate is equal to the previous period contribution rate plus the average of differences between actual and required rates from two previous periods.

Pensions and other benefits: Replacement rates, take-up rates and indexation

As described above, the pension module uses an assumed combined distribution of past service years and earnings to calculate new pensions. This assumed distribution is presented in table 9.6.

The replacement rate for *newly awarded old-age pensions* is set at the level of 46 per cent of the average reference wage. *Pensions in payment* are adjusted in line with the CPI. The invalidity rate is set at a constant 8.8 per cent of the contributing population throughout the projection period for status quo projections, and the number of survivors' pensions at 7.3 per cent of the number of old-age pensions. The number of disaster-related pensions is assumed to be 6.1 per cent of the total number of pensions. The average invalidity pension is assumed to be equal to the average old-age pension. The average survivors' pension is assumed to be 60 per cent of the average old-age pension, while average social pensions are held at 67 per cent of the average old-age pension, and average disaster pensions at 54 per cent.

The average replacement rate (ratio of average benefits in payment to average reference wage) for *unemployment benefits* is set at 37 per cent of the average reference wage. The take-up rate (ratio of beneficiaries to registered unemployed) for unemployment benefits is set at 55 per cent.

Replacement rates for *sickness and maternity benefits* are set at 88 per cent and 80 per cent, respectively. The average number of sick days per insured person is 4.8, and the average number of maternity days per women aged 15–45 is 4.1. These parameters are assumed to be constant throughout the projection period.

All family benefits are adjusted every year, according to changes in the CPI. Most Disaster Fund benefits and benefits classified as "other" are also adjusted in line with the CPI. The absolute poverty line is set at the level of 46 hryvyna for 1996 and then adjusted in line with price inflation.

9.2.5.4 Projection results: Status quo

Overall social expenditure and its fiscal dimension

Under the *basic scenario* (scenario 1 in figure 9.8), the share in GDP of total social benefit and service expenditure (excluding education) may still increase for the first few years of the projection period (until 1999), reaching 24.9 per cent (table 9.7). As soon as the economy achieves the expected high rate of growth, the share of social expenditure in GDP would start to decrease to 21.3 per cent in 2005, 19.5 per cent in 2010 and 18.4 per cent in 2015. A slowdown in this decreasing trend is seen in the period 2002–2006, when the unemployment rate will approach its peak.

For the *second scenario* (*stagnation*), we see that the share of social expenditure in GDP would continuously increase under status quo conditions. The major forces behind this increase would be expenditure on pensions (which

Table 9.6 Ukraine: Reference wage/past service matrix

Reference wage as % of average wage (two head columns)		Past service as a percentage of average past service (two top rows)									Total
		Up to 20	20–40	40–60	60–80	80–100	100–120	120–140	140–160	Above 160	
Classes	Mid-class	15	30	50	70	90	110	130	150	160	
Up to 40	20	5	4	2	1	0	0	0	0	0	12
40–80	60	2	3	5	4	1	2	0	0	0	17
80–120	100	1	1	5	4	3	3	0	0	0	17
120–160	140	0	0	5	4	3	4	2	0	0	18
160–200	180	0	0	2	2	2	5	3	2	0	16
200–300	250	0	0	1	1	2	4	2	2	0	12
300–400	350	0	0	0	0	2	2	1	1	0	6
400–500	450	0	0	0	0	2	0	0	0	0	2
500+	500	0	0	0	0	0	0	0	0	0	0
Total		**8**	**8**	**20**	**16**	**15**	**20**	**8**	**5**	**0**	**100**

Figure 9.8   Ukraine: Social expenditure (as a percentage of GDP)

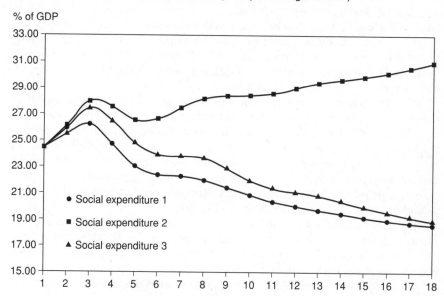

% of GDP

• Social expenditure 1

■ Social expenditure 2

▲ Social expenditure 3

would show no decrease in the first part of the period and an increase in the second), unemployment benefits and social assistance.

The results of the *third (optimistic) scenario* show a declining trend in social expenditure, similar to the one observed in the basic scenario. Here, GDP growth is assumed to be the same as in the basic scenario, but with a higher unemployment rate at the beginning of the period and then growing employment after 2005. While the share of social expenditure would be higher than in the first scenario for the first 12 years, afterwards it would decrease to slightly lower levels. The difference is accounted for by expenditure on unemployment benefits and social assistance.

Table 9.7   Ukraine: Contribution rates for the basic scenario 1998–2015 (status quo conditions)

	1998	1999	2000	2005	2010	2015
Total	**48.8**	**58.8**	**63.1**	**55.6**	**50.3**	**47.4**
Pension Fund	33.6	40.8	43.3	34.2	29.8	28.9
Employers	32.6	39.8	42.3	33.2	28.8	27.9
Employees	1.0	1.0	1.0	1.0	1.0	1.0
Social Insurance Fund	4.0	4.0	4.0	4.0	4.0	4.0
Employment Fund	1.2	1.9	3.0	6.9	7.4	6.2
Disaster Fund	10.0	12.1	12.8	10.5	9.1	8.2

How would these expenditures be financed? The model assumes that beginning in 1999 social security contribution rates will be adjusted (with some time lags) to the levels required to balance revenue with the expenditure of the social funds (the Pension, Employment and Disaster Funds). This would cause a sharp increase in current contribution rates in 1999 and a decrease in the Government's share of social protection financing (table 9.7). Afterwards, in the basic scenario, contribution rates will start to decrease.

It can be seen that in the long term, and assuming status quo conditions (which means, for example, adjusting pensions only to inflation despite a significant increase in real wages), that the rates for contributions to finance the pension system would decrease significantly. On the other hand, as unemployment will be growing, more resources will be needed to finance unemployment benefits and employment promotion expenditure. It is also important to note that, unless reformed, the Disaster Fund will continue to require contributions nearly as high as those today, even in the distant future.

The second scenario would, of course, require much higher contribution rates to finance social protection expenditure. In the third scenario, contribution rates would decrease even more than in the basic scenario, mainly because of much higher levels of employment. Figure 9.9 shows the development of pay-as-you-go (PAYG) contribution rates required to finance the expenditure of the social funds in all three scenarios.

Figure 9.9   Ukraine: PAYG total contribution rates (as a percentage of wage funds)

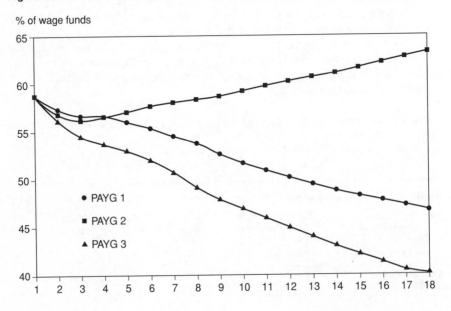

Figure 9.10   Ukraine: Public finance deficit (as a percentage of GDP)

% of GDP

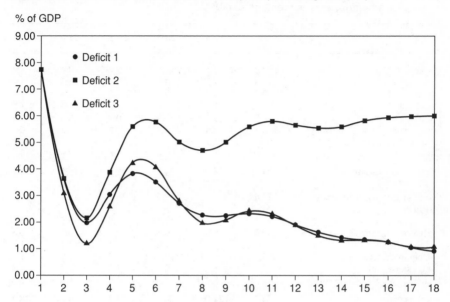

The next important question is: What are the implications of different levels of social expenditure for the overall balance of public finance? Since revenue and expenditure for most public budget categories (unconnected directly to social protection) are held at a constant proportion of GDP in the status quo projections, it is obvious that the calculated overall balance of public finances will follow the paths of social expenditure and revenue. In the relatively optimistic basic and third scenarios, the public budget deficit will decrease in the long term. The stagnation scenario, meanwhile, will not only prevent any long-lasting improvement in the public finances; it will also eventually lead to even larger deficits. Figure 9.10 shows public deficit measured as a percentage of GDP for all three scenarios. The initial decrease in the deficit seen in the first few years results from an assumed increase in contribution rates in 1999.

The Social Budget and individual social protection subsystems

Table 9.8 shows overall levels of expenditure (as a percentage of GDP) for the major social protection schemes in the context of an overall Social Budget for Ukraine (for the basic scenario). Table 9.9 shows the projected structural changes within the Social Budget.

Pension expenditure will of course continue to dominate overall social spending, but in the medium term its role might decrease slightly, in terms of its share in both GDP and total social expenditure. However, we must recall once again that status quo projections assume price indexation of pension

Table 9.8 Ukraine's Social Budget: Expenditure and income, 1998–2015 (basic scenario, as a percentage of GDP)[1]

Year	1998	1999	2000	2005	2010	2015
Pensions	12.2	12.1	11.8	9.2	8.4	8.2
Health care	4.3	4.3	4.3	4.2	4.3	4.4
Unemployment	0.7	0.8	0.9	1.8	1.8	1.5
Short-term benefits	1.6	1.7	1.6	1.5	1.4	1.4
Family benefits	0.9	0.9	0.9	0.7	0.6	0.5
Social assistance and housing	2.2	2.4	2.4	1.8	1.2	0.8
Disaster Fund benefits	1.7	1.7	1.7	1.4	1.2	1.1
Other	1.0	1.0	1.0	0.8	0.6	0.5
Total social expenditure	**24.7**	**24.9**	**24.5**	**21.3**	**19.5**	**18.4**
Social security contributions, of which:	13.4	16.6	17.7	14.3	12.8	11.9
Pension insurance	10.2	12.8	13.5	9.8	8.5	8.3
Health insurance	0.0	0.0	0.0	0.0	0.0	0.0
Short-term benefits	1.2	1.2	1.2	1.1	1.1	1.1
Unemployment insurance	0.3	0.5	0.8	1.7	1.9	1.6
Disaster Fund	1.7	2.1	2.2	1.6	1.4	1.3
Income from general revenues	11.2	8.3	6.8	7.0	6.6	6.1
Total income	**24.7**	**24.9**	**24.5**	**21.3**	**19.5**	**18.4**

[1] For clarity, changes in reserves and investment incomes are omitted.

benefits, while real wages are assumed to grow significantly in the basic scenario. Therefore, at the end of the projection period, the share of pension expenditure will start to increase again: this signals increasing demographic tensions and the fact that in the long term, pension expenditure might start to grow again because of the ageing of the population. This is particularly true if the current retirement age remains unchanged, as is assumed for the status quo simulations.

In the medium term, the proportion of spending on direct anti-poverty measures, such as unemployment benefits and social assistance, will increase as a result of economic restructuring and increasing unemployment and poverty. Projected figures based on current policy choices certainly under-estimate the financing needs of effective future poverty alleviation policies. This shows the necessity for the reform of current schemes, in order to allow the more effective allocation of resources within the social protection system.

Expenditure on health care will also probably increase to a greater extent than is shown in the status quo simulations, taking into account the need to improve the quality of these services. Major structural changes within the health care system will be necessary in order to meet increasing demands and to contain rising costs.

Table 9.9 Ukraine: Structure of social expenditure and revenue, 1998–2015 (percentages)

Year	1998	1999	2000	2005	2010	2015
Pensions	49.6	48.6	48.0	43.2	42.9	44.5
Health	17.6	17.4	17.5	19.7	21.9	24.2
Unemployment	2.7	3.2	3.7	8.6	9.2	8.3
Short-term benefits	6.6	6.7	6.6	6.8	7.3	7.6
Family benefits	3.7	3.7	3.6	3.3	2.9	2.5
Social assistance and housing	8.8	9.6	9.8	8.4	6.4	4.2
Disaster Fund benefits	7.0	6.8	6.7	6.4	6.1	5.8
Others	4.0	4.0	4.0	3.6	3.3	2.8
Total social expenditure	**100.0**	**100.0**	**100.0**	**100.0**	**100.0**	**100.0**
Social security contributions, of which,	54.5	66.8	72.3	67.1	66.3	67.0
Pension insurance	41.5	51.4	55.1	46.0	43.7	45.2
Health insurance	0.0	0.0	0.0	0.0	0.0	0.0
Short-term benefits	4.9	5.0	5.0	5.3	5.8	6.2
Unemployment insurance	1.3	2.1	3.3	8.0	9.5	8.7
Disaster Fund	6.8	8.3	8.9	7.7	7.3	7.0
Income from general revenues	45.5	33.2	27.7	32.9	33.7	33.0
Total income	**100.0**	**100.0**	**100.0**	**100.0**	**100.0**	**100.0**

Figures 9.11, 9.12 and 9.13 show the development of expenditure on pensions, unemployment and social assistance benefits, respectively, for the three alternative economic scenarios and under status quo conditions.

9.2.5.5 Sensitivity tests

Different types of growth could have an impact on the results of projections, as already seen when comparing the results from the scenarios analysed previously. The comparison of the basic scenario with scenario 2 above demonstrates that results are sensitive to economic growth. A comparison of scenarios 1 and 3, meanwhile, shows sensitivity to different types of growth. To observe this sensitivity more clearly, let us check three additional scenarios, using the same GDP growth rates but different labour productivity growth rates.

The assumptions and main results for these scenarios are shown in table 9.10. The first scenario has GDP, labour productivity and real-wage growth rates all equal to 2 per cent per year throughout the projection period. The second and third scenarios differ only with respect to the assumed labour productivity growth rates. In the second scenario, labour productivity grows by 1.8 per cent per year, while in the third it grows by 2.2 per cent per year.

Calculated employment remains unchanged in the first scenario, while it grows by 0.2 per cent per year in the second scenario, and decreases by

Figure 9.11   Ukraine: Pension expenditure as a percentage of GDP

% of GDP

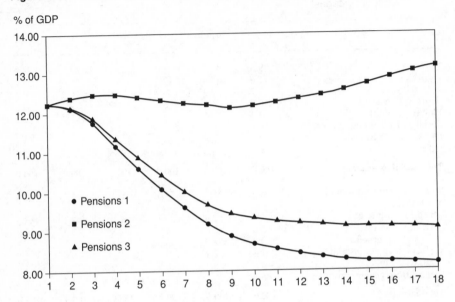

Figure 9.12   Ukraine: Unemployment benefit expenditure (as a percentage of GDP)

% of GDP

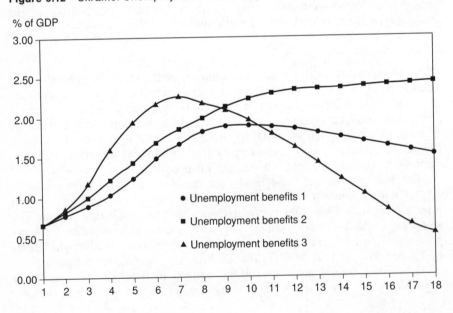

Figure 9.13 Ukraine: Social assistance and housing (as a percentage of GDP)

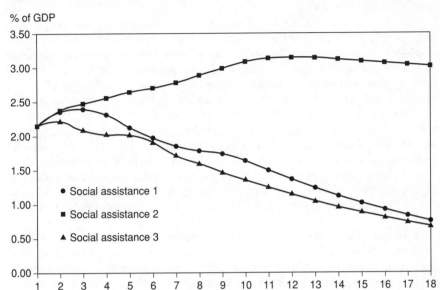

0.2 per cent per year in the third. The average unemployment rate over the period is 7.9 per cent in the first scenario. In the second, it is 1.7 percentage points lower (as employment increases), and in the third scenario it is 1.7 percentage points higher. The model's calculation of unemployment rates is therefore

Table 9.10 Ukraine: Sensitivity to labour productivity growth assumptions

Assumptions (% per year)	Scenario 1	Scenario 2	Scenario 3	Difference (2) – (1)	Difference (3) – (1)
GDP growth	2	2	2	0	0
Productivity growth	2	1.8	2.2	−0.2	0.2
Wage growth	2	2	2	0	0
Results					
Employment growth (% per year)	0	0.2	−0.2	0.2	−0.2
Unemployment rate (%)	7.9	6.2	9.6	−1.7	1.7
Labour costs (% of GDP)	52.3	52.9	51.8	0.5	−0.5
Social expenditure (% of GDP)	24.97	24.74	25.35	−0.23	0.38
Pensions (% of GDP)	12.09	12.13	12.06	0.04	−0.03
Unemployment benefits (% of GDP)	1.18	0.93	1.42	−0.25	0.24
Social assistance (% of GDP)	1.45	1.37	1.70	−0.08	0.24
PAYG contribution rate (%)	49.9	48.4	51.5	−1.5	1.6
Public finance deficit (% of GDP)	3.86	3.74	4.14	−0.12	0.28

highly sensitive to the combination of assumptions regarding GDP and productivity growth.

The direction of the impact of these scenarios on other results are in most cases as intuitively expected. Conditions of higher employment and lower unemployment would require less expenditure on unemployment benefits, social assistance and total social expenditure. Financing requirements, expressed by PAYG contribution rates, would also be lower, as well as the overall public budget deficit. The only result that is not intuitively clear is the reverse reaction of pension expenditure, which is higher when employment is higher and vice versa. A higher unemployment rate might be expected to push more persons out of the labour force and into early retirement. However, this type of behaviour is not mapped within the model, and further development work should aim at including this factor. In the present version of the model, the higher number of employed persons means a higher number of persons covered by pension insurance and therefore a higher number of persons retiring later.

Effects of the various assumptions on labour productivity would be similar in some respects to changing assumptions on labour force participation rates, as the major impact of both would be different paths of employment and unemployment.

It is also important to check the sensitivity of the model to wage growth assumptions. Table 9.11 shows the results of another set of three scenarios, in which GDP and productivity all grow over the projection period at a constant rate of 2 per cent per year, while real wages grow by 2 per cent, 1.8 per cent and 2.2 per cent per year, respectively.

Here, as well, most impacts are as would be intuitively expected. Lower wages result in lower expenditure on earnings-related contributory benefits

Table 9.11 Ukraine: Sensitivity to wage growth assumptions

Assumptions (% per year)	Scenario 1	Scenario 2	Scenario 3	Difference (2) – (1)	Difference (3) – (1)
GDP growth	2	2	2	0	0
Productivity growth	2	2	2	0	0
Wage growth	2	1.8	2.2	−0.2	0.2
Results					
Employment growth (% per year)	0	0.0	0.0	0.0	0.0
Unemployment rate (%)	7.9	7.9	7.9	0.0	0.0
Labour costs (% of GDP)	52.3	51.6	53.1	−0.8	0.8
Social expenditure (% of GDP)	24.97	24.84	25.11	−0.13	0.14
Pensions (% of GDP)	12.09	12.06	12.13	−0.04	0.04
Unemployment benefits (% of GDP)	1.18	1.16	1.20	−0.02	0.02
Social assistance (% of GDP)	1.45	1.50	1.41	0.04	−0.04
PAYG contribution rate (%)	49.9	50.5	49.3	0.6	−0.6
Public finance deficit (% of GDP)	3.86	3.87	3.85	0.01	−0.01

(such as pensions and unemployment benefits). However, since the contribution base (the wage fund) is also lower, it seems that the reduction in expenditure is still not enough to finance the benefits, and an increase in contribution rates is necessary. The share of social insurance contributions in overall labour costs increases, but the wage fund (net of contributions) decreases. The impact of the lower share of wages in GDP seems to be stronger, and eventually the share of total labour costs in GDP is lower. A lower wage also leads to higher spending on social assistance, as more wage earners fall below the poverty line. The size of the public finance deficit seems to be almost insensitive to these assumed changes. The slight increase shown in the deficit suggests that increased revenue from contributions and decreased expenditure on contributory benefits do not match a decrease in revenues from taxes and an increase in social assistance expenditure.

Changes in the real wage do not have any impact on employment and unemployment in the model. This link is not included automatically in the present version, but this should be borne in mind when designing scenario assumptions on GDP, productivity and wages.

9.2.5.6 Testing feedback between social expenditure and the economy

As described earlier in Part III, the model allows the use of three types of feedback from the social protection system into the economy as a whole. These feedback mechanisms were not activated in the projections described in the previous sections. Now, we test the reaction of the model to these sources of economic feedback (table 9.12).

The feedback mechanisms are modelled through elasticity parameters. First, it is assumed that a higher public finance deficit will have a negative impact on GDP growth, modelled through the elasticity of GDP growth relative to a percentage change in the share of the public deficit in GDP. Secondly, it is assumed that higher labour costs resulting from high contribution rates would lead to lower employment by reason of increased average labour productivity (choice of less labour-intensive production techniques). This link is modelled through the elasticity of labour productivity growth relative to the change in the share of labour costs in GDP. Thirdly, it is assumed that some social expenditure (such as for health, sickness, income-support benefits and

Table 9.12   Ukraine: Assumed values of elasticities for feedback tests

Elasticities	Scenario 1	Scenario 2	Scenario 3
GDP to public deficit	0	−1	−1
Productivity to labour costs	0	1	5
GDP to social expenditure	0	1	1

education) would have a positive impact on economic growth and employment. This is modelled through the elasticity of GDP growth relative to a change in the share of these categories of social expenditure to GDP. Each of these feedback mechanisms works with a time lag of one period, taking into account that in real life all the behavioural economic adjustments take time.

The definite size of the feedbacks for the Ukrainian economy, just as for most other economies, is not known; thus testing the sensitivity of the model and, it is hoped, the economy to the cost of social security is the only way to explore potential effects and build a case for further research. Figures 9.14 to 9.24 on the following pages show the results of a simulation of three different scenarios, with different assumed values for the above elasticities. All major economic assumptions are the same as in the basic scenario presented previously. The first scenario is simply a repetition of the basic scenario – all elasticities are equal to zero. The second activates the elasticities, giving them all a value of 1 (−1 in case of the elasticity of GDP to the public deficit). The third intensifies the elasticity of labour productivity growth and gives it a value of 5.

We see changes in the variables which are assumed to have an impact on GDP and productivity growth rates: the public finance deficit (figure 9.14), the share of labour costs in GDP (figure 9.15), and the share of social expenditure in GDP (figure 9.16).

The assumed adjustment mechanism for social insurance contribution rates is a lagged adjustment to average required PAYG contribution rates from the

Figure 9.14 Ukraine: Public finance deficit (as a percentage of GDP)

% of GDP

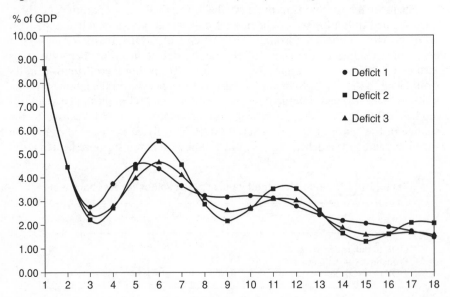

Figure 9.15 Ukraine: Share of labour costs in GDP

% share of GDP

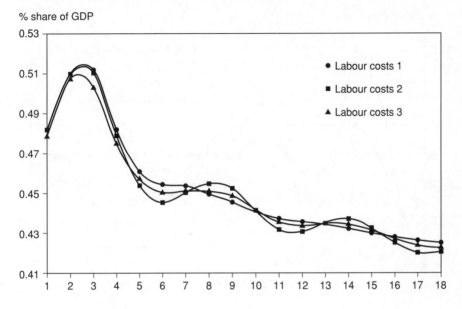

Figure 9.16 Ukraine: Employment-enhancing social expenditure (as a percentage of GDP)

% of GDP

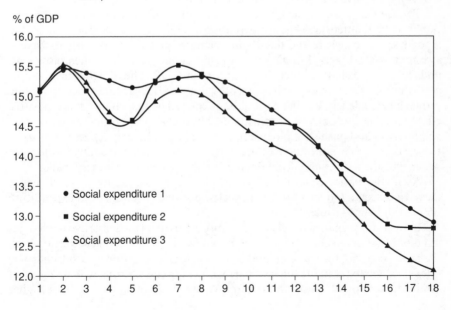

Figure 9.17   Ukraine: GDP growth rates (after feedback)

% of GDP growth rate

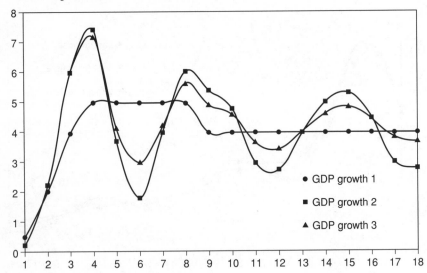

past two periods. Because of this lagged mechanism, there is some fluctuation in actual contribution levels even in the basic scenario, and thus in revenue from contributions, overall public revenue and labour costs.

The feedback effect, particularly the link of GDP growth to the size of the public deficit, intensifies these fluctuations. This can be clearly seen in the second scenario, where the fluctuating changes in the deficit seem to have a strong impact on actual GDP growth rates, employment and unemployment, and thus on the share of social expenditure in GDP. The initial adjustment of contribution rates from their current values to higher ones decreases the public finance deficit, but increases labour costs. The first change has a positive effect on GDP and thus on employment, but the second one increases average productivity and pushes employment down. The productivity effect seems to be too weak to stabilize the fluctuations. Further adjustments to contribution rates occur, but the amplitude of the fluctuation in the deficit becomes smaller.

As in the basic scenario, the share of social expenditure in GDP has a decreasing trend. On average, the expected positive effect of social expenditure on growth is not visible.

In the third scenario, the elasticity of productivity growth relative to changes in labour costs was set at a much higher value than in the second scenario. As in the basic scenario, the share of labour costs in GDP has a downward trend. The intensified feedback in the third scenario, however, has a strong stabilizing effect on the fluctuation of all variables. Employment levels are also on average higher

Figure 9.18 Ukraine: Employment growth (after feedback)

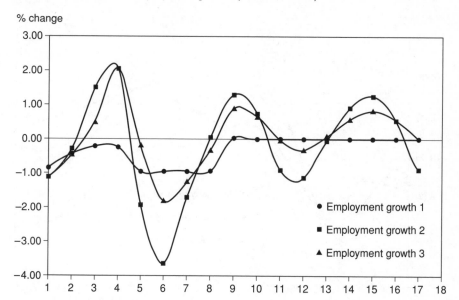

% change

than in the first two scenarios, while the unemployment rate is significantly lower.

The above results show that it would be worthwhile to continue research on the nature of the feedback between the economy and the social protection system, and on the actual numerical values of the respective elasticities.

9.2.5.7 Policy experiments

One of the main applications of the model is to analyse the potential impact of various changes in social policy on the country's Social Budget and its economic and fiscal environment. There are many parameters and assumptions in the status quo version of the model that reflect policy choices. A simulation of the effects of some policy proposals would mean changing these parameters and assumptions (such as the retirement age, replacement rates or adjustment mechanisms) in the model. In this section, we look at an example of such an analysis.

In the status quo projections, it is assumed that pension benefits will be adjusted in line with price increases. As in the basic scenario, it is assumed that real wages will increase beginning in 2001. The indexation of pensions in payment in line with prices will therefore mean that the ratio of the average pension to the average wage will continuously decrease. Under the basic scenario, average pensions would fall to close to 30 per cent of the average

Figure 9.19   Ukraine: Unemployment rate (after feedback)

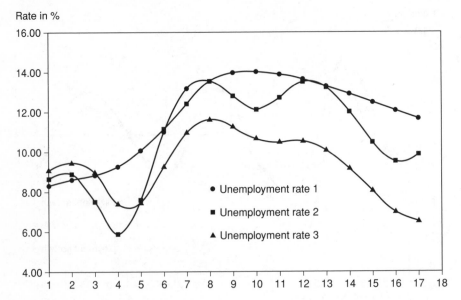

wage. It might be assumed that, in order to prevent such a fall, there would be a policy decision to change the indexation formula. There might be a full wage indexation introduced, or some mixture of price and wage indexation (pensions would be adjusted by a weighted average of the wage and price indices).

Let us check the impact of introducing full wage indexation of pensions beginning in the year 2000 (this would be a most costly solution). All other assumptions remain as in the basic economic scenario presented earlier. Figures 9.20–9.23 present the main results for three alternative scenarios. The first is a simple repetition of the basic scenario presented earlier. In the second, pensions in payment begin to be adjusted in line with average wages as of the year 2000. The third scenario is identical to the second, except that the feedback mechanisms have been activated.

In figure 9.20, we see that the optimistic outcome of the basic scenario with respect to falling expenditure disappears with the introduction of wage indexation. Pension expenditure as a percentage of GDP is no longer falling and even begins to increase, starting from the middle of the projection period. Pay-as-you-go (PAYG) contribution rates necessary to finance pension expenditure would have to be significantly increased, and would then fall to a much lower extent than in the basic scenario (figure 9.21). The level of labour costs would also be much higher than in the basic scenario (figure 9.22). Total social expenditure would decrease, but again to a lesser extent than in the basic scenario (figure 9.23).

Figure 9.20 Ukraine: Change of indexation – Pension expenditure (as a percentage of GDP)

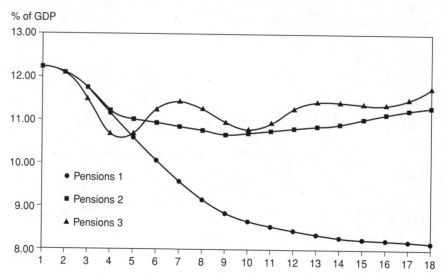

Figure 9.21 Ukraine: Change of indexation – PAYG contribution rate

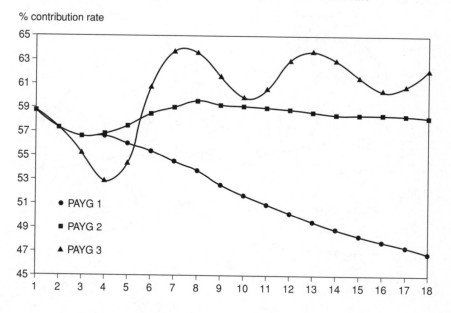

Figure 9.22   Ukraine: Change of indexation – Labour costs (as a percentage of GDP)

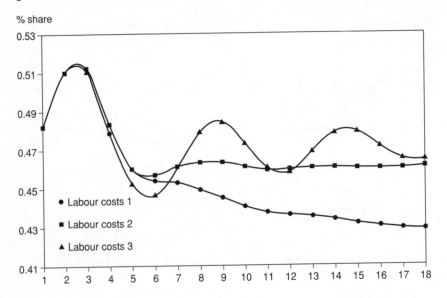

Figure 9.23   Ukraine: Change of indexation – Social expenditure (as a percentage of GDP)

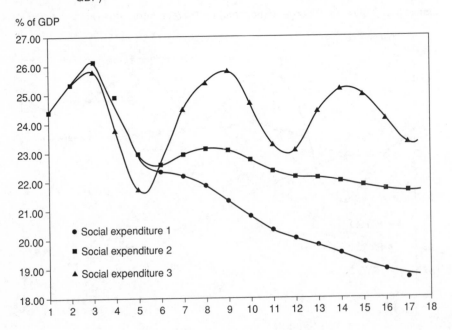

Figure 9.24   Ukraine: Pension expenditure – Effects of an increased retirement age

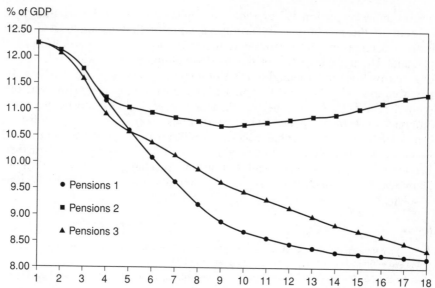

% of GDP

This example illustrates an important policy dilemma: how is it possible to keep pension benefits at adequate levels and at the same time hold the cost of pensions within affordable limits? The answer is obvious: it is not possible without significant changes in the current pension system. One unavoidable measure is to increase the retirement age. Another hypothetical scenario with a retirement age significantly higher than the present one would show that it allows pension levels to remain in a reasonable relationship to wages, while preventing an increase in total pension costs.

Figure 9.24 shows the results of such a simulation with respect to the share of pension expenditure in GDP (figure 9.24). The first scenario is the previously used basic scenario. The second includes indexation to wages beginning in 2000. The third scenario also includes wage indexation, but it contains higher assumed retirement ages as well – starting from 1998, the retirement age for both sexes is increased gradually to 65 at a rate of a one-year increase annually. Pension expenditure would be significantly lower than in the second scenario, although still higher than in the basic scenario. However, the decreasing trend in pension expenditure continues, as increasing the retirement age has long-lasting effects.

The results presented here should be treated as an example only, in order to illustrate the kind of policy options that may be analysed using the model. The detailed policy options that must be considered in creating a programme for the reform of the social protection system in Ukraine will almost certainly differ from the examples offered here.

9.2.6   Summing up

The example in section 9.2 presents an application of the Social Budgeting concept to the conditions of Ukraine, a country that is still in a difficult economic situation, and where many major economic and social reforms are pending. The main objective of this model-building exercise was to develop a quantitative tool to support the decision-making process in social policy. Its potential use for policy-makers could be demonstrated clearly. However, this is not the end of the development work. The model has to be firmly implemented into the Government's policy advisory structures: there is a need to establish an expert team in the Government which would not only use the present model version for policy analysis, but would also maintain and develop it further. Economic conditions and social legislation are changing quickly. Without maintenance and updating, this model – like any other – will soon become obsolete.

Notes

[1] At the time this book was written, no reliable information was available on any spillover effects of the Asian financial crisis on Panama's economy and labour market.

[2] Decree No. 394 on targeted cash benefits to low-income persons of June 1993, and joint Decree of 14 June 1993.

[3] The Ministry of Statistics is responsible for the statistical monitoring of the social assistance scheme, notably for in-kind and cash benefit payment activity.

[4] M. Rul et al. Phasing out subsidies for housing and communal services (Kyiv, Dec. 1994; mimeo).

[5] All figures show developments over an 18-year period, with 1998 shown as year 1 and 2015 shown as year 18.

PART V

GENERAL CONCLUSIONS

INTENDED MESSAGES **10**

The intention of this book is to convey several messages. Firstly, the financial analysis of any social protection system has to take into account the fact that it is embedded in a country's demographic and economic environment. The projection of the system's revenue and expenditure is meaningless if it is not based on underlying demographic and economic projections. Whoever wants to develop a view on the future of a national social protection system cannot avoid inventing a consistent view on the future development of the population to be covered and the underlying potential of the economy to support the system.

Secondly, social protection systems do not operate in isolation from fiscal and monetary systems. Many – if not most – social protection systems in the world are fiscally and legally intertwined with the government accounts. Planning a Social Budget is equivalent to planning parts of the government budget – and vice versa. Such planning also gives supplementary signals from the fiscal sphere to central banks as to whether monetary policy may be maintained or has to be changed – and, again, vice versa.

Thirdly, one of the most promising and reliable ways of planning social finances is to use a consistent model family that mathematically reflects the relevant physical and monetary links among the population, the economy and the social protection system. In order to do so, the modeller needs a methodologically consistent statistical data basis, as well as established and pragmatic modelling techniques. Therefore, much emphasis in this book has been placed on these issues. We are convinced that whoever analyses the data of a social protection system, puts them into a given methodological format, and then models the system will obtain a comprehensive understanding of its functioning in reality, both in general terms and in detail.

It is not the sender but the receiver who decides on the contents of a message. With this in mind, the authors have tried their best to formulate their views in as clear and as understandable a way as possible. The outcome is a textbook that is addressed not primarily to an academic readership but mainly to the experts in national administrations who are involved in the planning of public and/or more specifically – Social Budgets. This book is intended to contribute to improving governance in the field of social protection. Furthermore, in providing a tried and tested methodology for data compilation, it also contributes to enhancing the international comparability of social protection systems.

Social protection systems around the world are under scrutiny. In the developed world, where countries redistribute up to 35 per cent of GDP through social protection, the systems are accused of creating unemployment and insufficiently (no longer) reaching out to the poor. In the developing world, where countries often redistribute less than 10 per cent of GDP, the systems are said almost exclusively to support the relatively better off, binding resources that would better be channelled to the needy, and thus contributing to the widening of gaps in income inequality.

Whatever the conclusions drawn from this debate may be, the fiscal result will either be an increase, a stabilization or a downsizing of the present scope of systems in many cases accompanied by a reallocation of the resources within the given boundaries.

This book is a technical contribution to that debate. The authors, in their involvement with the analysis of social protection systems around the world, frequently observed that participants in the debate tended to focus on single aspects of (failure of) social protection or one of its branches only, taking the partial observation as an indicator for the whole. Reform proposals are also often discussed without comprehensive knowledge about how much they might cost in absolute terms, or in terms of reallocation of available resources, or without an understanding of the structure and size of the interrelations between different subsystems of the national social protection systems. A situation often looks different when embedded in a broader context. This is what this book tries to achieve; it aims to open the reader's eyes to the broader perspective *and*, simultaneously, to provide a set of tools that facilitate such a view in order to prepare for balanced reform decisions.

This book can help strengthen the argumentation of quantitative experts in social protection. The authors are aware of the fact that it represents another volume in an array of books on modelling. However, there are no modelling books focusing comprehensively on national social protection systems and, at the same time, based on vast analytical experience in many different countries around the world. Whether the objective of the book has been properly achieved, however, depends finally on its readers. The authors are eager to receive comments and constructive criticism. They are seeking a worldwide dialogue on the concept and techniques of social budgeting, which is long overdue.

ANNEXES

ISSUES BRIEF: INTERDEPENDENCIES BETWEEN MACROECONOMIC DEVELOPMENTS AND SOCIAL PROTECTION

Social Budgeting is modelling. Modelling is analysing the past and transforming the resulting insights into hypotheses about the future. Part II of this book has provided a variety of possibilities ("methods") on how the flow of funds of social protection systems can be systematically grouped in order to allow for rational historical analyses. Proposals on how to transform the analytical results into "modelling the future" were made in Part III (with two concrete applications explained in Part IV).

The fundamental hypothesis attributed to all parts of this book is that the development of social protection systems not only depends on the underlying macroeconomic developments but also, in turn, has impacts on economic development itself. It is this issue, the "interdependency" between the systems, on which we concentrate in this issues brief.

Social Budgeting is an element of social policy. Social policy means permanent public interaction between those taking decisions and those affected by them, whether directly (as beneficiaries) or indirectly (as enterprises). Policy proposals will be supported or challenged – often both at the same time but from different perspectives. Then, governments need analytical instruments that allow them to balance arguments and to stay on course.

Therefore, it is necessary to stake out the main areas of macroeconomic concern that might influence a country's social protection system, and vice versa. Preparing some economic background for modelling is the purpose of this issues brief. For a proper understanding, it might be helpful to note that we try to be as descriptive as possible, so as to avoid judgements as to whether a certain interdependency is "positive" or "negative" for social protection or the economy. We try also to take account of the fact that many seemingly obvious relations between economic and social finance developments depend on time and location. Established relations might change over time and from country to country. Only analysis of the past in concrete country cases can shed light on the most promising modelling approach.

Thus, in trying not to be limited to fruitless, possibly too narrow fixations, we keep the following paragraphs "open" in the sense that potential interdependencies are addressed but are not put in concrete terms. This has been left to Parts III and IV of the main body of the book.

It should also be noted that this issues brief is not a substitute for a full economic textbook. It mainly serves to sketch the main areas of interest for readers who are not familiar with social protection issues in a macroeconomic context. At the end of the book, we recommend some macroeconomic textbooks for further reading.

1. THE MACROECONOMIC FRAME

The interdependencies between the national economy, its structure and development, and the social protection system are manifold. On the one hand, it is mainly the level of national production and its dynamics that determine the amount of financial resources potentially available for social protection. On the other, the social protection system is not merely a mechanism of redistribution; the structure and development of its revenues and expenditures have numerous direct and indirect impacts on the current state and potential future development of the economy. Simply for analytical purposes, it is often helpful to separate both the economy and the social protection system. But this methodological requirement should not be misinterpreted. It is indispensable for analytical reasons, but in reality both systems together constitute a general equilibrium system in which interdependent economic and social activities involving countless transactions between different institutional units are carried out simultaneously, and within which feedback are continually taking place from one type of activity to another. In other words, in the following text, whenever the description of macroeconomic interdependencies is given a certain order (which is, of course, unavoidable), the sequence must not be misinterpreted as a "cause-result dependency" unless otherwise indicated.

In broad terms, the interdependencies between the economy and a social protection system might be presented as follows (Figure AI.1).[1]

Figure AI.1 Interdependencies[1] between the economy and a social protection system

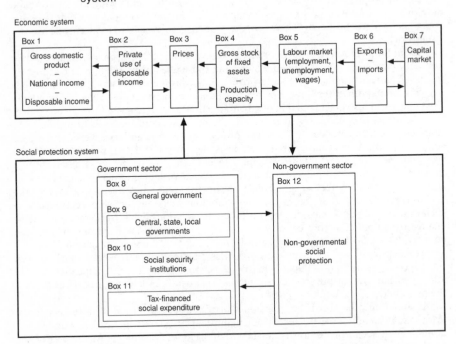

Note: [1] Arrows indicate the direction of interdependency.

The figure starts with a module indicating the production of GDP or, using a different point of view, the national income (box 1). National income is the aggregate income of the production factors, that is the sum of profits, interest and rental income, work income of the self-employed and labour income of dependent employment. After redistributive government activities (taxation, transfers), it is the source of the disposable income available to the different sectors of the economy, such as private households including non-profit institutions serving households (NPISHs), enterprises and government.[2]

Disposable income of private households is allocated between final consumption of goods and services and savings (box 2). In many countries, private household savings are one of the main financial sources for enterprise and government investments in fixed assets. Thus, in combination with household and government consumption, savings co-determine the expenditure structure of GDP.[3] In countries where the amount of private household savings is not sufficient to provide for the necessary investment resources, the other sectors of the economy have to help out: either enterprises have to refinance their investments internally to a high degree,[4] and/or the government sector has to run a primary budget surplus, and/or the country's capital account has to be negative.[5]

While the private use of disposable income determines to a large extent the demand side of an economy, the stock of fixed assets – and thus the economy's production capacity – shape the supply side. Prices (box 3) are usually influenced by demand and supply, although the impact of both sides of the market on price levels and price developments may differ with respect to its strength, depending on the particular situation.

Net investments, that is, gross investments minus depreciation (equals consumption of gross fixed assets) have a direct impact on the gross stock of fixed assets (box 4). Their level and quality (age structure), combined with employed labour,[6] determine the production capacity (which is not necessarily the actual production) of the economy.

The labour market (box 5) is of major importance for the analysis of social protection systems. Labour supply (equals that part of the total population which is either actually working or actively looking for employment) is determined by individual households' decisions, taking into account information on different economic and social factors (such as levels of wages, taxation, capital income and transfers, as well as individual preferences concerning leisure and consumption). The overall level and development of labour supply depend not only on demographic trends, the age and sex structure and the occupational qualifications of the population, but also on various other factors, including the effectiveness of the educational and the health system of the country. Labour demand (equals the number of gainful work places offered) is determined by firms' decisions and various other economic factors (such as unit labour costs relative to the costs of capital, where labour costs equal the level of wages plus other work-related payments – including contributions paid by employers to finance social protection benefits and services). Unemployment is the residual (balancing item) of labour supply and demand; it occurs when the number of those willing to work is higher than the number of those actually employed. It is mainly in the labour market that level and structure of wages are determined.[7]

The trade balance of a country (exports minus imports, box 6) is indirectly linked with its social protection system. Clearly, imports depend on aggregate demand directed to the rest of the world. It is the broadly based experience of countries all over the world that increasing national demand attracts higher imports. In many countries, the import elasticity of aggregate demand is even higher than 1, that is, imports of these countries grow faster over periods than national aggregate demand. There are examples of economies where expansionary social expenditure policies have resulted in a deterioration of the trade balance owing to imports growing faster than GDP. On the other hand, there are positive or negative impacts of social protection systems on the cost structure of enterprises and therefore on the international competitiveness of economies, but these are often overestimated. Thus, the state and development of a country's trade balance might be taken as one signal for determining a more expansionary or more cost-containing social policy.

Broadly speaking, a capital market (box 7) implies long-term financial assets.[8] It is in this market that the cost of capital is determined.[9] The direct and indirect interrelationships between a country's social protection system and its capital market may be manifold, depending on the financial design of the system. For example, if social protection incorporates a significant funded component, it may, depending on its size and structure, represent a major part of the continuous flow of resources to the national (and, in cases, international) capital market and, thus, influence the price (interest rate) for long-term capital. The system's revenues might then be heavily influenced by this same interest rate. On the other hand, if a system were in deficit, it might have to be subsidized through government transfers which, in turn, might have to be refinanced through the capital market. In case of insufficient capital supply, a crowding-out situation may occur, leading to increases in the level of interest rates, thus incurring additional expenditure to the government. Relative to labour costs (wages plus "overheads"), the price for capital might significantly contribute to shaping a country's production technology, as when the relative labour or capital intensity of national production influences labour market developments (employment levels, unemployment).

The general government (box 8) represents all activities of the central, state and local governments (box 9) plus those of the social security institutions (box 10). Depending on the actual institutional design, the social protection system may also comprise social expenditure financed from general revenue (box 11). Furthermore, non-governmental institutions paying (and financing) social benefits (enterprises, NPISHs, box 12) might exist and their transactions might be interrelated with the public sector.

2. GROSS DOMESTIC PRODUCT, DISPOSABLE INCOME AND PRIVATE CONSUMPTION

Gross domestic product (GDP) is the most commonly used macro measure for the level of output (income) produced by a country's economy in a given period.[10] It has to be understood that GDP is a *flow variable*, not a stock. In each given period, it has once again to be produced by combining a country's capital stock and labour force which, in economic terms, are both *stock variables*. The outcome of the production process is goods and services. The process is paralleled by the creation of income, the monetary equivalent of the goods and services produced. Its level and development is the only national source[11] available for the redistribution of income through the social protection system.

It has become practice to look at GDP from three different points of views, that is from the perspective of the economic sectors that produce GDP (the "supply side"), from the perspective of its allocation to different final expenditures (the "demand side": private and government consumption, investments, exports less imports), and from the perspective of its "primary distribution"[12] (the allocation of GDP to labour income, capital income and consumption of fixed capital *before* the impact of the government's redistributive measures). In the context of this book, we will focus primarily on the third perspective, GDP's primary distribution.[13]

Figure AI.2 Production of GDP, its use and primary distribution

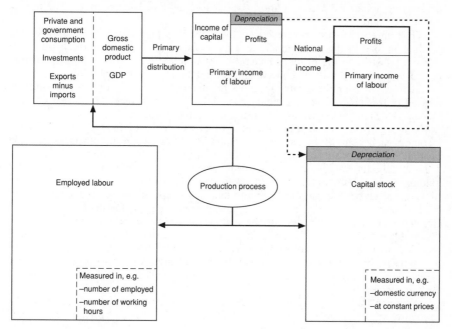

It is obvious that those who produce GDP should also receive the respective income equivalent; the production factor labour receives labour income and the production factor capital (the owners of fixed capital) receives capital income.[14] Before allocating primary income to the production factors, it is practice (just as it is usual practice in business accounting) to set aside "the costs of maintaining intact the stock of fixed assets used in production – that is, ... the costs of replacing assets used up in production".[15] To do so is reasonable, as the replacement of the used-up parts of the national stock of fixed assets is one important prerequisite for maintaining the economy's production potential. It might be worthwhile mentioning that no practice has developed in this context to take account explicitly of the costs of maintaining the production factor labour[16] "intact", which would represent an equivalent item to "consumption of fixed capital" (figure AI.2).

The primary income distribution and the expenditure structure of GDP are important for an evaluation of social protection revenue policies. If, as is typically the case, social security systems are predominantly financed out of labour income, then the labour income share in GDP provides a valuable first insight into the potential scope and limitations of the generosity of such a system. Countries with a low employee labour income share, say 25 to 30 per cent (as is, for instance, the case in Turkey),[17] can only afford a social protection system with a limited scope compared with those having a labour income share of, say, 70 per cent (which is the case in many OECD countries), unless the system is subsidized through general revenue or co-financed by earmarked taxes on capital income, for example.

Information on the expenditure structure of GDP is important for governments considering a shift from contribution (labour-income)-based financing to a more tax-financed design.

The primary incomes as produced by the economy do not normally remain with the production factors. The government and the social protection system (be it public or private) redistribute the primary incomes[18] for different purposes to different sectors of the economy by way of collecting income taxes, social contributions and other revenues, while using these same revenues for different outlays in the same period. As a result of this process, gross primary capital and labour incomes are turned into net incomes which might be increased by transfers received from the State, the social protection system or from abroad, and reduced by other transfers paid. In short, the disposable income of each sector of the economy is derived by adding all current transfers receivable by that sector and subtracting all current transfers payable by that same sector.[19] Theoretically, the households' disposable income may be interpreted "as the maximum amount that a household ... can afford to spend on consumption goods or services (during a given period) without having to finance its expenditures by reducing its cash, by disposing of other financial or non-financial assets or by increasing its liabilities."[20] But it should be recalled that in the context of macro accounting the concept of disposable income does not provide for information on single household or individual income distribution. Such information has to be derived from other sources. Still, on an aggregate basis the concept of disposable income gives valuable insight as to what extent aggregate consumption and savings are being "fuelled" out of different sources, such as social protection.

Although the concept of disposable income principally applies to all sectors of the economy, we are mainly interested here in the disposable income of private households, because the expenditures of a social protection system are, by definition, directed towards households. For example, a country's share of social benefits in total private households' disposable income might provide valuable insights for national as well as international comparisons.

The technical (accounting) terms of the different components of private households' disposable income are summarized in figure AI.3. First, the household sector receives all profits transferred by the enterprise sector. Profits that remain within enterprises, those which are not distributed, are not taken into account. The transferred profits are normally income taxable – the amount of income tax on profits has to be deducted from gross profits transferred to private households. Another important part of disposable income is the sum of net wages received by employees. Furthermore, social cash benefits received from the social protection system have to be added, as well as any other transfers received from the other sectors of the economy. As a result of international economic and financial interdependency, many households may also receive transfers from abroad ("rest of the world"). Such received transfers may, for example, be (net) profits or social benefits. In order to achieve a complete picture of the nationally available (net) disposable income, the following deductions are required: transfers are payable by the household sector to other sectors of the economy, for instance fines and penalties to be paid to the government or current (though voluntary) transfers paid to the NPISHs. And there might be (voluntary or compulsory) transfers payable to the rest of the world, for example, remittances of employed persons whose family members live abroad.[21]

The analysis of private households' disposable income is interesting, as the same absolute amount might have a very different structure depending on the design of the social protection system. For example, when there are income tax and social contribution

Figure AI.3   Private households' disposable income, consumption and savings

	Disposable income	Private
=	Profits transferred to private households	households'
minus	Taxes on transferred profits	consumption
plus	Net wages	
plus	Social cash benefits	
plus	Other received transfers	
plus	Transfers from the rest of the world	Private
minus	Other transfers payable	households' savings
minus	Transfers payable to the rest of the world	(residual)

```
┌──────────────────────────────┐
│        Capital market        │
├──────────────────────────────┤
│ • Supply of long-term financial │
│   assets for investment        │
│ • Demand for long-term financial │
│   assets                       │
│ • Interest rates (price for capital) │
└──────────────────────────────┘
```

rates, the share of net profits and net wages in disposable income may be relatively low, whereas the share of social benefits and other government transfers may be high. On the other hand, the same absolute amount of households' disposable income under a regime of low income tax and contribution rates may result in a high share of net profits and net wages in disposable income, and a low share of social benefits and other government transfers.[22] In the first case, the economic and social system may be characterized on a macro level as highly redistributive, whereas this would not apply in the second case. Such an analysis of the degree of redistribution might be useful for international comparisons, and also at the national level to support social policy and tax system reforms as well as other macroeconomic policy decisions.

Private households' disposable income reflects resources that are available for a *free choice* of goods and services. This is one reason why social transfers in kind are not included in the concept of disposable income but are considered part of government consumption (see section 8, "Government budget").

The residual of households' disposable income and private consumption (disposable income minus private consumption) represents households' aggregate savings. These may be positive or negative, depending on whether disposable income exceeds private consumption, or vice versa. When saving is positive, the unspent income must be used to acquire assets or reduce liabilities. To the extent that unspent income is not used deliberately to acquire financial or non-financial assets or to reduce liabilities, it must materialize as an increase in cash, itself a financial asset. If saving is negative, some assets must have been liquidated, cash balances run down or liabilities increased. Thus, the savings behaviour and savings capacity of private households directly affects the amount of resources available on the capital market (see section 7, "The capital market").

3. PRICES AND INFLATION

For many reasons, prices of goods and services and their movements constitute core areas to be considered when evaluating a country's social protection system and its interdependencies with the economy. The main analytical interest is focused on purchasers' (consumer) prices which, for simplicity, can be considered as constituting the sum of producers' prices and the costs of transportation and storage to make the goods and services available for the purchaser at the required time and place. Producers' prices are those which reflect the cost of production (labour and capital cost of production, including a profit component), and purchasers' prices are those which have to be paid by the final consumer.[23] Depending on legislation, the price levels of goods and services are usually also influenced by taxes payable and subsidies receivable on these units as a consequence of their production or sale (see also box on price indices, pp. 249–250).

The purchasing power of a given level of nominal social benefits depends on the level of consumer prices at the time when the benefit is paid. If prices increase due to *inflation* (measured, for example, by the CPI) while the benefit remains constant, its purchasing power decreases and vice versa.[24] Thus, the real income position of beneficiaries' households might be directly influenced by inflationary price movements, and the social protection system has to react accordingly in order to fulfil its income protection function. If, in an inflationary situation, this function can only be maintained through contribution and/or tax rate increases, the "financiers" of the protection system might be affected twice, first, through the inflation-induced real income loss and, second, by the inflation-induced tax rate increase.

Regular and/or ad hoc indexation of social benefits is one of the most commonly used measures in social protection systems in order to protect benefits against losses of purchasing power through inflation. Although inflation seems to follow a cyclical pattern, it has been reduced worldwide since the early 1970s and 1980s (figure AI.4).

Figure AI.4 Long-term development of the world inflation rate, 1961–97

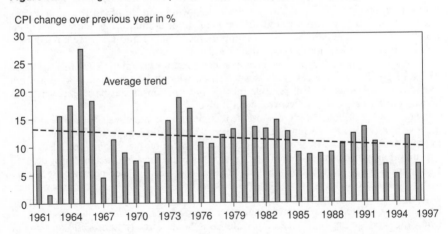

Source: World Bank.

Figure AI.5 Number of countries affected by hyperinflationary waves (with annual CPI inflation above 30 per cent and above 50 per cent)

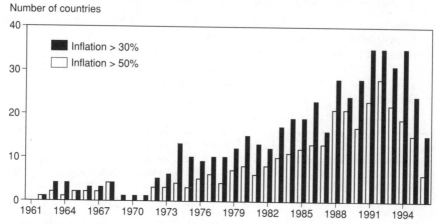

Source: World Bank and ILO.

Within this general trend, inflationary waves occur again and again on a regional or national basis, as in the Eastern European countries in transition at the beginning of the 1990s, in Bulgaria between 1996 and 1997, and in Southeast Asia between 1997 and 1998.

In fact, very much in contrast to the overall success in price stabilization, the last three to four decades of the twentieth century have seen a significantly growing number of countries suffering from hyperinflationary waves (figure AI.5) posing threats to their respective social protection systems.

In total, according to the available price statistics 83 different countries have, since the early 1960s, suffered from annual inflationary waves with CPI rates higher than 30 per cent (55 countries higher than 50 per cent). This is almost half the present member States of the International Labour Organization or the International Monetary Fund. In order to avoid misunderstandings, this is not to say that inflation is on average a worldwide growing problem (see figure AI.4) but that an increasing number of governments have to deal with the disastrous impacts of inflation on the operation of social protection systems – irrespective of the reasons that have led to the inflationary waves.[25]

Whenever such price waves occur, the purchasing power of social benefits paid is under threat – even if explicitly linked to (past) price developments – and any fiscal balance of social protection systems may then be destroyed because important fiscal system variables are formally linked to past price (or wage) developments. In general, any legally defined built-in formulae for the adjustment of system variables of social protection systems designed under the assumption of, at worst, moderate and non-volatile price developments tend to become obsolete in sudden inflationary periods if linked to past price (or wage) developments.

This is mainly caused by time-lag-induced problems of administration which stem from the time difference between the statistical information available on past price (or wage) developments and the minimum administrative procedures required to use that information for the adjustment of social protection system variables.[26]

Examples of such regular bound system variables are:

- lower/upper earnings limits which determine the range of income subject to contribution payments; these may be linked to past wage developments; or
- benefits in payment; these may be linked to past wage or price developments; or
- any other instrumental variable, such as legal minimum wage, which is used to steer automatically the finances of the system that may be linked to past wage or price developments.

In order to avoid such disturbances of social protection systems, a macroeconomic and monetary policy aiming at price stability or, at least, stable inflation rates[27] may be considered one of the most valuable "assets" of (indirect) social policy. Thus, it is important to note that it is not social protection systems that trigger off inflation – in general, their scope is just too small to expect any major inflationary impacts. It is normally the other way around: social protection systems are threatened by inflation. Still, it cannot be denied that social protection systems, if of a significant "minimum size", might well have some measurable, though moderate, impact on price levels and movement by affecting the economy's aggregate demand ("demand-pull effects") and/or by impacts on production costs ("cost-push effects"). Demand-pull effects might occur in a situation when benefits are being increased and, at the same time, the economy is operating near full-capacity utilization. Retailers might then try to increase sales profits. Equally, cost-push effects might occur through benefit-induced higher tax/contribution rates on labour income under conditions of lax monetary policy.

Although there are theoretical interdependencies between a social protection system and the general price level of an economy, their intensity has to be assessed in each country's individual case. While the impacts of the economy on the social protection system's finances – via employment, wages and prices – are obvious, the reverse impacts, that is, those of the protection system on the economy, are not always equally so. For example, an expansionary social policy might have both demand-pull and cost-push effects on an economy's price level, negatively influencing its international competitiveness. There is some empirical evidence, however, that the same policy might have adverse effects on the economy's exchange rate (in terms of currency devaluation), thus re-establishing international competitiveness. Also, a deflationary (cost-containment) social policy might, in a "first round", positively affect national price levels (reduce inflation or even reduce absolute price levels), and thus enhance international competitiveness. But the same policy might, by means of "second round" effects, be offset by a currency appreciation. This is to say that, although the financial regulations governing a social protection system might have impacts on an economy's competitiveness, these effects should not be overestimated or, rather, should be carefully assessed only in the concrete economic context. It is normally something other than social policy variables that most influence international competitiveness, for example labour productivity, the quality of goods, delivery in time, the quality and sustainability of services, exchange rates, and so on.

Furthermore, any price effects of social protection depend on the general rules and standards, and the intensity, governing a country's competition among market participants. If competition is high, any demand-pull and/or cost-push effects on prices would probably be only marginal.[28]

Price indices

A major prerequisite for the profound analysis of social protection systems in an economic context is the availability of price statistics. In a Social Budget context, consumer price statistics are of predominant importance. Statistical offices might regularly compile and publish:

- *cost-of-living indices* for different types of households for different social policy reasons and analytical purposes; and/or
- a *consumer price index* (CPI) based on national accounts; and
- values and structures of *consumer baskets* for different types of households for different social policy reasons and analytical purposes.

The actual choice as to which type of indices statistical offices prefer to calculate and publish would normally depend on a number of considerations (see below). Social protection legislation would then have to be based on the information provided, for example if the regular or ad hoc adjustments of benefits in payment were linked to price developments. With respect to such adjustment policies, it is important to understand the implications of different price measurement concepts. This is why some further thought is given to this issue.

The two most commonly used price indices are the *Laspeyres* and *Paasche* indices. Both may be defined as weighted averages of price relatives,[1] the weights being the values[2] of the individual goods and services in one or the other of the two periods compared in relation to the total value of all goods and services included.

While the Laspeyres index is defined as a weighted arithmetic average of the price relatives using the values of a base period as weights, the Paasche index is defined reciprocally to the Laspeyres index by using the values of a later period (i.e. not the base period) as weights and a harmonic average of the price relatives instead of an arithmetic average.[3]

The actual choice of either of the two indices is not especially important for the *practice of social budgeting,* but it is important to understand some of the theoretical implications of the indices for a proper interpretation of projection results, for example.

A comprehensive overview of the theoretical and practical implications of the two indices and their behaviour vis-à-vis each other is given in the *SNA 1993.*[4]

Empirically, Laspeyres indices tend to register larger increases over time than Paasche indices. It can be shown mathematically that this relationship holds whenever the price and quantity relatives (both weighted by values) are negatively correlated. Such negative correlation is to be expected and in fact observed in the vast majority of situations that are covered by index numbers, for instance for consumers who react to changes in prices by substituting goods and services that have become relatively less expensive for those that have become relatively more expensive.

In economic theory an index may be defined "as the ratio of the minimum expenditures required to enable a consumer to attain the same level of utility under the two sets of prices. It is equal to the amount by which the money income of a consumer needs to be changed in order to leave the consumer as well off as before the price changes occurred."[5] With respect to this approach to index numbers, it can be shown that the Laspeyres index provides an upper bound to the theoretic index, whereas the Paasche index provides a lower bound. Suppose, for example, the consumer's income were to be increased by the same proportion as the Laspeyres index (which may be practice, for instance, in old-age systems with respect to pensions in payment). It follows that the consumer must be able to buy the same quantities as in the base period and must therefore be at least as well off as before. However, by substituting products that have become relatively less expensive for ones that have become relatively more expensive, the consumer should be able to obtain a higher level of utility. This substitution is equivalent to setting up a negative correlation between price and quantity relatives. In other words, the consumer can thereby attain a higher level of utility and the Laspeyres must exceed the theoretic index.[6]

As the Laspeyres and the Paasche indices may be considered non-symmetric with respect to economic theory, attempts have been undertaken to overcome this deficiency by constructing "symmetric indices", a famous approach being Fisher's Ideal Index, defined as the geometric mean of the Laspeyres and the Paasche indices. Although the theoretical attributes of Fisher's Index are considered to be superior to the Laspeyres and Paasche indices, it does not play a major role in statistical offices' practice (as opposed to economic research), mainly for three reasons.[7] First, its advantage in terms of accuracy of measurement of price developments is not significant as long as the spread between the Laspeyres and the Paasche indices is not very great; in that case, Fisher's Index would measure some average development of Laspeyres and Paasche. Second, it is demanding in its data requirements, as both the Laspeyres and the Paasche indices have to be calculated, thereby not only increasing costs but also possibly leading to a delay in calculation and publication, which is especially relevant if price indices are published on a monthly basis in order to support policy decisions (monetary policy, social benefit adjustments, etc.). Third, this index is not as easy to understand as the Laspeyres and the Paasche indices.

Price statistics, including the underlying statistical data and concepts, provide important information for the administering of social protection systems. For example, they might serve as a basis for the application of poverty lines, the construction of consumer baskets for different types of households (which might be used for purposes of social assistance) and the indexation of poverty lines, benefits in payment and possibly other social protection variables.

[1] A price relative is defined as the ratio of the price of a specific product in a period t to the price of the same product in the base period. See SNA 1993, p. 382.
[2] Value is equal to the price per unit multiplied by the number of quantity units. ibid., p. 380.
[3] ibid., p. 382.
[4] ibid., pp. 383–384.
[5] ibid., p. 383.
[6] With respect to the Paasche index (lower bound to the theoretic index), the reasoning runs along the same lines as used for the Laspeyres index. ibid., p. 383.
[7] ibid., p. 384.

4. CAPITAL STOCK, PRODUCTION CAPACITY AND CAPACITY UTILIZATION

In this section we address aspects of the economic relations between an economy's capital stock and its social protection system. The notion "capital stock", which will be explained in some detail, should not be confused with the stock of financial assets. Some interdependencies between an economy's financial assets and social protection will be addressed in section 7 ("The capital market").

Here, the notion "capital stock" is used in the sense of the non-financial assets available for an economy's production process. Two different categories might be distinguished: produced and non-produced assets. They are regarded as "produced" if they come into existence as outputs from the production process and, accordingly, "non-produced" if they exist for reasons other than the production process.[29]

Produced assets consist of fixed assets, inventories and valuables. *Fixed assets* are defined as produced assets that are themselves used repeatedly, or continuously, in the production process over an extended period (for more than one year). They include the following types:

- tangible fixed assets, such as dwellings, other buildings and structures, machinery and equipment; and cultivated assets – trees, livestock – that are used to produce goods such as fruit, rubber, milk, etc.;
- intangible fixed assets, such as mapped mineral exploration, computer software, entertainment and literary or artistic originals (for example, original films, sound recordings, manuscripts, tapes and similar assets); and
- land.

Military equipment in terms of destructive weapons such as missiles, rockets, and bombs cannot be treated as fixed assets, because they are not in fact used in production.

Inventories consist mainly of stocks of outputs that are still held by the unit that produced them prior to their being processed further.

Valuables may be goods of considerable value that are not used primarily for production purposes or consumption but are held as stores of value over time, such as precious stones and metals, recognized works of art and antiques.

It is mainly an economy's fixed assets that act as the capital base for production. Its level and quality (measured, for instance, by its age structure), when combined with the employed labour force, determine the production capacity (not necessarily the actual production) of the economy. It is obvious that, given a certain level, structure and quality of the capital stock, an economy's output level (measured in terms of GDP) will depend on a number of prerequisites. For example, the skills of the employed labour force would have to meet the necessary requirements in order to make efficient use of the capital stock. A modern capital stock combined with an unskilled labour force would only lead to poor production results, and the same would hold true if an outdated capital stock were combined with a skilled labour force. This is why investments in the maintenance and modernization of the level, structure and quality of the national capital stock may be idle unless accompanied by matching investments in "human capital" and vice versa. In order to maximize an economy's output (GDP), both efforts have to come together.

However, the level and quality of the capital stock, together with adequately skilled labour, only determine the production potential of the economy (its capacity) at any given point of time. Actual production is determined by a number of further factors, mainly by aggregate (domestic plus external) demand. Social protection systems, as mentioned earlier, can have a crucial impact on domestic demand. In many countries, large parts of the social protection systems (for example, unemployment benefits) have been explicitly designed to play the role of so-called "automatic stabilizers". Such an anticyclical stabilizing role of social expenditure may be seen in figure AI.6. Examples of major driving forces behind the anticyclical development of the western German Social Budget are time lags in the benefit adjustment practice (as described in the previous section) and movements in the number of recipients of unemployment benefits.

Social protection systems may also play a role in maintaining and enhancing the production potential of a country directly or indirectly. Direct positive impacts on labour productivity are to be expected from effective rehabilitation and employment promotion measures, and from health protection and promotion. These fields of social policy aim at re-establishing, maintaining and/or improving individual work capacity – physically and mentally – either so intended (in case of rehabilitation and employment promotion) or as "windfall gains" to the economy (in case of health protection and

Figure AI.6   Anticyclical development of the western German Social Budget, 1961–97

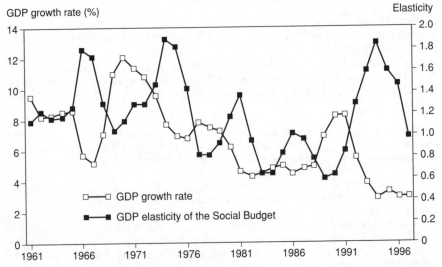

Note: The GDP elasticity of the Social Budget has been calculated for each year as the annual percentage change in total social expenditure over the annual percentage change in nominal GDP. For reasons of graphical presentation, both the GDP elasticity and the GDP growth rate have been smoothed by using a moving average of the order 3 (MA3).

promotion). Of course, the main role in improving the quality of labour is played by the educational system, but different social protection provisions often aim at facilitating or enhancing access to education at all levels.

Indirect impacts on the structure and quality of the capital stock are to be expected through the financing method of social protection. For example, if social protection were predominantly financed through levying contributions on labour income, then the imposed additional costs might cause businesses to invest in efficiency improvements of the employed capital, thus potentially reducing employment demand. The same effect might be expected if major parts of social protection were fully funded, as when benefits are paid out of the economy's return on capital (profits). Alternatively, if social protection were financed through other sources (such as indirect taxation), then induced lower labour costs might result in additional demand for labour.

5.   THE LABOUR MARKET

It is in the labour market where the decision is made as to how much labour is actually employed in an economy. Given the capital stock, this market simultaneously determines the amount of goods and services (GDP) produced, the nominal wages (the "price for labour") and, as a result, the real wages, which are nominal wages divided by the general price level.

In a Social Budget context, we are mainly interested in the average behaviour of aggregate labour supply and demand,[30] not so much in structural questions (flexibility, spread of wages, working conditions, etc.), although it might be important to understand these in specific circumstances, especially when considering interdependencies between disaggregate labour market developments and social protection legislation. In order to address such issues quantitatively, however, several distinguished labour market models would be needed. It would be necessary to investigate their respective inter-relationships, and the relationships between these sub-labour markets and specific social protection legislations, which is beyond the scope of this book.

Labour is not a commodity like any other, because it is (a service) provided by human beings. Thus, when analysing labour markets, it is not just economic and technical questions that have to be considered; social aspects are of equal importance. Still, with respect to the dominant macroeconomic focus of this book, it seems appropriate to perceive private households as pure economic actors ready to supply a certain amount of labour at a certain wage level and enterprises (employers) as being ready to demand a certain, presumably different, amount at that given wage.

The degree to which private households are prepared to participate in the labour market – to compete for jobs – depends on a number of variables. Under pure economic considerations, one of the most influential variables is the level of real wages, that is, the amount of goods and services which can be purchased per unit of nominal wage earned. Thus, the level of real wages depends on both prices for goods and services and nominal remuneration. The more units of goods the household can expect to buy, the more labour it will be prepared to offer. However, this probably only holds true up to a certain level of real wages; once this level has been surpassed, the household might change its behaviour and reduce its effective labour supply. Such potential behavioural changes might also be influenced by the availability of other sources of income. Furthermore, cultural aspects, education and individual expectations of future economic and political developments might also codetermine individual household decisions on labour market participation. When there is sufficient (statistical and other) information, these theoretical considerations might be used in order to explain the behaviour of the labour market participation rate by means of a model.

Labour demand is determined by the process of competition for workers between enterprises.[31] At a given level of real wages, labour demand will be positively correlated with the expected development of sales, that is, economic growth expectations; and, at a given level of sales, demand for labour will be higher if real wages are lower and vice versa. Apart from this most simple economic model, labour demand will in reality also depend on the technology used and on the level of qualification of labour supply; again, cultural aspects as well as political expectations might be highly influential on the hiring behaviour of enterprises.

The average labour income and the total amount paid are determined in the labour market. Paid total labour income plays a dominant and direct role in the financing of social protection systems, and very often a direct or indirect role in the design of social benefits; therefore, some considerations concerning its components are necessary. Usually, labour income is defined as presented in figure AI.7.

Labour income ("primary income of labour"; "total compensation of employees") has two main components:[32] (a) wages and salaries payable in cash or in kind; and (b) the value of the social security contributions (actual or imputed) payable by employers to social security systems or to privately funded social insurance systems to secure social benefits for their employees, or to cover unfunded social benefits (imputed contributions). Other employees' fringe benefits payable by the employer are also to be taken into account (see "Further labour costs" in figure AI.7).

Figure AI.7 The composition of primary labour income

Primary income of labour	minus	Employers' social security contributions • pensions insurance • unemployment insurance • employment accident insurance • other
	minus	Further labour costs • health care services expenditures • health care cash expenditures • cost of maternity care and benefits • other
	equals	Gross wages
	minus	Employees' social security contributions • pensions insurance • unemployment insurance • other
	minus	Employees' income tax
	equals	Net wages

Wages and salaries include the values of any social contributions, income taxes and so on payable by the employee, even if they are actually withheld by the employer for administrative convenience or other reasons and paid directly to social insurance systems or tax authorities, on behalf of the employee. Wages and salaries may be paid in various ways, including payments in kind as well as in cash. A comprehensive and detailed list of possible wage components can be found in *SNA 1993*.[33]

The sum of net wages is total labour income minus fringe benefits minus employers' contributions minus employees' contributions minus employees' income taxes. This amount is part of the private household sector's disposable income. Average net wages may be of major importance when assessing the appropriateness of the level(s) of income provided by the social protection system.

For an in-depth analysis as well as projections of the Social Budget, it is helpful to use average labour income (average wages) by the different categories of employees as represented in the labour market balance. The actual labour market balance should be designed so that it meets the structure of available statistical information on wages. This might sometimes be in conflict with the requirement to reconcile the labour market balance with the available categories of contributors (see Part III). In such cases estimations might be necessary.

6. EXPORTS AND IMPORTS

A country's international trade relations, and the related amounts and structure of flows of goods and services across borders, seem to have only limited common grounds with its social protection system. This is in contrast to the recurring World Trade Organization (WTO) negotiations which prove that governments, businesses and trade unions internationally attach more and more linkages to the two policy areas.

Different factors determine the extent to which the costs of social protection affect the price levels of traded goods and services. One such potential factor is the revenue structure of a country's Social Budget, as follows (other things being equal): the more social protection is financed out of (employers') social contributions levied on wages and less out of general taxation, such as turnover tax or value added tax (VAT), the higher the labour cost content of production will be at a given time. By contrast, a Social Budget being financed predominantly out of indirect taxation, such as VAT, might result in lower labour costs and thus in lower production costs. As exports are usually exempt from national VAT, a switch in the financing regime from contributions to VAT could lead to improved price competitiveness of domestic production in the world markets. Of course, this holds true only under the assumption that macroeconomic labour costs do react to different Social Budget financing structures, that is that labour costs are lower under a VAT-dominated regime of financing as compared to a contribution-dominated regime. There are reasons to assume that this will not be the case, because VAT is normally added to the national producer price level, thus increasing retail prices. Therefore, in order to avoid losses in purchasing power, it is to be expected that under a "VAT regime" wage levels would be increased accordingly. The extent to which this could happen depends on the prevailing national economic circumstances, especially the bargaining power of workers in wage negotiations.

Another essential factor influencing international competitiveness is labour productivity. Given a certain level of (nominal) labour costs (all other variables unchanged), actual price levels depend on the number of items produced per labour cost unit ("labour unit costs"). The higher labour productivity, the cheaper goods can be offered on the markets. Thus, whatever the national cost of social protection might be, if the cost level is accompanied by a sufficient labour (and capital) productivity level the country's exports will not be negatively affected.

The third major factor determining the price level of national products on world markets is the currency exchange rate. There is as yet no substantial research on the interlinks between exchange rate levels (movements) and social protection. But conventional economic wisdom suggests that (too) high social protection would result in a devaluation of a country's currency, because of its demand effects on the domestic and external markets. Thus, increasing social expenditure could result in fostering export performance. By contrast, (too) low social transfers might lead to a currency appreciation because it could contribute to excessively low domestic demand, thus hampering exports. Empirical evidence is unclear. Germany might be considered as a test case to check empirically whether its continuously high social expenditure ratio (since the 1970s close to 30 per cent of GDP)[34] has contributed to maintaining an average exchange rate position of its currency among the other leading world currencies, thus contributing to the country's continuous trade surplus. On the other hand, the 1997–98 financial and economic turbulence in East Asia proved that low social expenditure shares (and labour income shares) in GDP by no means guarantee stability or appreciation of exchange rate positions achieved. The virtual absence of social protection, if maintained over too long periods of time, might even contribute to currency devaluations.[35]

A country's *imports* depend on the level of domestic aggregate demand, which is the sum of private and government consumption, private and public investments, and exports. Other fundamental factors are also important, as whether a country pursues liberal trade policies or whether it introduces import restrictions or indirect barriers for certain types of goods and services. Again, the exchange rate – and the convertibility of the national currency – are of major importance.

Private household demand is principally directed towards goods and services irrespective of their origin, that is, of whether they have been produced nationally or abroad. The same holds true for investment goods purchased by enterprises and the government. In many cases, the production of export goods and services is only possible on the basis of imported goods and services that serve as necessary input to national production; in other words, there is normally a certain import content in exports.

Whether the relative consumer goods (investment goods) content in total imports is high or low depends on national macroeconomic policies. When demand for national investments in tangible assets can be satisfied out of national production, the import content of investment goods may be kept low and the consumer good content high. When the national investment industry is underdeveloped or uncompetitive, countries might wish to import investment goods and the consumer goods content of total imports will be relatively low.

Whatever the macroeconomic trade policies of a country might be, experience shows that there are normally direct *short-term* interdependencies between social expenditures and imports (of course, only as long as both social expenditures and imports are of any significance in relation to GDP). For example, when there are expansionary social policies[36] (especially when combined with expansionary wage policies), imports of consumer goods and services tend to increase, resulting in a deterioration of the trade balance, and probably also negatively affecting the exchange rate; such problems may become crucial if, as is the case in many countries, the import elasticity of aggregate demand is higher than 1, a situation where imports in these countries grow faster than national aggregate demand. Additional problems often occur when a deterioration of the exchange rate runs out of control and then has direct negative impacts on the domestic consumer price level. These are some of the main reasons why conflicts between national social policies, national investment strategies and, thus, trade policies might arise.[37] A Social Budget might serve as a tool for policy information that helps balance such possible conflicting national policies by means of finding "compromises" between income policies and other policy areas.

However, over the longer term empirical evidence does not support views that generously designed social protection provisions would prevent countries from successfully participating in world trade. By contrast, countries with generous social protection systems may be as successful in trading as countries with less generous systems. Compare, for example, the cases of Japan and Germany,[38] presented in figures AI.8 and AI.9.

Both countries maintained high trade balance surpluses at significantly differing social expenditure ratios, the Japanese ratio being only about half the level of Germany's.

At the same time, a low social expenditure ratio does not necessarily safeguard countries from running high long-term trade deficits; this is proved by the United States case as reflected in figure AI.10, where the social expenditure ratio was about the same as in Japan but accompanied by a persistent trade deficit.

In the long-term perspective, a country's structure and level of exports depend on its international marketing efforts, the quality of the goods and services delivered, investment strategies of national industries abroad, the degree that national production

Figure AI.8 Japan: Social expenditure ratio and trade balance, 1980–97

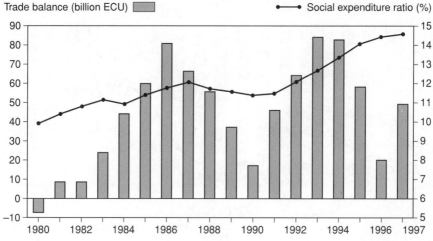

Source: 1980 to1985: OECD; 1996 and 1997: authors' estimates.

Figure AI.9 Germany: Social expenditure ratio and trade balance, 1980–97

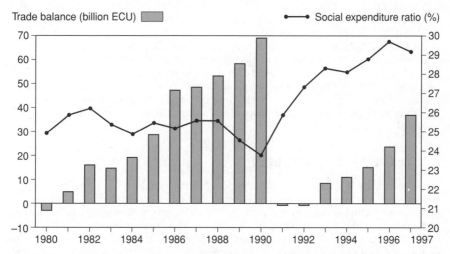

Note: Structural break in trade surplus and increase in social expenditure ratio in 1991 due to reunification.
Source: 1980 to1993: OECD; 1994 to 1997: authors' estimates based on national information.

matches the level and structure of international demand, and so on. Of course, the success or failure of export policies also depends on the prices of the goods and services offered, of which social protection is one cost component. The exchange rate of the national currency in relation to the currencies of the trading partners is the other

257

Figure AI.10   United States: Social expenditure ratio and trade balance, 1980–97

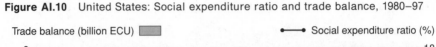

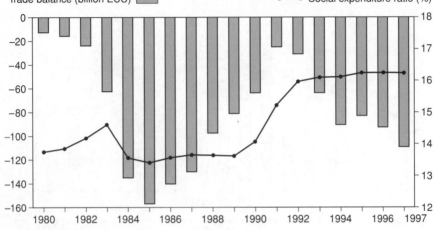

Source: 1980 to1995: OECD; 1996 and 1997: authors' estimates.

important factor determining success or failure in world markets. Both national production costs and the currency exchange rate are directly or indirectly influenced by national labour productivity, and national labour productivity in relation to international labour productivity.

All in all, under a Social Budgeting perspective, the possible (positive and/or negative) correlations between trade flows and social expenditures are mainly of a short-term macroeconomic nature. The level of social expenditures compared to GDP may indirectly co-determine a country's currency exchange rate, which in turn directly co-determines the levels of trade flows. Over the longer term, however, it seems that the trade position of countries in the world market is not affected by spending levels on social expenditures, but by other factors.

7.   THE CAPITAL MARKET

The capital market is the market for supply and demand of long-term financial assets.[39] It is in this market that the cost of capital (the interest rate) is determined.[40] The finances of social protection systems may directly or indirectly play a prominent role in national and international capital markets, depending on the system's design. Most obvious, partially or fully funded pension schemes may have a direct impact on the supply side of the capital market. In this case, social protection co-determines the structure and possibly the level[41] of funds supplied to the capital market. Furthermore, from a capital market point of view, it would make a difference if contributions to funded schemes were obligatory or voluntary. In the first case, the capital market could rely on a permanent inflow of comparatively cheap monies, whereas in the second the amount of inflow would depend on possibly varying savings behaviour of private households, the variations depending, inter alia, on the savings incentives coming from the capital market institutions. Such incentives might (or might not) stem from the investment products offered, the returns paid and the administration fees charged. If funded schemes have to wind up their reserves in order to meet benefit payments, the demand side of the capital market might be affected through enhanced competition for liquidity. Under such conditions, funds and other investors might find themselves competing for narrowing capital supply, unless the pension scheme's withdrawal from the capital market were replaced by other savings.

Accordingly, it might be argued that the *absence* of funding has impacts on capital markets. In that case, opportunity costs for capital market institutions might be considerably higher than in the case of obligatory contributions to a funded pension system. Occasionally, the introduction of funded pensions has been advocated for the purpose of increasing available risk capital for new business. Obviously, from the capital market's perspective, the existence of (compulsory) funded schemes is convenient, whereas it probably requires substantial efforts to attract the same supply of savings in the absence of obligatory funded schemes.

However, boosting capital markets is of course not the prime purpose of national social protection systems. A Social Budget, on its aggregate level, may serve as a tool for information as to how many resources the social protection system of a country provides to the national (and international) capital markets, or to what degree it draws on the capital market's resources if underfunded or in deficit.

8. GOVERNMENT BUDGET

A country's Social Budget typically has close links to the government budget. All items of the Social Budget paid on the own account of public bodies constitute part of the government consolidated budget. Those items which are paid by non-government institutions are not included in the consolidated budget.

In the framework of national accounts, the public sector comprises alternatively the revenues and expenditures of the following institutional units:[42]

Alternative 1:

- central government;
- state governments;
- local governments;
- social security institutions.

Alternative 2:

- central government plus social security institutions operating at the central government level;
- state governments plus social security institutions operating at the state government level;
- local governments plus social security institutions operating at the local government level.

With respect to *Alternative 1*, a typical blueprint structure of the public sector's accounts is designed as shown in the following sequence of five figures (AI.11–AI.15).

On the revenue side (upper half of figures AI.11 to AI.14), all government levels include *transfers received* from other government institutions, and on the expenditure side (lower half of figures AI.11 to AI.14) *transfers paid* to other government institutions.

Figure AI.11 General government accounts: Central government (blueprint)

Item	Year 1	Year 2	. . .	Year t	Year $t+1$	. . .	Year $t+n$
	National currency						
Revenue	Statistics				Projections		
Received capital income							
From enterprises							
From other government levels							
Received transfers							
Received current transfers							
Taxes							
Indirect taxes							
Direct taxes							
Imputed social security contributions							
Other current transfers							
Transfers received from other government levels							
Received transfers of wealth							
Other revenues							
Expenditure							
Interest payments on public debt							
Interest on national debt							
Interest on international debt							
Paid transfers							
Paid current transfers							
Subsidies							
Social benefits							
Other current transfers							
Transfers paid to other government levels							
Paid transfers of wealth							
Government consumption							
Net purchase of goods and services							
Gross wages and salaries							
Other consumption expenditures							
Gross investments							
Net lending/net borrowing (balance)							

These items have been explicitly included in order to explain the process of "consolidation" as follows: it is obvious that the sum of all transfers received by all government institutions must equal the sum of all transfers paid to all institutions during a given period, for example during one year.[43] "Consolidation" means to eliminate (deduct) these payments on the revenue side, as well as on the expenditure side of the public sector when summing up the revenues and expenditures of all government levels. The result is called the "consolidated government budget" (figure AI.15). In other words, when analysing the budgets of single government levels (institutions), the intergovernmental flows of funds have to be included, as they have impacts on the single institution's budget situation; but when the analytical interest switches to the revenues and expenditures of the overall government sector, these flows should be excluded.

Figure AI.12 General government accounts: State (provincial) governments (blueprint)

Item	Year 1	Year 2	...	Year t	Year $t+1$	...	Year $t+n$
	National currency						
Revenue	Statistics				Projections		
Received capital income							
From enterprises							
From other government levels							
Received transfers							
Received current transfers							
Taxes							
Indirect taxes							
Direct taxes							
Imputed social security contributions							
Other current transfers							
Transfers received from other government levels							
Received transfers of wealth							
Other revenues							
Expenditure							
Interest payments on public debt							
Interest on national debt							
Interest on international debt							
Paid transfers							
Paid current transfers							
Subsidies							
Social benefits							
Other current transfers							
Transfers paid to other government levels							
Paid transfers of wealth							
Government consumption							
Net purchase of goods and services							
Gross wages and salaries							
Other consumption expenditures							
Gross investments							
Net lending/net borrowing (balance)							

It is on the basis of this framework that the purpose of a Social Budget (in terms of accounting) becomes most obvious. It "extracts" all those revenues and expenditures from the public sector considered part of the country's social protection system, "adds" the financial flows of those parts of the social protection system which are not under the legal responsibility of public bodies (for example, under direct responsibility of private employers) and presents this information in a special format.

There are numerous financial links by definition between the social security institutions and the other government levels. The financial status of the social security institutions (at a given point of time or during a given period) directly co-determines the overall structure and fiscal situation of the government consolidated budget. If the social security

Figure AI.13 General government accounts: Consolidated local (municipality) governments (blueprint)

Item	Year 1	Year 2	. . .	Year t	Year t+1	. . .	Year t+n
				National currency			
Revenue			Statistics			Projections	
Received capital income							
From enterprises							
From other government levels							
Received transfers							
Received current transfers							
Taxes							
Indirect taxes							
Direct taxes							
Imputed social security contributions							
Other current transfers							
Transfers received from other government levels							
Received transfers of wealth							
Other revenues							
Expenditure							
Interest payments on public debt							
Interest on national debt							
Interest on international debt							
Paid transfers							
Paid current transfers							
Subsidies							
Social benefits							
Other current transfers							
Transfers paid to other government levels							
Paid transfers of wealth							
Government consumption							
Net purchase of goods and services							
Gross wages and salaries							
Other consumption expenditures							
Gross investments							
Net lending/net borrowing (balance)							

institutions are in surplus, they would add a positive contribution to the consolidated budget's balance; when there is a deficit, they would add a negative contribution. Surpluses or deficits might be of a "structural" (long-term) nature[44] or might be only temporary.[45]

Those parts of the social protection system not managed by public bodies may or may not be linked to the consolidated government budget. Normally, such links do exist through tax regulations. For example, non publicly managed social protection schemes might be favoured by tax exemptions, thus directly influencing the revenue side of the consolidated budget.

Figure AI.14 General government accounts: Consolidated social security institutions
(blueprint)

Item	Year 1	Year 2	...	Year t	Year $t+1$	...	Year $t+n$
	National currency						
Revenue	Statistics				Projections		
Received capital income							
From enterprises							
From other government levels							
Received transfers							
Received current transfers							
Taxes							
Indirect taxes							
Direct taxes							
Imputed social security contributions							
Other current transfers							
Transfers received from other government levels							
Received transfers of wealth							
Other revenues							
Expenditure							
Interest payments on public debt							
Interest on national debt							
Interest on international debt							
Paid transfers							
Paid current transfers							
Subsidies							
Social benefits							
Other current transfers							
Transfers paid to other government levels							
Paid transfers of wealth							
Government consumption							
Net purchase of goods and services							
Gross wages and salaries							
Other consumption expenditures							
Gross investments							
Net lending/net borrowing (balance)							

The analytical advantages of a Social Budget become most obvious in the context of short-, medium- and long-term projections and scenario calculations, that is, in the process of managing a country's public finances in macroeconomic and labour market terms. Possible future impacts and repercussions of a country's social protection system's finances on the overall public finances and on the economy may only be adequately analysed when combined with macroeconomic forecasts. In fact, this can only be achieved if the non-social-protection parts of the different government sector finances are as well projected. Otherwise, an interpretation of future social protection finances might lead only to partial analyses and wrong conclusions.

Figure AI.15 General government accounts: Consolidated (blueprint)

Item	Year 1	Year 2	. . .	Year t	Year $t+1$	. . .	Year $t+n$
	National currency						
Revenue	Statistics				Projections		
Received capital income							
From enterprises							
From other government levels							
Received transfers							
Received current transfers							
Taxes							
Indirect taxes							
Direct taxes							
Imputed social security contributions							
Other current transfers							
Received transfers of wealth							
Other revenues							
Expenditure							
Interest payments on public debt							
Interest on national debt							
Interest on international debt							
Paid transfers							
Paid current transfers							
Subsidies							
Social benefits							
Other current transfers							
Paid transfers of wealth							
Government consumption							
Net purchase of goods and services							
Gross wages and salaries							
Other consumption expenditures							
Gross investments							
Net lending/net borrowing (balance)							

9.   THE SOCIAL PROTECTION SYSTEM, ITS BUDGET AND THE ECONOMY: A SUMMARY

Depending on their specific design, social protection systems may turn over very large flows of funds. These flows depend on resources provided by the economy, but they may influence (positively or negatively) the market behaviour of all economic actors as well. Social protection systems depend on labour market developments, but there may also be repercussions. Such systems have an impact on the production process and on the demand for goods and services produced by the economy, whether they are new or matured systems, large or small in their financial scope, well or badly managed. Disposable income of private households, and their consumption and savings are equally affected. Interdependencies between social protection and price developments are obvious: the costs of production depend partially on the costs of social protection; the purchasing power of social benefits in payment depends directly on the level and development of consumer prices.

Social protection systems, to the convenience or disadvantage of actors in capital markets, co-determine the level and structure of an economy's capital stock and the extent to which it is utilized for production. They might influence countries' trade relations in the short term, but not so much in the long term. Depending on their prevailing design, they might positively or negatively influence capital markets and the developments of the price for capital (the interest rate). Social protection systems are directly interwoven with the fiscal performance of government budgets.

All this has been described to some extent in the present annex. The reader should keep in mind that this is not primarily a textbook on the economic foundations of social protection. Therefore, many issues that relate social protection to economic considerations, and vice versa, have had to be omitted.

Notes

[1] Definitions of the macroeconomic terms used in this chapter are closely related to the *SNA 1993*.

[2] Government transfers paid and received may also influence the income disposable to "the rest of the world"; here, to simplify, we disregard such interdependencies.

[3] From an expenditure point of view, GDP equals household consumption plus government consumption plus gross investment in fixed assets plus exports minus imports.

[4] By convention of the *SNA 1993*, corporations (enterprises) do not make final consumption expenditures, i.e. their disposable income is equal to their savings. See *SNA 1993*, p. 203.

[5] Capital imports have to be higher than capital exports.

[6] See explanations to box 5 in the following paragraph.

[7] Wages incorporate characteristics that clearly distinguish them from other (market) prices. This is why the term "wages" is being introduced here in the labour market context rather than in combination with box 3 (prices). In economic price theory, wages are sometimes regarded as the price for labour, labour being just one "commodity" among all the others.

[8] By convention, we distinguish the (long-term) capital market from the money market, which is the market for short-term capital. This distinction has sometimes been questioned in recent years, as the borderline between short-term money and long-term capital cannot always be easily drawn. See Norbert Kloten and Johann Heinrich von Stein (eds.): *Obst/Hintner – Geld-, Bank- und Börsenwesen, Ein Handbuch* [Money, banks and stock exchanges: A handbook]. *38.* (Stuttgart, C. E. Poeschel Verlag, 38th ed., 1988), p. 934.

[9] Frank J. Fabozzi and Franco Modigliani: *Capital markets: Institutions and instruments* (London, Prentice-Hall, 1992), p. 2.

[10] Other income concepts might be used instead, for example net domestic product, national income or others. For the purposes of explaining interdependencies between the economy and a Social Budget, the use of GDP has proved helpful.

[11] Theoretically, a country could do without its own production of GDP and, instead, tap the GDP of other countries. Up to a certain degree, this happens in reality via the trade relations between countries because, whenever a country's trade balance is negative (imports higher than exports), it taps the GDP of at least one other nation. But such a policy is not considered applicable and sustainable for most countries and, therefore, kept out of further consideration. See section 6, "Exports and imports".

[12] *SNA 1993*, pp. 157–182, 66–67.

[13] It should be noted that many countries fail to organize the statistical reporting system so that it shows GDP under the primary distribution and disposable income perspectives. Setting up a Social Budget database may help to improve statistical reporting systems in this respect. Without national accounts providing such information, an in-depth interpretation of the social protection system's finances will always remain of a preliminary nature.

[14] This term is equivalent to the term "operational surplus" as used in the *SNA 1993* instead of "profit", plus (parts of) "mixed income". See *SNA 1993*, pp. 11, 175.

[15] ibid, p. 11.

[16] Workers' recreational expenditures plus expenditure on occupational rehabilitation plus adult training expenditure might be taken as an estimate for the "consumption of labour".

[17] ILO: *Republic of Turkey: Social security and health insurance reform project. Social security*. Final report, (Geneva, March 1996).

[18] Gross incomes would equal net incomes only under a regime fully relying on indirect taxation (i.e. no income-tax collection).

[19] A more systematic explanation of the concept of "disposable income" and its links with economic theoretic concepts may be found in *SNA 1993*, p. 186.

[20] *SNA 1993*, p. 187.

[21] ibid, p. 200.

[22] This holds true as long as low income tax rates are not counterbalanced by accordingly high indirect tax rates (e.g. in a VAT regime).

[23] A more precise differentiation of price concepts is provided, for example, in *SNA 1993*, pp. 151–154. The notions "producers' prices" and "purchasers' prices" as used in this section are not exactly the same as defined in the *SNA 1993*. For example, the *SNA* allows for intermediate consumption at purchasers' prices.

[24] It is important to note that the CPI generally measures *inflation* only. In case prices increase only for reasons of quality improvements in consumer goods, for example, then the CPI does not change, i.e. "real value of benefit" calculations would show no change (constant benefit assumed) despite higher prices observed in the markets.

[25] It is left for further research to determine to what extent such price waves may have been triggered off by structural adjustment programmes, i.e. price liberalization without simultaneous implementation of proper competitive structures.

[26] Wolfgang Scholz and Anne Drouin: "Regular adjustment of financial parameters of social protection systems in volatile inflationary environments", in *International Social Security Review* (Geneva, ISSA), 1/98, pp. 47–71.

[27] Theoretically, prices are regarded as stable if the price index does not change over time (zero inflation rate); a stable inflation rate means positive inflation, the rate not changing.

[28] But the same competitive process may equally have an impact on the factor combination in the production process, i.e. on the relative use of capital and labour.

[29] *SNA 1993*, p. 218.

[30] Supply and demand of labour might be measured in numbers of persons, in time (hours), by skills or other systematic categories. Such information could also be differentiated by gender and/or types of employment and/or sectors of the economy, etc. In this book we pursue a pragmatic approach, i.e. we focus mainly on labour supply and demand in terms of numbers of persons. The authors' experience of cooperation with many governments proves that national statistical institutions are normally able to provide the most detailed, consistent and reliable labour market information in terms of numbers of persons.

[31] State demand for labour is being disregarded for reasons of simplicity; this does not affect the basic argument. Also, we limit our considerations to dependent employment.

[32] *SNA 1993*, p. 166.

[33] ibid., pp. 166–167.

[34] Rate based on national statistical methodology.

[35] It might be argued that inadequate social infrastructures contributed to the massive devaluations of that region's currencies, as such deficiencies revealed a fundamental weakness of past growth performance, unsustainable if not supplemented by major structural reforms, including improvements of the social protection infrastructure. cf. Wolfgang Scholz: "Economic crisis, employment and social protection – The case of Southeast Asia", in *ASIEN, Deutsche Zeitschrift für Politik, Wirtschaft und Kultur* (Hamburg, German Association for Asian Studies), No. 70, 1999, pp. 48–53.

[36] We say "expansionary social policy" if social expenditure growth exceeds the simultaneous growth of the national production potential (both either in real or in nominal terms).

[37] France, at the beginning of the 1980s, is an example of such a policy conflict. The attempt to pursue expansionary social expenditure policies resulted in a rapid deterioration of the trade balance and an exchange rate crisis. The case of Germany's reunification may serve as another illustrative example. After 1990 different macroeconomic impacts took place simultaneously: social expenditures grew faster than GDP, thus contributing

to accelerating imports and redirecting previous export streams to satisfy domestic demand for consumer and investment goods. Both effects simultaneously resulted in a short-term deterioration of the trade surplus. Only later was trade performance able to adjust to previous (pre-reunification) levels.

[38] The German case is taken as an example for the European Union, which complies with the same pattern, although less significantly.

[39] Kloten and von Stein, op. cit., p. 934.

[40] Fabozzi and Modigliani, op. cit., p. 2.

[41] Though whether pension funds co-determine the level of nationally and internationally available capital market resources is disputed in the literature.

[42] *SNA 1993*, p. 103.

[43] In practice, a standard problem of statistical offices in consolidating government accounts is that the cash flow reports received from different government levels do not match. For example, transfers reported to be paid in year t by the central government to the state level are not necessarily reported to be received by the state level in that same year. Such differences may occur because of delays caused by banking procedures or because of degrees of freedom permitted in the accounting provisions of different government levels. In order to overcome the related problems of consolidating the government accounts, it is normally assumed by statistical offices that paid transfers have been received by the addressed institution in that same period.

[44] For example, the United States social security surplus might be called structural, thus contributing positively to the consolidated government budget balance on a long-term basis.

[45] For example, the typically cyclical development of the German public health insurance balance temporarily contributes either positively or negatively to the consolidated government budget.

GLOSSARY OF THE NATIONAL ACCOUNTS DEFINITIONS[1]

Throughout this book, reference has been made to economic issues and repeatedly to the relation between social expenditure (revenue) and GDP. It is hoped that readers will have achieved a relatively clear methodological and conceptual view of "social expenditure". This may not be the case, however, for the macroeconomic concept of production (GDP), although "social expenditure" in social sciences as well as in politics is often related to this worldwide successfully established statistical construct. Therefore, this annex concentrates on only some of the basic definitions and concepts of measurement of GDP, and a few of its derivatives. Interested readers may refer to the *SNA 1993*, which is recommended to all those who would like to understand comprehensively the interdependencies between economies and social protection systems.

Those who do will realize that not all "economic" labels used in this book are actually identical with the ones used in the SNA. The following comparative listing of notions might help to understand the links of some of the labels used in this text to the ones used in the SNA:

In the text	*SNA*
Subsidies	Transfers
Private organizations	Non-profit organizations serving households (NPISHs)
Enterprises (sector)	Corporations
Government (sector)	General government
Private households	Households
Economic sector	Industry
Capital market	Financial market
Investment(s)	Capital formation
Capital income	Property income
Operational surplus	Operating surplus
GNP	GNI

Fixed capital   The value of a fixed asset to its owner at any point of time is determined by the present value of the future rentals that can be expected over its remaining service life. The sum of values of all economic fixed assets of an economy is called its fixed capital (capital stock). Fixed assets are entities over which ownership rights are enforced either individually or collectively, and from which economic benefits may be derived by their owners by holding or using them over a period of time. The level and quality of the fixed capital co-determines the level and quality of an economy's *output*. For more details see Annex I ("Issues brief"), section 4.

Consumption of fixed capital   Consumption of fixed capital is the value of previously created fixed assets used up in the production process as a result of physical deterioration, normal obsolescence or normal accidental damage. Thus, it is a cost of production. It is defined in a way that is theoretically appropriate and relevant for the purposes of economic analysis. Its value may deviate considerably from depreciation as recorded in business accounts or as allowed for taxation purposes, especially during periods of inflation. It is measured by the decrease, between the beginning and the end of the current accounting period, in the present value of the remaining sequence of rentals to be expected from a fixed asset. The extent of the decrease will be influenced not only by the amount by which the efficiency of the asset may have declined during the current period but also by the shortening of its service life and the rate at which its economic efficiency declines over its remaining service life. The actual calculation of the consumption of fixed capital requires that statisticians estimate the present value of the stock of fixed assets, the lifetime of various types of assets, patterns of depreciation, and so on.

Output   Output consists (only) of those goods and services produced within an establishment that become available for use outside that establishment. This includes output of goods and services produced for own final use (own-account agricultural production, own-account capital formation, etc.). The output of the whole economy is equal to the sum of the outputs of its establishments. Output is measured at *basic prices* or, if these are not available, at *producers' prices*.

Intermediate consumption (input)   Intermediate consumption consists of the value of the goods and services consumed as inputs by the process of production, excluding fixed assets whose consumption is recorded as *consumption of fixed capital*. The goods or services may be either transformed or used up by the production process. The input is measured at *purchasers' prices*.

Gross (net) value added   Gross value added is the difference between the value of *output* and the value of *intermediate consumption*. It is an unduplicated measure (avoiding "double counting") of output in which the values of the goods and services used as intermediate inputs are eliminated from the value of output. The production process itself can be described by a vector q of the quantities of goods and services intermediately consumed or produced in which the inputs carry a negative sign. By associating a price vector p with this quantity vector, gross value added is obtained as the inner product $p'q$ of the two vectors. Thus, from an accounting point of view, gross value added is essentially a balancing item, and there is no actual set of goods and services that can be identified with the gross value added of an individual producer, sector or industry. Net value added is defined as gross value added less *consumption of fixed capital*.

GDP   Gross domestic product (GDP) at *market prices* represents the final result of the production activity of resident producer units. GDP is a concept of value added. It is the sum of results of all resident producer units (institutional sectors/industries) plus that part of taxes, less subsidies, on products which is not included in the valuation of output. If *basic prices* are used for valuing output, GDP is equal to the sum of *gross* *value added* of all resident producer units plus all taxes on products (less subsidies). If *producers' prices* are used for valuing output, GDP is equal to the sum of gross value added of all resident producer units plus taxes and duties on imports (less import subsidies) and value added type taxes. Next, GDP is also equal to the sum of the final uses of goods and services (all uses except *intermediate consumption*) measured in *purchasers' prices*, less the value of imports of goods and services. Finally, GDP is also equal to the sum of *primary incomes* distributed or retained by resident producer units. GDP is not a measure of welfare but merely an indicator of overall production activity.

NDP Net domestic product (NDP) at *market prices* is obtained by deducting the *consumption of fixed capital* from GDP. Although, on a conceptual basis, it is more relevant for various types of economic analysis than GDP, this aggregate (NDP) is less often used in practice because of the statistical and methodological problems related to the estimation of the consumption of fixed capital.

GNP (GNI) *Primary incomes* generated in the production activity of resident producer units are distributed mostly to other resident institutional units; however, part of them may go to non-resident units. Symmetrically, some primary incomes generated abroad may go to resident units. This leads to the definition of gross national income (GNI; commonly denominated GNP (*SNA 1993*)). GNP (GNI) is equal to GDP less taxes (less subsidies) on production and imports, less compensation of employees and property income payable to the rest of the world plus the corresponding items receivable from the rest of the world. GNP (GNI) is not a concept of value added but of income.

Primary incomes Primary incomes are incomes that accrue to institutional units as a consequence of their involvement in processes of production or ownership of assets that may be needed for purposes of production. They are payable out of the value added created by production. The primary incomes that accrue by lending or renting assets to other units for use in production are described as property income. Receipts from taxes on production or imports are treated as primary incomes of governments. More concrete, primary incomes comprise: (a) compensation of employees receivable by households; (b) operating surplus, or mixed income, of enterprises; (c) interest, dividends and similar incomes receivable by the owners of financial assets; (d) rents receivable by owners of land leased to other units; and (e) taxes (less subsidies) on production or imports receivable (payable) by government units. For more details, especially on employees' compensation, see Annex I ("Issues brief"), sections 2 and 5.

Basic prices The basic price is the amount receivable by the producer from the purchaser for a unit of goods or services produced as output minus any tax payable, and plus any subsidy receivable, on that unit as a consequence of its production or sale. It excludes any transport charges invoiced separately by the producer. The basic price measures the amount retained by the producer and is, therefore, the price most relevant for the producer's decision making. It is this price definition which requires adding taxes (less subsidies) to measured value added in order to achieve the correct market price level of GDP (see *GDP*).

Producers' prices The producer's price is the amount receivable by the producer from the purchaser for a unit of goods or services produced as output minus any value added tax (VAT), or similar deductible tax, invoiced to the purchaser. It excludes any transport charges invoiced separately by the producer.

Purchasers' prices   The purchaser's price is the amount paid by the purchaser, excluding any deductible VAT or similar deductible tax. It includes any transport charges paid separately by the purchaser to take delivery at the required time and place.

Market prices   Market prices are the current prices observed in the economy. The amounts charged by non-market producers (public services) may not be economically significant. Such prices are not used to value the output sold at such prices. Instead, such output is valued by its costs of production. This remark refers, mutatis mutandis, also to the concepts of *basic prices* and *producers' prices*.

Note

[1] All the definitions are either direct quotations or are equivalent to the explanations given in the *SNA 1993*. As this information is taken from different parts of the *SNA 1993*, we do not give explicit citations here. For a full understanding of national accounts, the reader should refer to that publication.

GLOSSARY OF THE SOCIAL ACCOUNTING SYSTEM

1. REVENUES BY LEGAL CATEGORY

The notion "legal category" is used to stress that the relevance of revenues subsumed under this categorization and the cause of their payment are normally stipulated by legislation (as opposed to the revenue categorization by sector of the economy, which primarily – but not solely – addresses a sectoral view irrespective of legal definitions; see below).

In a disaggregated breakdown of the Social Budget, revenues by legal category might be presented by each sector of the economy separately (see section 2, "Revenues by sector of the economy").

Social contributions   Social contributions comprise actual contributions paid in order to acquire rights to social protection benefits and imputed contributions.

Actual contributions are paid by the insured population and by employers on behalf of the insured population. Contributions paid by the insured population are paid by employees, self-employed persons, recipients of social benefits and other persons, and by social or other institutions in lieu of the recipients of social benefits. Employees' contributions comprise all contributions paid either directly by themselves or by employers in lieu of their employees according to legislation (deductions from individual gross wages). Contributions paid by self-employed persons comprise all contributions paid on their own account. Contributions paid by recipients of social benefits include all contributions deducted from their respective individual gross benefits, for example contributions paid by pensioners or recipients of unemployment benefits. Other persons' contributions include all contributions paid by those who are not social protection beneficiaries and who are not included in the labour force, for example contributions paid by homemakers or students. Social institutions' contributions paid in lieu of their respective beneficiaries comprise contributions paid "on top" of individual gross social benefits in order to maintain or to acquire rights to (other) social benefits, for example contributions paid by unemployment insurance for unemployed persons to pension insurance.[1]

Imputed contributions are non-actual, thus "notional" employers' contributions are included in a Social Budget in order to balance benefits directly received by employees and other qualifying persons from their present or former employers. These contributions might either be set equal to the actual amount of benefits paid or, when an equivalent contributory system exists, be estimated on the basis of the provisions of that contributory system.[2]

Received current transfers (subsidies)   "A transfer is defined as a transaction in which one institutional unit provides a good, service or asset to another unit without receiving from the latter any good, service or asset in return as counterpart. A cash transfer consists of the payment of currency or transferable deposit by one unit to another without any counterpart."[3] Under this item we subsume cash transfers received by the social protection system from general government institutions – public institutions "outside" the social protection system (inter-system transfers). First, we distinguish current (cash) transfers paid by the different levels of government to the social protection system and, second, current (cash) transfers paid by other sources to the social protection system. The "other sources" are part of "general government".

Received current transfers do not include transfers of funds committed to finance the social protection system's gross fixed capital formation, such transfers being treated as capital transfers[4] (included in *Other revenues*).

Other revenues   These include government transfers of funds committed to finance gross fixed capital formation of the social protection system, returns on financial investments, fines and others.

Transfers received from other institutions   This item includes all received current transfers of an SAS institution from the other institutions included in the same SAS (intra-system transfers). These payments affect the balance of each single institution (where applicable). On a consolidated level (aggregate SAS), transfers from other institutions received and transfers to other institutions paid are equal, and therefore their effect on the consolidated balance is equal to zero.

2.   REVENUES BY SECTOR OF THE ECONOMY

This is a presentation of the Social Budget showing the funds of each (mutually exclusive) sector of the economy[5] that flow into the social protection system. The sectors of the economy as distinguished in the Social Budget are enterprises (including public enterprises), general government (according to the *SNA 1993*, federal level, provincial level, local level, social security institutions), non-profit institutions serving households (NPISHs), private households and the "rest of the world". The enterprises sector, general government, NPISHs and private households comprise all institutional units that are resident in the economy; the sector "rest of the world" comprises units that are resident abroad. A Social Budget does not require accounts to be compiled in respect of flows of funds taking place in the rest of the world, but all flows of funds between resident and non-resident units have to be recorded in order to obtain a complete accounting for the resident units.

In a disaggregated breakdown of the Social Budget, the revenues by sector of the economy might, for each sector, be presented by their legal categorization, principally contributions, received current transfers and other revenues separately (see section 1, "Revenues by legal category").

Enterprises   The Social Budget reports all funds (contributions, received current transfers, other revenues) flowing from the enterprises sector to the social protection system.

The enterprises sector comprises all resident non-financial and financial corporations and quasi-corporations. In practice, they make up most of the sector. In addition, it includes non-profit institutions (NPIs) engaged in the market production of goods (for example, hospitals or schools that charge fees that enable them to recover their current production costs), or in market production of financial services (for example, insurance), including those financed by subscriptions from enterprises whose role is to promote and serve the interests of those enterprises. For example, the enterprises sector's flows of funds into the Social Budget could comprise the actual and imputed employers' contributions for all employees working in this sector, current transfers from public and private enterprises and investment returns, fees, charges, and so on (other revenues by legal category).

Received transfers from other intra Social Budget institutions would not be recorded as, by definition, the Social Budget's institutions are regarded as separate from this sector.

General government   The Social Budget reports all funds (contributions, received current transfers, other revenues) flowing from the general government sector to the social protection system. "The general government sector consists mainly of central, state and local government units together with social security funds imposed and controlled by those units. In addition, it includes NPIs engaged in non-market production that are controlled and mainly financed by government units or social security funds."[6]

For example, the general government sector's flows of funds into the social protection system could comprise the actual contributions of the employees working in this sector, current transfers from the different government levels and other revenues by legal category. Received transfers from other intra-SAS institutions would not be recorded.

Non-profit institutions serving households (NPISHs)   The Social Budget reports all funds (contributions, received current transfers, other revenues) flowing from the NPISH sector to the social protection system.

"The non-profit institutions serving households sector consists of all resident NPIs, except those controlled and mainly financed by government, that provide non-market goods or services to households."[7] They do not include NPIs engaged in market production of goods and services (included in the enterprises sector).

For example, the NPISH sector's flows of funds into the Social Budget could comprise the actual and imputed employers' contributions for all employees working in this sector and other revenues by legal category. Received transfers from other intra Social Budget institutions would not be recorded as, by definition, the Social Budget's institutions are regarded as separate from this sector.

Private households   The Social Budget reports all funds (contributions, received current transfers, other revenues) flowing from the private households sector to the social protection system.

"The households sector consists of all resident households. These include institutional households made up of persons staying in hospitals, retirement homes, convents, prisons, etc. for long periods of time."[8] They do not include NPIs engaged in market production of goods and services (included in the enterprises sector).

For example, the private households sector's flows of funds into the Social Budget could comprise the actual employees' contributions, the contributions paid by self-employed persons, the contributions paid by other persons (including the contributions paid by social security institutions or other institutions in lieu of recipients of social benefits), the employers' actual and imputed contributions for all employees working in this sector, and other revenues by legal category. Received transfers from other intra Social Budget institutions would not be recorded as, by definition, the Social Budget's institutions are regarded as separate from this sector.

Rest of the world   The Social Budget reports all funds (contributions, received current transfers, other revenues) flowing from the rest of the world to the social protection system. For example, the flows stemming from the rest of the world could comprise employees' and employers' contributions for employees residing abroad ("non-resident units"), but who are cross-border commuting to the economy on a short-term basis. Also, bilateral or international donations, grants, transfers, and so on would be recorded under this heading.

3.   EXPENDITURES BY ECONOMIC CATEGORY

The notion "economic category" is used in order to stress the predominantly economic perspective under which potential users of a Social Budget might consider its information on expenditures under this categorization (as opposed to the expenditure categorization by function, which primarily addresses the broad social purpose of a Social Budget's outlays (see below).

Income replacements   Under this heading a Social Budget reports all cash benefits paid in order to replace a loss of current (wage) income. Payments are recorded gross, and include all amounts of contributions or taxes, if any, that might be deducted from the individual gross benefit by the individual recipient, or that might be paid "on top" of the gross individual benefit by an institution. It also includes indirect expenditures, that is, tax reductions for social reasons or reductions of interest rates for social reasons. The sum of income replacements and reimbursements (see *Reimbursements*, below) corresponds to the "social (cash) benefits" as used in the national accounts (with the exception that national accounts do not record indirect benefits).

Reimbursements   This comprises the costs of goods and services bought by entitled households or single persons to the extent that these costs are reimbursed through the social protection system.

In the *SNA 1993* these benefits are classified as "social benefits in kind" based on the following reasoning.[9] Social transfers in kind:

> consist of individual goods and services provided as transfers in kind to individual households by government units (...) and NPISHs, whether purchased on the market or produced as non-market output by government units or NPISHs.... Social security benefits in kind are subdivided into two types: those where beneficiary households actually purchase the goods or services themselves and are then reimbursed, and those where the relevant services are provided directly to the beneficiaries....
>
> The reimbursement by social security funds of approved expenditures made by households on specified goods or services is a form of social benefit in kind. Examples of expenditure that may be reimbursable are expenditures on medicines, medical or dental treatments, hospital bills, optometrists' bills, etc.
>
> When a household purchases a good or service for which it is subsequently reimbursed, in part or in whole, by a social security fund, the household can be regarded as if it were an agent

acting on behalf of the social security fund. In effect, the household provides a short-term credit to the social security fund that is liquidated as soon as the household is reimbursed. The amount of the expenditure reimbursed is recorded as being incurred directly by the social security fund at the time the household makes the purchase, while the only expenditure recorded for the household is the difference, if any, between the purchaser's price paid and the amount reimbursed. Thus, the amount of the expenditure reimbursed is not treated as a current transfer in cash from the social security fund to households.

Goods and services   The term "goods and services" reflects the monetary equivalent of goods and services in kind delivered to households directly by the Social Budget's institutions or through "third parties" (doctors, pharmacies, hospitals, etc.).

In the *SNA 1993* in-kind benefits are described as follows:[10]

These consist of individual goods and services provided as transfers in kind to individual households by government units (including social security funds) and NPISHs, whether purchased on the market or produced as non-market output by government units or NPISHs. They may be financed out of taxation, other government income or social security contributions, or out of donations and property income in the case of NPISHs. If it is not possible to segregate the accounts of social security funds from those of other subsectors of government, it may not be possible to divide social benefits into those provided by social security and others. Social security benefits in kind are subdivided into two types: those where beneficiary households actually purchase the goods or services themselves and are then reimbursed and those where the relevant services are provided directly to the beneficiaries....

The number and type of social transfers in kind provided to households by government units reflect their general economic and social policy concerns. While the recipients of current cash transfers may dispose of them as they wish, the recipients of social transfers in kind have little or no choice.

General services   These reflect the monetary equivalent of all services provided by the social protection system's institutions to the covered population which cannot be attributed to individual beneficiaries. General services are subdivided into administration, measures and grants. In the *SNA 1993* terminology, these expenditures may be cash benefits or benefits in kind.

Administration   "Administration" reports all expenditures of the Social Budget's institutions that are necessary to meet its obligations, and to maintain and improve the service standards of the social protection system. It includes the social protection institutions' staff remuneration, all costs related to self-governing bodies, investments in tangible assets, and so on. These expenditures are classified as "benefits", without which the social protection system would fail to work. The amount of administration expenditures is no indicator of the administration's quality. Administration costs are regarded as benefits in kind.

Measures   These are advisory, supervisory and/or supportive services provided by the social protection system's institutions which are not part of "normal" administration, and which cannot be attributed to individual beneficiaries. In terms of the *SNA 1993* these expenditures are benefits in kind.

Grants   These are transfers to "third parties" that are not included in the set of the SAS institutions, for example transfers or subsidies paid by social protection institutions to private institutions with social functions in the field of social assistance. In terms of the *SNA 1993* these expenditures may be treated as cash benefits.

Transfers paid to other institutions   These include all current transfers of a Social Budget institution as paid to the other institutions included in the Social Budget (intra-system transfers). They affect the balance of each Social Budget's single institution (where applicable). On a consolidated level (aggregate Social Budget), transfers to other institutions paid and transfers from other institutions received are equal, so their effect on the consolidated Social Budget's balance is equal to zero.

4.   EXPENDITURES BY SOCIAL FUNCTION[11]

Old age   This function covers all institutions' benefits payable to persons who have attained a specified standard retirement age, as defined by the statutes of the scheme or by national law, following which insured active persons cease normal covered employment. Benefit payments to persons who took advantage of early retirement provisions or who continued to work after reaching the legal retirement are included. In most countries the standard retirement age is between 55 and 65 years of age; for example, in Switzerland it is currently 65 for men and 62 for women. The administrative expenditures related to the expenditures under this function are also included.

Examples of benefits included are:

- periodic family allowances for dependants paid to beneficiaries of old-age pensions;
- disability benefits paid to beneficiaries who have reached the legal age of retirement of the scheme, even though in certain schemes they continue to be recorded under the invalidity function (as in Trinidad and Tobago);
- partial retirement pensions which are to be included under either the normal retirement pension or the early retirement pension;
- special old-age benefits provided to public employees through special schemes.

Examples of benefits not included are:

- programmes of early retirement for labour market reasons which are classified under the unemployment function, and programmes of early retirement for health reasons which are classified under the invalidity function. Expenditures on benefits of both programmes should be recorded under "old age" once the beneficiary has reached the legal retirement age;
- medical benefits to retired persons, which are recorded under the sickness and health function;
- allowances for assistance in subsidizing rent, not specifically related to the retired status of the beneficiary, which are recorded under the housing function.

Survivors   This covers benefits paid to survivors (widows, widowers, orphans) of a protected person of an age up to the legal retirement age, and arising from the death of a protected person. The administrative costs related to the expenditures under this function are also included.

Examples of benefits included are:

- periodic family allowances for dependants paid to beneficiaries of survivors' pensions;
- pensions paid to disabled orphans beyond the prescribed age for receipt of orphans' pensions;
- funeral benefits.

Examples of benefits not included are:

- medical care offered to survivors, which should be recorded under the "sickness and health" function;
- any survivors' benefits paid to persons of legal retirement age and over, which should be recorded under "old age".

Prevention This includes all institutions' benefits paid to eligible persons aiming at the prevention of diseases, work accidents, occupational diseases, and occupational and general disability. Rehabilitation provided through medical care to disabled/ invalid persons is recorded (usually benefits in kind). The administration costs related to "prevention and rehabilitation" expenditures are reported under this function.

Sickness This covers any benefit provided "with a view to maintaining, restoring or improving the health of the person protected and his ability to work and to attend to his personal needs" (ILO Medical Care and Sickness Benefits Convention, 1969 (No. 130), article 9). It includes benefits paid for the loss of earnings due to absence from work necessitated by an acute condition due to disease or injury requiring medical treatment or supervision (ILO Income Security Recommendation, 1944 (No. 167), article 9).

Examples of benefits included are:

- continued salaries and wages paid to employees during periods of inability to work;
- periodic family allowances for dependants paid to beneficiaries of sickness benefits;
- sick leave taken by parents during illness of a child/dependant;
- prosthetic and orthopaedic appliances which are to be recorded either under outpatient or inpatient care, depending on the type of service under which they were provided;
- medical care provided to beneficiaries of old-age, invalidity, survivors' and unemployment benefits, which are all included under this function;
- all public health campaigns which provide medical care and medical support.

Examples of benefits not included are:

- reimbursement of health care costs of the poor, which is included under the social assistance function;
- health care related to work injury, which is recorded under the employment injury function;
- sickness benefit for a single illness, which is generally paid for a limited period of time (e.g. for a maximum of 52–78 weeks in Mexico). Following this maximum prescribed period, if the disability/sickness continues and invalidity benefits are paid, these should then be registered under the invalidity function.

Work injury and occupational diseases This covers any benefit paid by a work injury programme for work-related injury, disease, incapacity and death of a protected person. It also covers the injury, disease, incapacity and death of a protected person if it occurs following the cessation of the employment which caused the state. The administration costs related to "work injury and occupational diseases" expenditures are reported under this function.

Invalidity   This covers any benefit arising from the partial or total inability of protected person to participate in gainful employment because of a non-occupational chronic condition owing to disease or injury, or by reason of the loss of a limb or one of its functions. The administration costs related to "invalidity" expenditures are reported under this function.

Examples of benefits included are:

- benefits provided by programmes of early retirement due to invalidity;
- periodic family allowances for dependants paid to beneficiaries of invalidity pensions.

Examples of benefits not included are:

- benefits paid to invalid orphans (even if they continue beyond the prescribed age for receipt of an orphans' pension), which are to be recorded under the survivors' function;
- partial or total invalidity arising from work-related causes, which is recorded under the work injury function;
- medical care (prosthesis and medical rehabilitation), which are registered under the sickness and health function;
- pension payments to recipients of invalidity benefits on attaining the standard retirement age, which are to be recorded under the old-age function.

Children and youth   This covers benefits provided to families in order to meet the costs and needs related to child-raising. Generally these benefits are provided for children up to a certain age limit (usually linked to the compulsory school-leaving age or the age at which higher studies are completed). Furthermore, in many countries no age limit is set for family benefits provided for the support of a handicapped child. The administration costs related to "children and youth" expenditures are reported under this function.

Examples of benefits included are:

- periodical child benefits, child-raising allowances;
- the cost of kindergartens;
- payments and measures under public youth assistance schemes (the costs of youth-related social programmes, street workers and youth-related anti-drug programmes, etc.);
- any paternal benefit paid to a father who stays at home to look after an infant child;
- birth grants and nursing allowances paid at the time of childbirth.

Examples of benefits not included are:

- family allowances provided to recipients of benefits under the old-age, invalidity, survivors', employment injury, sickness and health, and unemployment functions, which are to be recorded under their respective function;
- health care services provided during maternity, which are to be included under the sickness and health function;
- allowances for assistance in subsidizing rent or accommodation linked to helping families support the costs of housing, which are recorded under the housing function;
- services provided towards family planning, which are to be recorded under the sickness and health function;

- sick leave taken by a protected person during the illness of a child/dependant, which is to be recorded under the sickness and health function.

Maternity   This covers benefit payments related to pregnancy and delivery. The administration costs related to "maternity" expenditures are reported under this function.

Examples of benefits included are:

- nursing allowances paid at the time of childbirth;
- any benefit paid to the mother during the first days after childbirth and during rest periods, if any (includes employers' benefits, accordingly, if any).

Examples of benefits not included are:

- medical check-ups of mother and child, which should be recorded under the "sickness" function.

Other family functions   This should cover all family-related expenditures (including administrative expenditures) that cannot be subsumed under *children and youth* or *maternity*.

Unemployment   This covers any benefit provided to a protected person arising from involuntary loss of gainful employment. These expenditures are also known as "passive labour market expenditures". The administration costs related to "unemployment" expenditures are reported under this function.

Examples of benefits included are:

- early retirement programmes established for labour market reasons and not financed by pension funds;
- periodic family allowances for dependants paid to beneficiaries of unemployment benefits;
- means-tested unemployment assistance in cash or in kind provided to the unemployed;
- subsidies provided by the government in order to support the costs of employment (e.g. tax reductions or subsidies to enterprises employing the unemployed).

Examples of benefits not included are:

- benefits paid on loss of gainful employment due to invalidity or sickness, which are to be recorded under their respective functions;
- cash benefits provided during maternity leave, which are recorded under the family function (e.g. Quebec's maternity benefits are in part provided through the unemployment programme and should as such be recorded under the maternity function).

Occupational training   This covers all expenditures on vocational training, support of training on the job, career advice, and so on, as provided by the different institutions included in the SAS. These expenditures are also known as "active labour market measures". The administration costs related to "occupational training" expenditures are reported under this function.

Examples of benefits included are:

- training for youths who have never been employed, in the form of cash allowances or in-kind benefits;
- staff training provided to employees for career development and for job training.

Mobility This includes all direct expenditures on measures to provide for work incentives, to change workplace, to create jobs (including public work programmes), and so on, financed by the institutions included in the SAS.

These expenditures are also known as "active labour market measures". The administration costs related to "mobility" expenditure are reported under this function.

Housing Any expenditures provided in order to directly or indirectly help a household meet the costs of housing or to improve housing conditions (maintenance). The benefit may be means or income tested. The administration costs related to "housing" expenditures are reported under this function.

Examples of benefits included are:

- the market value of the property and the actual price which the household pays;
- the commercial rent which should be charged for the property and the actual rent which the household pays;
- commercial mortgage interest and the mortgage interest charged to the household.

Examples of benefits not included are:

- housing benefits linked directly to one of the other functions (such as the accommodation of old-age benefit recipients in nursing homes, accommodation provided to the unemployed), which are to be recorded under the specific function to which they relate.

General neediness (poverty) This is defined as benefits in cash or in kind provided to individuals who require specific assistance in order to obtain a defined minimum level of income, or to meet minimum subsistence requirements. These benefits are provided on a means-tested basis to individuals whose income (whether from active employment, benefits or other sources) falls below the poverty-line level. The administration costs related to "general neediness" expenditures are reported under this function.

Examples of benefits included are:

- periodical means-tested cash benefits provided under social assistance legislation;
- rehabilitation of drug and alcohol abusers not covered by measures provided by social insurance;
- accommodation provided to certain vulnerable and needy categories of society (such as shelters for refugees).

Examples of benefits not included are:

- means-tested benefits which are provided to recipients of benefits under the other functions and thus linked to other risks (e.g. unemployment assistance, food, clothing, housing provided on a means-tested basis to beneficiaries of unemployment benefit);
- housing benefits provided to households to meet the costs and needs related to their accommodation requirements;
- benefits and assistance provided by private charitable organizations (such as benefits-in-kind provided by the International Red Cross/Crescent Organization), unless they are included in the institutions of the SAS.

Other functions These cover all expenditures that cannot be subsumed under one of the other functions. It should only be used in exceptional cases where benefits may be paid that do not at all comply with the definitions of one of the other functions. The administration costs related to "other functions" expenditures are reported under this function.

Notes

[1] *SNA 1993*, p. 196.

[2] ibid., p. 197. This *SNA 1993* concept has been criticized because it does not explain how any notional technical reserves should be treated in the system's financial accounts and balance sheets.

[3] ibid., p. 188.

[4] ibid., p. 200.

[5] In order to obtain a full in-depth understanding of the sectoral classification of a Social Budget, the reader is directed to the *SNA 1993*, Chapter IV, "Institutional units and sectors", pp. 87–112.

[6] ibid., p. 88.

[7] ibid., p. 88.

[8] ibid., p. 88.

[9] ibid., p. 201.

[10] ibid., p. 201.

[11] This part of the glossary relates closely to ILO: *The Cost of Social Security. Nineteenth International Inquiry* (Geneva, 1997), pp. 30–40.

GLOSSARY OF TERMS USED FOR PROJECTIONS

Catchment ratio The ratio of the average insurable earnings of a social security scheme (in a given period) to the average wage of the total economy (in that same period).

Contribution ceiling The minimum and/or maximum amount of individual wages that is subject to contributions to a social security scheme. The (upper) ceiling usually (but not always) reflects the maximum amount on which benefits are calculated.

Contributor ratio The ratio of the contributing population (persons with at least one contribution paid in a given period) to the total number of employed persons (in that same period).

Coverage ratio The ratio of the total number of registered insured persons (persons with an insurance record but not necessarily active) to the total labour force.

Defined benefit The benefit paid in a defined benefit scheme. It is usually formula based, the formula taking into account the individual number of contribution or insurance years and the individual amount of earnings during the same period. The formula-bound amount is guaranteed to each person who meets defined entitlement conditions.

Defined contribution The contribution to be paid in a defined contribution (pension) scheme. In a defined contribution scheme the benefits paid depend exclusively on the amount of contributions accumulated in an individual account.

Density The ratio of the number of contributions actually paid during a given period to the potential maximum number of contributions in the same period.

Eligibility conditions The set of legally defined conditions which stipulate if and when a person has the right to claim a benefit.

Insurable earnings The wages received for services rendered to an employer and which are subject to the payment of contributions to a social security scheme. Insurable earnings generally include a base salary and may or may not include additional components awarded to an insured person. See also *Contribution ceiling*.

PAYG (cost) rate   The ratio of the total expenditure of a scheme to the sum of insurable earnings of that scheme. It reflects the contribution rate to be charged if a scheme were financed on a pure assessment (pay-as-you-go) basis.

Poverty line   The level of income defining the borderline of poverty. If persons (households) are in a position to dispose of less than this amount, they are poor. There are different (absolute, relative and subjective) approaches to define a poverty line.

Replacement rate   The ratio of the amount of cash benefits to the underlying insurable earnings, calculated either individually or as an average for a group of persons, or for all beneficiaries of the scheme.

Scaled premium   The contribution rates to be paid in a scaled premium system. In their most generic definition, they include all systems of contribution rates which are increased throughout the life-cycle of a scheme on a step-by-step basis (where the duration of the individual "steps" are called the periods of equilibrium.) Scaled premium systems are (pension) systems of partial funding.

Social assistance intervention line   This line is equivalent to the minimum income guaranteed by the State to each citizen through the social assistance scheme. It is usually lower than the poverty line.

Time horizon   Starting from the last statistically observed base period, the maximum number of periods up to which the results of a projection are accessible to meaningful interpretation. The time horizon varies with the specific scheme(s)/economy under consideration.

Unit cost   The cost of a unit of service or goods in a given category of services (such as a hospital day). This concept is often used in health modelling.

Utilization frequency   The number of cases of treatment or units of care per insured or protected person in a given category of social services (in a given period). This concept is often used in health modelling.

SOCIAL BUDGETING DATA REQUIREMENTS: A CHECKLIST

The following list provides a standard frame for the data set required for a typical version of the ILO Social Budget model. The list may equally be regarded as a "minimum" or a "maximum" frame – *minimum* if, in a concrete country case, the data basis and modelling environment are much richer than assumed in this book, and *maximum* if circumstances allow for only a limited social budgeting approach. If not specifically mentioned otherwise, the data should be collected for at least three observation years, for the start year of the projections and at least two preceding years. Of course, the analytical basis for projections will often improve with the length of the available time-series on past observations. This is especially important concerning the economic and labour market data.

In section 2 of this annex the list comprises a certain number of assumptions on future developments. These are essentially the factors driving the projections. The list can only serve only as a first rough frame to check how laborious the development of a methodological and statistical basis for a Social Budget, including the modelling part, would probably be, or to indicate where improvements might be required. It has to be adjusted to the prevailing realities in each individual country's case.

1.   STATISTICAL DATA

1.1   Demographic and household data

1.1.1 Demographic data

(1)   Population by sex and age group
(2)   Mortality table by sex and age group
(3)   Fertility rates by age group
(4)   Net international migration by sex and age group
(5)   Marriage rate by sex and age group

1.1.2 Household data

Census data (or similar source)

(6)   Total number of households by household size

(7) Number of households and household members by socio-economic group (classi-fied by labour market status of the breadwinner: households headed by employees, self-employed, farmers, pensioners, unemployed and others)

Household income and expenditure survey data

(8) Number of households (and number of persons) by average monthly per capita household income (total and for each of the socio-economic groups). Income brackets can be expressed as a ratio of average monthly per capita income to the national monthly average wage. Ideally, the size of the income bracket should be at least 5 per cent of the average wage.

(9) Composition of the total household income by source: income from employment, self-employment, and agricultural activity; from different social benefits by type (pensions, other social insurance benefits, family benefits, unemployment benefits, social assistance and all the other income-tested benefits); other income – for each of the socio-economic groups and for all the income brackets.

1.2 Economy

(10) GDP in current prices by economic sector (National Accounts = SNA)
(11) GDP in constant prices by economic sector (SNA)
(12) Sectoral GDP deflators
(13) GDP in current prices by expenditure component (SNA)
(14) GDP in constant prices by expenditure component (SNA)
(15) GDP expenditure deflators
(16) Primary factor income distribution (SNA)
(17) Employers' social security contributions (SNA)
(18) Sum of gross wages (SNA)
(19) Income tax on sum of wages (SNA)
(20) Employees' social security contributions on sum of wage (SNA)
(21) National gross average wage by economic sector and average grand total (SNA)
(22) National net average wage by economic sector and average grand total (SNA)
(23) Consumer price index (CPI) – year-to-year basis
(24) Monthly consumer price index (CPI) for at least three observation years
(25) Short- and long-term interest rates (market)
(26) Short- and long-term interest rates (policy instruments)
(27) Exchange rate versus US$/euro/yen (annual average)
(28) Monthly exchange rates for at least three observation years

1.3 Labour force and employment

(29) Labour force participation rates (or labour force) by sex and single age (labour force survey (LFS) data)
(30) Number of employed by age, sex and main sector of the economy (if different coverage and social security systems for different sectors) and by public and private sector (if different coverage and social security systems for public and private employees) (LFS data)
(31) Employees by age, sex and main economic sector (LFS data)
(32) Self-employed by age, sex and main economic sector (LFS data)
(33) Unemployed by age and sex (LFS data)
(34) Registered unemployed by age and sex (administrative data)

1.4   Government accounts

(35) Accounts of central government (SNA)
(36) Accounts of state/provincial governments (SNA)
(37) Accounts of local governments (SNA)
(38) Accounts of social security system (SNA)
(39) Consolidated public sector accounts (SNA)

1.5   Social protection

1.5.1 Financial accounts

(40) Revenue and expenditure of the pension scheme(s)
(41) Revenue and expenditure of the public health scheme(s)
(42) Revenue and expenditure of the unemployment benefit scheme
(43) Revenue and expenditure of the social assistance scheme
(44) Revenue and expenditure of family benefit scheme(s)
(45) Revenue and expenditure of sickness benefit scheme(s)
(46) Revenue and expenditure of other short-term benefit schemes
(47) Revenue and expenditure of other social protection schemes
(48) Revenue and expenditure of other social purpose schemes

1.5.2 Contributions and contributors

(49) Average insurable earnings of the pension scheme(s) by sex and age group, and average grand total
(50) Average insurable earnings of the health insurance scheme(s) by sex and profession, and average grand total
(51) Average insurable earnings of the unemployment insurance by sex and profession, and average grand total
(52) Average insurable earnings of the other social security schemes by sex and profession, and average grand total
(53) Contribution collection and/or insurance ceilings on earnings in the pension scheme(s)
(54) Contribution collection and/or insurance ceilings on earnings in the health insurance scheme(s)
(55) Contribution collection and/or insurance ceilings on earnings in the unemployment insurance
(56) Contribution collection and/or insurance ceilings on earnings in other social security schemes
(57) Legal contribution rates in the pension scheme(s)
(58) Legal contribution rates in the health insurance scheme(s)
(59) Legal contribution rates in the unemployment insurance
(60) Legal contribution rates in other social security schemes
(61) Number of contributors to pension scheme(s) by sex and age group, and grand total
(62) Number of contributors to pension scheme(s) by sex and profession, and grand total
(63) Number of contributors to health insurance scheme(s) by sex and profession, and grand total

(64) Number of contributors to unemployment insurance by sex and profession, and grand total
(65) Number of contributors to other social security schemes by sex and profession, and grand total
(66) For the pension scheme(s): number of dependent spouses and children per contributor by sex and age group, and grand total
(67) For other schemes(s): number of dependent spouses and children per contributor by sex and profession of contributor, and grand total
(68) Average co-payments to health care per patient
(69) Number of patients

1.5.3 Average benefits/costs, beneficiaries and providers

Pensions

(70) Average amount of old-age pensions by sex and age group
(71) Average amount of old-age pensions by pre-retirement profession
(72) Average amount of invalidity pensions by sex and age group
(73) Average amount of invalidity pensions by pre-retirement profession
(74) Average amount of survivors' pensions by sex and age group
(75) Average amount of survivors' pensions by pre-invalidity profession
(76) Average amount of minimum/social pensions by sex and age group
(77) Average amount of minimum/social pensions by pre-retirement profession
(78) Number of old-age pension(er)s by sex and age group
(79) Number of old-age pension(er)s by pre-retirement profession
(80) Number of invalidity pension(er)s by sex and age group
(81) Number of invalidity pension(er)s by pre-retirement profession
(82) Number of survivors' pension(er)s by sex and age group
(83) Number of survivors' pension(er)s by pre-retirement profession
(84) Number of minimum pension(er)s by sex and age group
(85) Number of minimum pension(er)s by pre-retirement profession
(86) Total pension benefit expenditure by type of pension

Health care

Government health care scheme

(87) Total costs per public hospital
(88) Total costs per public hospital bed
(89) Total costs per ambulatory clinic/health centre
(90) Total costs per employed physician
(91) Total costs per other health care staff
(92) Dental care expenditure per case
(93) Pharmaceutical expenditure per prescription
(94) Number of public hospitals
(95) Number of public hospital beds
(96) Number of public hospital days
(97) Number of hospital days per patient by sex and three age groups: children/youth, actives and pensionable ages
(98) Number of ambulatory clinics/health centres

(99)   Number of ambulatory care cases by sex and three age groups: children/youth, actives and pensionable ages
(100) Number of employed physicians
(101) Number of other health care staff
(102) Number of dental care cases per patient by sex and three age groups: children/youth, actives and pensionable ages
(103) Number of prescriptions
(104) Number of prescriptions per patient by sex and three age groups: children/youth, actives and pensionable ages

Social insurance health scheme

(105) Number of ambulatory care cases
(106) Number of cases per capita by sex and three age groups: children/youth, actives and pensionable ages
(107) Number of hospital days
(108) Number of hospital days per capita by sex and three age groups: children/youth, actives and pensionable ages
(109) Number of dental care cases
(110) Number of cases per capita by sex and three age groups: children/youth, actives and pensionable ages
(111) Number of prescriptions
(112) Number of prescriptions per capita by sex and three age groups: children/youth, actives and pensionable ages

Private health care

(113) Number of private hospital beds
(114) Number of private practitioners and specialists

Sickness and maternity benefits

(115) Average daily sickness benefit by sex and age group
(116) Number of sickness days per year and insured person by sex and age group
(117) Number of work days per year
(118) Average maternity benefit per day
(119) Number of maternity benefit cases per woman
(120) Number of maternity days per maternity case

Unemployment benefits

(121) Average benefit by sex and age group
(122) Number of beneficiaries by sex and age group
(123) Average duration of benefit payment per case
(124) Severance pay by sex and age group
(125) Severance pay per capita by economic sector
(126) Number of dismissals
(127) Number of severance pay cases

Family benefits

(128) Average benefit per case
(129) Number of child benefit cases
(130) Average benefit per case
(131) Number of cases of parental leave

Social assistance (means-tested benefit)

(132) Average monthly benefits per recipient unit by type of benefit
(133) Number of benefit recipients by type of benefit
(134) Minimum subsistence levels for different recipient units

Housing benefits

(135) Average benefit per case
(136) Number of cases

Tax benefits

(137) Estimated total tax benefits (tax credits with a "social purpose")

Other benefits

(138) Other benefits per case
(139) Cases of other benefits

2. ASSUMPTIONS

(A1) (Official) population projection
(A2) Projection of labour force participation rates by sex and single age group
(A3) Projection of GDP at constant prices
(A4) Projection of labour productivity
(A5) Projection of labour productivity by economic sector
(A6) Projection of GDP deflators
(A7) Projection of interest rate(s)
(A8) Projection of household composition and average household size

3. LEGISLATION

(L1)   Laws on pension scheme(s)
(L2)   Laws on health scheme(s)
(L3)   Laws on unemployment scheme(s)
(L4)   Laws on social assistance scheme(s)
(L5)   Laws on family benefit scheme(s)
(L6)   Laws on sickness benefit scheme(s)
(L7)   Laws on other short-term benefit schemes
(L8)   Laws on other social protection schemes
(L9)   Laws on other social purpose schemes
(L10) Tax laws with a "social purpose"
(L11) Supplementary agreements between employers and employees, etc.

ANNEX VI

BLUEPRINTS FOR THE TABLE STRUCTURE OF AN SAS

Figure AVI.1 Revenue by legal category and institution (year t)

| Institution | Revenue Total Year t (National currency) | Social contributions | | | | | Subsidies | | Other revenue | Transfers from other institutions |
| | | By the insured | | Others | By the employers | | General government | Other sources | | |
		Employees	Self-employed		Actual	Imputed				
1. Basic systems										
1.1 National systems										
1.1.1 Child benefits										
1.1.2 Child-raising allowances										
1.2 General systems										
1.2.1 Health insurance										
1.2.2 Pension insurance										
1.2.3 Occupational accidents and diseases insurance										
1.2.4 Unemployment insurance										
1.2.5 Continued payment of wages in case of illness										
1.3 Special systems										
1.3.1 Statutory system										
1.3.1.1 Civil service pensions										
1.3.1.2 Civil service family supplements to wages and salaries										
1.3.1.3 Civil service health assistance										
1.3.2 Other occupation-related systems										
1.3.2.1 Old-age assistance for farmers										
1.3.2.2 Old-age insurance for the liberal professions										
1.3.3 Systems related to war victims and others										
1.3.3.1 War veterans' pensions and related benefits										
1.3.3.2 Reparations and related payments										
1.3.3.3 Other compensatory benefits										

2. Supplementary systems				
2.1 National systems				
2.1.1 Youth-related assistance				
2.1.2 Public health services				
2.2 General systems				
2.2.1 Supplementary (occupational) pensions by private employers				
2.2.2 Other general systems				
2.3 Special systems				
2.3.1 Supplementary (occupational) pensions by public employers				
2.3.2 Other general systems				
2.4 Voluntary systems				
2.4.1 Employers' contractual and voluntary benefits				
2.4.2 Other voluntary systems				
3. Other social protection systems				
3.1 Public social assistance				
3.2 Promotion of training				
3.3 Housing allowances				
3.4 Unemployment assistance				
Total Social Budget				

Note: The institutional table structure is related to the Eurostat classification of the German Social Budget but extended by a few generalizing items.

Figure AVI.2 Revenue by sector of the economy and institution (year t)

Institution	Revenue Total Year t (National currency)	Enterprises	Governments Central	State	Local	Social insurance	Private Households	Institutions	Rest of the world
1. Basic systems									
1.1 National systems									
1.1.1 Child benefits									
1.1.2 Child-raising allowances									
1.2 General systems									
1.2.1 Health insurance									
1.2.2 Pension insurance									
1.2.3 Occupational accidents and diseases insurance									
1.2.4 Unemployment insurance									
1.2.5 Continued payment of wages in case of illness									
1.3 Special systems									
1.3.1 Statutory system									
1.3.1.1 Civil service pensions									
1.3.1.2 Civil service family supplements to wages and salaries									
1.3.1.3 Civil service health assistance									
1.3.2 Other occupation-related systems									
1.3.2.1 Old-age assistance for farmers									
1.3.2.2 Old-age insurance for the liberal professions									
1.3.3 Systems related to war victims and others									
1.3.3.1 War veterans' pensions and related benefits									
1.3.3.2 Reparations and related payments									
1.3.3.3 Other compensatory benefits									

2. Supplementary systems

2.1 National systems

  2.1.1 Youth-related assistance

  2.1.2 Public health services

2.2 General systems

  2.2.1 Supplementary (occupational) pensions by
       private employers

  2.2.2 Other general systems

2.3 Special systems

  2.3.1 Supplementary (occupational) pensions by
       public employers

  2.3.2 Other general systems

2.4 Voluntary systems

  2.4.1 Employers' contractual and voluntary benefits

  2.4.2 Other voluntary systems

3. Other social protection systems

3.1 Public social assistance

3.2 Promotion of training

3.3 Housing allowances

3.4 Unemployment assistance

Total Social Budget

Note: The institutional table structure is related to the Eurostat classification of the German Social Budget but extended by a few generalizing items.

Figure AVI.3 Revenue by legal category, sector of the economy and institution *i* (year *t*)

Economic sector	Revenue Total Institution *i* Year *t* — National currency	Social contributions					Subsidies		Other revenues
		By the insured			By the employers		General government	Other sources	
		Employees	Self-employed	Others	Actual	Imputed			
Enterprises									
Central government									
State governments									
Local governments									
Social insurance									
Private households									
Private organizations									
Rest of the world									
Total revenue of institution *i*									

Figure AVI.4 Expenditure by economic category and institution (year *t*)

Institution	Expenditure	Total	Income replacements	Reimbursements	Goods and services	General services			Transfers to other institutions
	National currency					Administration	Measures	Grants	
1. Basic systems									
1.1 National systems									
1.1.1 Child benefits									
1.1.2 Child-raising allowances									
1.2 General systems									
1.2.1 Health insurance									
1.2.2 Pension insurance									
1.2.3 Occupational accidents and diseases insurance									
1.2.4 Unemployment insurance									
1.2.5 Continued payment of wages in case of illness									
1.3 Special systems									
1.3.1 Statutory system									
1.3.1.1 Civil service pensions									
1.3.1.2 Civil service family supplements to wages and salaries									
1.3.1.3 Civil service health assistance									
1.3.2 Other occupation-related systems									
1.3.2.1 Old-age assistance for farmers									
1.3.2.2 Old-age insurance for the liberal professions									
1.3.3 Systems related to war victims and others									
1.3.3.1 War veterans' pensions and related benefits									
1.3.3.2 Reparations and related payments									
1.3.3.3 Other compensatory benefits									

2. **Supplementary systems**
   2.1 National systems
     2.1.1 Youth-related assistance
     2.1.2 Public health services
   2.2 General systems
     2.2.1 Supplementary (occupational) pensions
           by private employers
     2.2.2 Other general systems
   2.3 Special systems
     2.3.1 Supplementary (occupational) pensions
           by public employers
     2.3.2 Other general systems
   2.4 Voluntary systems
     2.4.1 Employers' contractual and voluntary
           benefits
     2.4.2 Other voluntary systems

3. **Other social protection systems**
   3.1 Public social assistance
   3.2 Promotion of training
   3.3 Housing allowances
   3.4 Unemployment assistance

Total Social Budget

Note: The institutional table structure is related to the Eurostat classification of the German Social Budget but extended by a few generalizing items.

Figure AVI.5 Expenditure by social function and institution (year *t*)

Institution	Total Year *t*	Old age and survivors		Health					Family			Employment			Subtotals			
Social function / National currency		Old age	Survivors	Prevention, rehabilitation	Sickness	Work injury	Invalidity		Children, youth	Maternity	Other	Occupational training	Mobility	Unemployment	Housing	Poverty	Other functions	

1. Basic systems
1.1 National systems
  1.1.1 Child benefits
  1.1.2 Child-raising allowances
1.2 General systems
  1.2.1 Health insurance
  1.2.2 Pension insurance
  1.2.3 Occupational accidents and diseases insurance
  1.2.4 Unemployment insurance
  1.2.5 Continued payment of wages in case of illness
1.3 Special systems
  1.3.1 Statutory system
    1.3.1.1 Civil service pensions
    1.3.1.2 Civil service family supplements to wages and salaries
    1.3.1.3 Civil service health assistance
  1.3.2 Other occupation-related systems
    1.3.2.1 Old-age assistance for farmers
    1.3.2.2 Old-age insurance for the liberal professions
  1.3.3 Systems related to war victims and others

1.3.3.1 War veterans' pensions and related benefits
1.3.3.2 Reparations and related payments
1.3.3.3 Other compensatory benefits

2. Supplementary systems
2.1 National systems
2.1.1 Youth-related assistance
2.1.2 Public health services
2.2 General systems
2.2.1 Supplementary (occupational) pensions by private employers
2.2.2 Other general systems
2.3 Special systems
2.3.1 Supplementary (occupational) pensions by public employers
2.3.2 Other general systems
2.4 Voluntary systems
2.4.1 Employers' contractual and voluntary benefits
2.4.2 Other voluntary systems

3. Other social protection systems
3.1 Public social assistance
3.2 Promotion of training
3.3 Housing allowances
3.4 Unemployment assistance

Total Social Budget

Note: The institutional table structure is related to the Eurostat classification of the German Social Budget but extended by a few generalizing items.

Figure AVI.6 Expenditure by social function, economic category and institution (year *t*)

Institution / Social function	Total Year *t* (National currency)	Old age and survivors			Health			Family			Employment			Housing			Poverty			Other		
		Replacements, reimbursements	Goods and services	General services	Replacements, reimbursements	Goods and services	General services	Replacements, reimbursements	Goods and services	General services	Replacements, reimbursements	Goods and services	General services	Replacements, reimbursements	Goods and services	General services	Replacements, reimbursements	Goods and services	General services	Replacements, reimbursements	Goods and services	General services
1. Basic systems																						
1.1 National systems																						
1.1.1 Child benefits																						
1.1.2 Child-raising allowances																						
1.2 General systems																						
1.2.1 Health insurance																						
1.2.2 Pension insurance																						
1.2.3 Occupational accidents and diseases insurance																						
1.2.4 Unemployment insurance																						
1.2.5 Continued payment of wages in case of illness																						
1.3 Special systems																						
1.3.1 Statutory system																						
1.3.1.1 Civil service pensions																						
1.3.1.2 Civil service family supplements to wages and salaries																						
1.3.1.3 Civil service health assistance																						
1.3.2 Other occupation-related systems																						

1.3.2.1 Old-age assistance for farmers

1.3.2.2 Old-age insurance for the liberal professions

1.3.3 Systems related to war victims and others

1.3.3.1 War veterans' pensions and related benefits

1.3.3.2 Reparations and related payments

1.3.3.3 Other compensatory benefits

2. Supplementary systems

2.1 National systems

2.1.1 Youth-related assistance

2.1.2 Public health services

2.2 General systems

2.2.1 Supplementary (occupational) pensions by private employers

2.2.2 Other general systems

2.3 Special systems

2.3.1 Supplementary (occupational) pensions by public employers

2.3.2 Other general systems

2.4 Voluntary systems

2.4.1 Employers' contractual and voluntary benefits

2.4.2 Other voluntary systems

3. Other social protection systems

3.1 Public social assistance

3.2 Promotion of training

3.3 Housing allowances

3.4 Unemployment assistance

Total Social Budget

Note: The institutional table structure is related to the Eurostat classification of the German Social Budget but extended by a few generalizing items.

Figure AVI.7 Expenditure by economic category, social function and institution *i* (year *t*)

Social function	Economic category		Income replacements	Reimbursements	Goods and services	General services		
	Total Institution *i* Year *t*	National currency				Administration	Measures	Grants
1. Old age and survivors								
1.1 Old age								
1.2 Survivors								
2. Health								
2.1 Prevention and rehabilitation								
2.2 Sickness								
2.3 Work injury and occupational diseases								
2.4 Invalidity								
3. Family								
3.1 Children and youth								
3.2 Maternity								
3.3 Other family functions								
4. Employment								
4.1 Occupational training								
4.2 Mobility								
4.3 Unemployment								
5. Housing								
6. General neediness (poverty)								
7. Other functions								
Total expenditure of institution *i*								

Figure AVI.8 Transfers between institutions (year _t_)

Paying institutions \ Receiving institutions	1 Child benefits	2 Child-raising allowances	3 Health insurance	4 Pension insurance	5 Occupational accidents insurance	6 Unemployment insurance	7 Continued payment of wages in case of illness	8 Civil service pensions	9 Civil service family supplements to wages and salaries	10 Civil service health assistance	11 Old-age assistance for farmers	12 Old-age insurance for the liberal professions	13 War veterans' pensions and related benefits	14 Reparations and related payments	15 Other compensatory benefits	16 Youth-related assistance	17 Public health services	18 Supplementary (occupational) pensions by private employers	19 Other supplementary private systems	20 Supplementary (occupational) pensions by public employers	21 Other supplementary public systems	22 Employers' contractual and voluntary benefits	23 Other voluntary systems	24 Public social assistance	25 Promotion of training	26 Housing allowances	27 Unemployment assistance
1 Child benefits	X																										
2 Child-raising allowances		X																									
3 Health insurance			X																								
4 Pension insurance				X																							
5 Occupational accidents insurance					X																						
6 Unemployment insurance						X																					
7 Continued payment of wages in case of illness							X																				
8 Civil service pensions								X																			
9 Civil service family supplements to wages and salaries									X																		
10 Civil service health assistance										X																	
11 Old-age assistance for farmers											X																

National currency

		X (position)
12	Old-age insurance for the liberal professions	×
13	War veterans' pensions and related benefits	×
14	Reparations and related payments	×
15	Other compensatory benefits	×
16	Youth-related assistance	×
17	Public health services	×
18	Supplementary (occupational) pensions by private employers	×
19	Other supplementary private systems	×
20	Supplementary (occupational) pensions by public employers	×
21	Other supplementary public systems	×
22	Employers' contractual and voluntary benefits	×
23	Other voluntary systems	×
24	Public social assistance	×
25	Promotion of training	×
26	Housing allowances	×
27	Unemployment assistance	×
28	**Total payments**	

Figure AVI.9   Revenue by legal category

Legal category	National currency	Year 1	Year 2	Year 3	...	Year t	...	Year $t+n$
		Statistical results					Projection	
1. Social contributions								
1.1 Contributions by the insured population								
1.1.1 Employees' contributions								
1.1.2 Contributions by self-employed persons								
1.1.3 Contributions by beneficiaries								
1.1.4 Contributions by other persons								
1.1.5 Contributions paid by public institutions in lieu of beneficiaries								
1.2 Employers' contributions								
1.2.1 Actual contributions								
1.2.2 Imputed contributions								
2. Subsidies								
2.1 Subsidies paid by the government								
2.2 Subsidies paid from other sources								
3. Other revenues								
Total expenditure by legal category								

Figure AVI.10   Revenue by sector of the economy

Economic sector	National currency	Year 1	Year 2	Year 3	...	Year t	...	Year $t+n$
		Statistical results					Projection	
Enterprises								
Central government								
Provincial governments								
Local governments								
Social insurance								
Private households								
Private organizations								
Rest of the world								
Total revenue by economic sector								

Figure AVI.11 Expenditure by economic category

Economic category	National currency	Year 1	Year 2	Year 3	...	Year t	...	Year $t+n$
				Statistical results			Projection	

1. Income replacements (cash benefits)
2. Reimbursements (cash)
3. Goods and services (in-kind benefits)
4. General services
   4.1 Administration
   4.2 Measures
   4.3 Grants								

Total expenditure by economic category								

Figure AVI.12 Expenditure by social function

Social function	National currency	Year 1	Year 2	Year 3	...	Year t	...	Year $t+n$
				Statistical results			Projection	

1. Old age and survivors
   1.1 Old age
   1.2 Survivors								

2. Health
   2.1 Prevention and rehabilitation
   2.2 Sickness
   2.3 Work injury and occupational diseases
   2.4 Invalidity								

3. Family
   3.1 Children and youth
   3.2 Maternity
   3.3 Other family functions								

4. Employment
   4.1 Occupational training
   4.2 Mobility
   4.3 Unemployment								

5. Housing								
6. General neediness (poverty)								
7. Other functions								
Total expenditure by social functions								

Figure AVI.13 Expenditure by institution

Institution	National currency	Year 1	Year 2	Year 3	...	Year t	...	Year $t+n$
		Statistical results						Projection
1. Basic systems								
1.1 National systems								
1.1.1 Child benefits								
1.1.2 Child-raising allowances								
1.2 General systems								
1.2.1 Health insurance								
1.2.2 Pension insurance								
1.2.3 Occupational accidents and diseases insurance								
1.2.4 Unemployment insurance								
1.2.5 Continued payment of wages in case of illness								
1.3 Special systems								
1.3.1 Statutory system								
1.3.1.1 Civil service pensions								
1.3.1.2 Civil service family supplements to wages and salaries								
1.3.1.3 Civil service health assistance								
1.3.2 Other occupation-related systems								
1.3.2.1 Old-age assistance for farmers								
1.3.2.2 Old-age insurance for the liberal professions								
1.3.3 Systems related to war victims and others								
1.3.3.1 War veterans' pensions and related benefits								
1.3.3.2 Reparations and related payments								
1.3.3.3 Other compensatory benefits								
2. Supplementary systems								
2.1 National systems								
2.1.1 Youth-related assistance								
2.1.2 Public health services								
2.2 General systems								
2.2.1 Supplementary (occupational) pensions by private employers								
2.2.2 Other general systems								
2.3 Special systems								
2.3.1 Supplementary (occupational) pensions by public employers								
2.3.2 Other general systems								
2.4 Voluntary systems								
2.4.1 Employers' contractual and voluntary benefits								
2.4.2 Other voluntary systems								
3. Other social protection systems								
3.1 Public social assistance								
3.2 Promotion of training								
3.3 Housing allowances								
3.4 Unemployment assistance								
Total Social Budget								

Figure AVI.14 The SAS fiscal balance

Year	Year 1	Year 2	Year 3	...	Year t	...	Year $t+n$
Total revenue and expenditure	National currency	Statistical results				Projection	
A. Total revenue by legal category							
1. Social contributions							
1.1 Contributions by the insured population							
1.1.1 Employees' contributions							
1.1.2 Contributions by self-employed persons							
1.1.3 Contributions by beneficiaries							
1.1.4 Contributions by other persons							
1.1.5 Contributions paid by public institutions in lieu of beneficiaries							
1.2 Employers' contributions							
1.2.1 Actual contributions							
1.2.2 Imputed contributions							
2. Subsidies							
2.1 Subsidies paid by the government							
2.2 Subsidies paid from other sources							
3. Other revenues							
4. Transfers from other institutions	–	–	–	–	–	–	–
minus							
B. Total expenditure by economic category							
1. Income replacements (cash benefits)							
2. Reimbursements (cash)							
3. Goods and services (in-kind benefits)							
4. General services							
4.1 Administration							
4.2 Measures							
4.3 Grants							
5. Transfers to other institutions	–	–	–	–	–	–	–
C. = Fiscal balance (net lending/net borrowing)							
D. Total revenue by economic sector							
1. Enterprises							
2. Central government							
3. Provincial governments							
4. Local governments							
5. Social insurance							
6. Private households							
7. Private organizations							
8. Rest of the world							

Figure AVI.14 Continued

Total revenue and expenditure	Year	Year 1	Year 2	Year 3	...	Year t	...	Year $t+n$
	National currency	Statistical results					Projection	
minus								
E. Total expenditure by social function								
1. Old age and survivors								
1.1 Old age								
1.2 Survivors								
2. Health								
2.1 Prevention and rehabilitation								
2.2 Sickness								
2.3 Work injury and occupational diseases								
2.4 Invalidity								
3. Family								
3.1 Children and youth								
3.2 Maternity								
3.3 Other family functions								
4. Employment								
4.1 Occupational training								
4.2 Mobility								
4.3 Unemployment								
5. Housing								
6. General neediness (poverty)								
7. Other functions								
C. = Fiscal balance (net lending/net borrowing)								

Note: This table might be set up for each institution; in that case, inter-institutional transfers may exist.

BIBLIOGRAPHY

Barr, Nicholas. *The economics of the welfare state* (London, Weidenfeld and Nicolson, 2nd ed., 1993).

Bonss, Wolfgang. *Die Einübung des Tatsachenblicks. Zur Struktur und Veränderung empirischer Sozialforschung* [Exercising our views on reality: About the structure of and changes in empirical social research] (Suhrkamp, Frankfurt am Main, 1982).

Cichon, Michael; Newbrander, Bill; Yamabana, Hiroshi; Weber, Axel; Normand, Charles; Dror, David; Preker, Alexander. *Modelling in health care finance – A compendium of quantitative techniques for health care financing*, Quantitative Methods in Social Protection Series (Geneva, ILO/ISSA, 1999).

Cichon, Michael; Pal, Karuna. *Reflections on lessons learned: Financing old-age, invalidity and survivors' benefits in Anglophone Africa* (Geneva, ILO, Apr. 1997; mimeo.).

Commission of the European Communities – Eurostat, International Monetary Fund, Organisation for Economic Co-operation and Development, United Nations, World Bank. *System of National Accounts 1993 (SNA 1993)* (Brussels/Luxembourg, New York, Paris, Washington, DC, 1993).

Drouin, Anne, et al. *Actuarial practice in social security*, Quantitative Methods in Social Protection Series (Geneva, ILO/ISSA, forthcoming).

Fabozzi, Frank J.; Modigliani, Franco. *Capital markets: Institutions and instruments* (London, Prentice-Hall, 1992).

Federal Ministry of Labour and Social Affairs [Bundesministerium für Arbeit und Sozialordnung], Germany. *Ausgaben und Einnahmen des Sozialschutzes*, ESSOSS 1993 [Expenditure and revenue of social protection, ESSOSS, 1993] (Bonn, 1994).

——. *Materialband zu Deutscher Bundestag: Sozialbericht 1997* [Statistical Annex to Federal Parliament: Social Report 1997]. Drs. 13/10142 of 17 Mar. 1998. http://www.bma.de

——. *Social security in Germany. Expenditure and revenue 1960–1993* (Bonn, Printing Office of the Federal Ministry of Labour and Social Affairs, 1994).

Government of Ireland. *1996 – Statistical information on social welfare services* (Dublin, 1996).

Gujarati, Damodar N. *Basic econometrics* (New York, St. Louis, 2nd ed., McGraw-Hill, 1998).

International Labour Office (ILO). *Modelling results – Basic scenarios and options*, Interim report prepared for the Government of Turkey (Geneva, 1996).

——/United Nations Development Programme (UNDP). *Bulgaria – Short-term budget projections for the National Social Security Institute*, Report to the Government (Geneva, Sofia, 1998).

——. *Panama – Valuación financiera y actuarial integral de la Caja de Seguro Social y elaboración de un modelo de cuentas sociales (informe y anexos)* [Panama – Integrated financial and actuarial evaluation of the Social Security Fund and development of a Social Budget model (results and annexes)] (Geneva, San José, Lima, 1998).

——. *Preliminary actuarial assessment of the Unemployment Insurance Fund in South Africa – A technical guide* (Geneva, Sep. 1996).

——. *Republic of Turkey – Social security and health insurance reform project. Social security, Final report* (Geneva, Mar. 1996).

——. *Saint Lucia – Report to the Government on the Sixth Actuarial Review of the National Insurance Board as of 30 June 1996 and Supplement on the Study of Reform Measures Concerning Old-age Pensions* (Geneva, 1999).

——. *Social budgeting in Ukraine* (Budapest, 1998).

——. *Social protection in Egypt, Preliminary report* (Geneva, Nov. 1998).

——. *Thailand – Assessment of the feasibility of introducing an Unemployment Insurance Scheme in Thailand. Report to the Government* (Geneva, 1998).

——. *The Cost of Social Security, Nineteenth International Inquiry* (Geneva, 1997).

——. *The ILO pension model – Draft technical guide* (Geneva, 1997).

——. *The ILO population projection model – A technical guide* (Geneva, 1998).

——. *The ILO Social Budget model, version 6* (Geneva, 1999).

——. *World Employment Report 1998–99: Employability in the global economy – How training matters* (Geneva, 1998).

——. *Yearbook of Labour Statistics 1995*, 54th issue (Geneva, 1995).

——. *Yearbook of Labour Statistics 1997*, 56th issue (Geneva, 1997).

International Monetary Fund (IMF): *A manual on government finance statistics* (Washington, DC, 1986).

Iyer, Subramaniam. *Actuarial mathematics of social security pensions*, Quantitative Methods in Social Protection Series (Geneva, ILO/ISSA, 1999).

Kloten, Norbert; von Stein, Johann Heinrich (eds.). *Obst/Hintner – Geld-, Bank- und Börsenwesen, Ein Handbuch* [Money, banks and stock exchanges: A handbook] (Stuttgart, C. E. Poeschel Verlag, 38th ed., 1988).

Rul, M., et al. *Phasing out subsidies for housing and communal services* (Kyiv, Dec. 1994; mimeo.).

Scholz, Wolfgang. "Economic crisis, employment and social protection – The case of Southeast Asia", in *ASIEN, Deutsche Zeitschrift für Politik und Kultur,* No. 70 (Hamburg, 1999).

——; Drouin, Anne. "Regular adjustment of financial parameters of social protection systems in volatile inflationary environments", in *International Social Security Review* (Geneva, ISSA), Vol. 51, 1/98.

Statistical Office of the European Communities (Eurostat). *Social protection expenditure and receipts 1980–1993. Population and social conditions,* 3C (Luxembourg, 1995).

UNICEF. *Central and Eastern Europe in transition: Public policy and social contributions,* Regional Monitoring Report, No. 1, Nov. 1993.

United Nations. *World Population Prospects: The 1996 revision* (New York, 1996).

INDEX

Page numbers in bold refer to major text sections; those in italic to tables, figures and boxed examples. The letter *g* appended to a page number indicates a glossary entry.

The International Labour Organization

The *International Labour Organization* was founded in 1919 to promote social justice and, thereby, to contribute to universal and lasting peace. Its tripartite structure is unique among agencies affiliated to the United Nations; the ILO's Governing Body includes representatives of government, and of employers' and workers' organizations. These three constituencies are active participants in regional and other meetings sponsored by the ILO, as well as in the International Labour Conference – a world forum which meets annually to discuss social and labour questions.

Over the years the ILO has issued for adoption by member States a widely respected code of international labour Conventions and Recommendations on freedom of association, employment, social policy, conditions of work, social security, industrial relations and labour administration, among others.

The ILO provides expert advice and technical assistance to member States through a network of offices and multidisciplinary teams in over 40 countries. This assistance takes the form of labour rights and industrial relations counselling, employment promotion, training in small business development, project management, advice on social security, workplace safety and working conditions, the compiling and dissemination of labour statistics, and workers' education.

ILO Publications

The *International Labour Office* is the Organization's secretariat, research body and publishing house. The *Publications Bureau* produces and distributes material on major social and economic trends. It publishes policy statements on issues affecting labour around the world, reference works, technical guides, research-based books and monographs, codes of practice on safety and health prepared by experts, and training and workers' education manuals. It also produces the *International Labour Review* in English, French and Spanish, which publishes the results of original research, perspectives on emerging issues, and book reviews.

Catalogues and lists of new publications are available free of charge from ILO Publications, International Labour Office, CH-1211 Geneva 22, Switzerland. Please visit us at the World Wide Web at: www.ilo.org

Other ILO publications

Social security pensions: Development and reform
Edited by Colin Gillion, John Turner, Clive Bailey and Denis Latulippe
This manual provides detailed policy analysis of issues of social security pension reform while acting as an excellent reference guide to social security pension systems around the world. There is an ongoing debate over the type of reform countries should undertake, and the book investigates the various systems and presents valuable information. It offers methods of improving governance and measuring performance, gives design guidelines and parameters, and includes a survey of economic and labour market implications.
ISBN 92-2-110859-7   2000   120 Swiss francs

Modelling in health care finance: A compendium of quantitative techniques for health care financing
Quantitative Methods in Social Protection Series
Michael Cichon, William Newbrander, Hiroshi Yamabana, Charles Normand, David Dror and Alexander Preker
This book provides a solid understanding of the basics of modelling and assists health care professionals in grasping its uses in policy-making processes. A valuable guidebook for health system and health insurance managers alike, it offers the quantitative and analytical tools needed for sound resource allocation and financial governance of health systems. It bridges gaps between quantitative health economics, health financing and actuarial science while presenting methods for improving the efficiency, and lowering the costs, of current health systems.
ISBN 92-2-110862-7   1999   85 Swiss francs

Actuarial mathematics of social security pensions.
Quantitative Methods in Social Protection Series
Subramaniam Iyer
This informative book provides a much-needed resource on the actuarial foundation of the financing and management of social security pensions. By focusing on the underlying mathematical theory and techniques, it offers a ready reference for social security actuaries. The theoretical presentation emphasizes the principles and interrelationships and elucidates the impact of the different funding approaches. The volume elaborates on the projection technique of valuation as well.
ISBN 92-2-110866-X   1999   55 Swiss francs

Social Security Series
This series of five manuals, produced by the ILO's Social Security Department, provides the reader with information on all the major elements of social security. Each manual is a self-contained publication. The manuals will be particularly useful in countries where social security systems are not yet operational, are undergoing change or need to be improved:

Social security principles. Social Security Series No. 1. Edited by T. Whitaker
ISBN 92-2-110734-5   Price: 16 Swiss francs

Administration of social security. Social Security Series No. 2. Edited by T. Whitaker
ISBN 92-2-110735-3   Price: 16 Swiss francs

Social security financing. Social Security Series No. 3. Edited by T. Whitaker
ISBN 92-2-110736-1   Price: 16 Swiss francs

Pension schemes. Social Security Series No. 4. Edited by T. Whitaker
ISBN 92-2-110737-X   Price: 16 Swiss francs

Social health insurance. Social Security Series No. 5. Edited by T. Whitaker
ISBN 92-2-110738-8   Price: 16 Swiss francs

Other ILO publications

World Labour Report 1999–2000: Income security in a changing world
An important, flagship ILO study, the *World Labour Report 1999–2000* examines the changing context in which women and men are trying to achieve income security for themselves and their families. Drawing on detailed, worldwide data, the report assesses the impact of globalization and liberalization, and considers the vital role played by social protection in supporting, supplementing and replacing market incomes. In the process, it re-evaluates the relationship between social protection and the economy, and addresses the challenge of finding the most effective means to bring social protection to the majority who still go without.
ISBN 92-2-110831-7   2000   45 Swiss francs

Social security for the excluded majority: Case studies of developing countries
Edited by Wouter van Ginneken
The large majority of workers in the developing countries of Benin, China, El Salvador, India and the United Republic of Tanzania are excluded from social security protection. This book examines this problem, and explores ways in which governments and organizations can work together to bring social security benefits to those most in need such as children, the disabled and retired people. Through a series of case studies, it reviews various approaches to the extension of formal sector social insurance to informal sector workers, highlighting the most successful schemes.
ISBN 92-2-110856-2   1999   25 Swiss francs

Prices are subject to change without notice.